Irish
Found in South Carolina
1850 Census

Abstracted by
Margaret Peckham Motes

CLEARFIELD

Other books by the author:

Laurens & Newberry Counties, S.C.: Saluda and Little River Settlements 1749-1775, co-authored with Jesse H. Motes, III Winner of the National Genealogical Society 1995 Award for Excellence (Methods and Sources)

South Carolina Memorials: Abstracts of Land Titled - Vol. 1, 1774-1776, co-authored with Jesse H. Motes, III.

Free Blacks and Mulattos in South Carolina - 1850 Census

Blacks Found in the Deeds of Laurens and Newberry Counties, SC: 1785 to 1827: Listed in Deeds of Gift, Deeds of Sale, Mortgages, Born Free and Freed

Butcher, Baker, Candlestick Maker and Other Occupations in Newburyport, Massachusetts - 1850 Census

Printed for
Clearfield Company, Inc. by
Genealogical Publishing Co., Inc.
Baltimore, Maryland
2003

International Standard Book Number: 0-8063-5203-5

Made in the United States of America

CONTENTS

PREFACE

There were several migrations of Irish immigrants into South Carolina. In Robert L. Meriwether's book, *The Expansion of South Carolina 1729-1765*, one reads of the immigration from Ireland to South Carolina in the early 1700's when land was being offered to Protestants from Great Britain, Ireland, or the American colonies to encourage the settlement of the Province of South Carolina. The British were encouraging the settlement of the frontier by offering land to males of military age, with fees paid, and the promise of exemption from taxes for a period of four years.

A second wave of Irish immigrants arrived after the South Carolina Assembly passed the Bounty Act on July 25, 1761. The Act was modified that only Protestants could apply for bounty lands. These new arrivals also were to became the soldiers and patriots during the Revolutionary War. In Janie Revill's *A Compilation of the Original Lists of Protestant Immigrants To South Carolina 1763-1773*, the author compiled an extensive list immigrants who were leaving Ireland during this period of settlement.

In my earlier work, using the South Carolina Colonial Surveys, the land grants given by the Crown to settlers into the Province prior to the Revolution, the following information was found on the surveys: the name of the land owner and the bounding names, unless land was vacant. It was not unusual to find noted on the surveys, "name not known--Irish," "surname--Irish" or just "Irish Bounty Land."

With the tragedy of the potato famine in Ireland between 1845-1850 and the large numbers of Irish dying, many communities were totally eliminated, with many Irish were being forced from their homes by their landlord. They left Ireland by the thousands to sail to America, but many died on the voyage. Many Irish immigrants settled in the port cities of the East Coast and moved on to seek work in other areas.

The abstracted material for this book covers 4,000 Irish listed in South Carolina by the time of the 1850 census. The majority, 2,400, were located in the Charleston area. The population of the counties had a range of under 10 to over 250. There were 2,293 males and 1,825 females. In the grouping of Irish by age, the data show that most males were between 25 and 40, while the females ages ranged between 25 and 50. For the total listing, ages ranged from ninety-nine to under one year. A few mulattos are listed as having been born in Ireland. These names are listed at the end of the surname index.

Many families from New England, the Mid-Atlantic States and Europe migrated to South Carolina to take advantage of the growth and new business opportunities in the South. Many of these families had Irish in their households as servants or laborers.

Thirteen reels of microcopy were read, covering the 29 counties in the 1850 South Carolina Federal Census. The abstracted data were put into a database. The information abstracted was for all those who were born in Ireland and includes the following data: name, age, sex, occupation, white, unless listed as M (mulatto), birthplace, household number, dwelling number and the county in which they were living. Persons born in Ireland who were found in other households, hotels, convents, and on board ship were noted.

The Irish were found working in varied occupations. The majority were laborers, stonemasons, brick masons, bricklayers, clerks, farmers, merchants, shoemakers, policemen and servants; a few were priests and ministers. In my work on *Free Blacks in South Carolina in 1850,* the occupations of the free blacks and mulattos were surprisingly more varied than the Irish during this census. The blacks and mulattos were working as barbers, butchers, hair dressers, laundresses, carpenters, fishermen, painters, paper hangers, and market women, as well as servants, farmers and laborers.

Every effort has been made to keep the spelling of first and last names as they appeared in the census record. The spelling of names is always difficult, and variations appear for the same surnames.

Special thanks to Jesse H. Motes, III for his support during this project.

Margaret P. Motes
Newburyport, Massachusetts
November 2002

MICROCOPY RECORDS:

The 1850 South Carolina Census Reels

M432-848	Abbeville and Anderson Counties
M432-849	Barnwell and Beauford Counties
M432-850	Charleston County
M432-851	Chester, Chesterfield, Colleton and Darlington Counties
M432-852	Edgefield and Fairfield Counties
M432-853	Georgetown and Greenville Counties
M432-854	Horry, Kershaw and Lancaster Counties
M432-855	Laurens and Lexington Counties
M432-856	Marion, Marlboro and Newberry Counties
M432-857	Orangeburg and Pickens Counties
M432-858	Richland and Spartanburg Counties
M432-859	Sumter and Union Counties
M432-860	Williamsburg and York Counties

The Microcopy used was purchased from American Genealogical Lending Library, Bountiful, Utah.

ABSTRACT FORMAT:

Last name, first name, age, sex, occupation (if indicated), color (, -) all are white unless listed as m for mulatto, birthplace, dwelling #, family #, county. Notes if any apply. See examples below

Example: Conner, Margaret, 19, F, Servant, -, Ireland, 355, 327, CHAS. In HH of Col. W. S. King 48 m born CT.

A few mulattos are found in the census records as being born in Ireland. These names are listed together at the end of the surname index on pg. 203.

vi

COUNTY CODES:

Abbreviation, county and the date the census was taken.. Two census were recorded in January 1851.

ABB:	Abbeville. 20 July to 14 December 1850.
AND:	Anderson. Western Division.17 July to 12 Octtober 1850.
AND*:	Anderson. Easter Division. 22 July to 19 October 1850.
BARN:	Barnwell. 16 July to 22 November 1850.
BEAU:	Beaufort, St. Helena Parish: 3 October to 10 December 1850. (Note: last page out of order)
BEAU*:	Beaufort, Prince Williams Parish (Whites). 6 September to 16 December 1850.
BEAU#:	Beafort, Prince Williams Parish (Free Black). 6 September to 16 December 1850. Pages 35-36)
BEAU+:	Beaufort, St. Lukes Parish. 16 September to 16 November 1850.
BEAU-:	Beaufort, St. Peters Parish. 12 July to 12 September 1850.
CHAS:	Charleston. City of Charleston, Ward 1, Parishes of St. Philips & St. Michael's. 1 August to 16 August 1850.
CHAS*:	Charleston. City of Charlteston, Ward 2. The Parish of St. Philips & St. Michael's. 20 August to 18 Auuust 1850.
CHAS-:	Charleston. City of Charleston, Parishes of St. Philips and St. Michael's, Ward 4. 10 October to 12 November 1850.
CHAS%:	Charleston. Charleston Neck, Parish of St. Philips & St. Michael's. 9 November to 22 December 1850.
CHAS#:	Charleston, Parish of St. James Santee. 23 July to 18 August 1850.
CHAS!:	Charleston, St. Andrews Parish. 26 August to 18 October 1850.
CHAS$:	Charleston. Christ Church Parish. 1 August to 20 September 1850. CHAS & Charleston, Parish of St.

Thomas and St. Dennis. November to 16 November 1850.

CHAS^:	Charleston, Parish of St. Johns, Colleton. 13 August to 23 October 1850.
CHAS-:	Charleston, St. Johns Berkley. 2 September to 12 October 1850.
CHAS2:	Charleston, St. Stephens Parish. 21 August to 19 November 1850.
CHAS3:	Charleston, St. James Goosecreek. 25 July to 26 November 1850.
CHES:	Chester. 22 July and 16 November 1850.
CHFD:	Chesterfield. 30 July to 13 January 1851.
COLL:	Colleton, St. Bartholomew's Parish. 14 August and 25 December 1850.
COLL*:	Colleton, St. George's Parish. 28 October to 16 November 1850.
COLL+:	Colleton, St. Paul's Parish. 21 October to 24 December 1850.
DARL:	Darlington, First Division. 26 July to January 1851.
EDGE:	Edgefield. 11 July to 19 December 1850.
EDGE*:	Edgefield. 23 October to 19 December 1850.
FAIR:	Fairfield. 13 July and 23 November 1850.
GEOR:	Georgetown, City of George Town. 19 August 1850.
GEOR*:	Georgetown, Prince George, Winyaw. 20 August to 22 August 1850.
GEOR+:	Georgetown, Lower All Saints. 23 August to 23 August 1850.
GREE:	Greeville. 22 July to 13 December 1850.
HORR:	Horry. 24 July and 4 November 1850.
KERS:	Kershaw. 19 July and 16 December 1850.

LANC:	Lancaster. 11 November to 16 November 1850.
LAU:	Laurens. 23 July to 13 December 1850.
LEX:	Lexington. 27 July to 13 October 1850.
MAR:	Marion. 19 July to 26 November 1850.
MARL:	Marlboro. 29 July and 15 October 1850.
NEWB:	Newberry. 18 July to 16 November 1850.
ORNG:	Orangeburg, between the River Road from Orangeburgh CH to Branchville and Four Hole Swamp. 13 December to 18 January 1851.
ORNG*:	Orangeburg, between Santee and Edisto North of Bellville Road. 12 November to 26 December 1850.
ORAN+:	Orangeburg, Orangeburg District. 29 July to 25 Dec. 1850.
PICK:	Pickens, Western Division. 26 July to 25 December 1850.
PICK+:	Pickens, Eastern Division. !9 July to 12 October 1850.
RICH:	Richland, Town of Columbia. 3 October to 28 October 1850.
RICH+:	Richland. 20 July to 1 October 1850.
SPART:	Spartanburg. 15 July to 18 December 1850.
SUMT:	Sumter. 19 July to 22 November 1850.
UNION:	Union. 17 July to 23 November 1850.
UNN+:	Union: 29 October to 21 November 1850.
WILL:	Williamsburg. 22 July to 22 November 1850.
YORK:	York. 29 July to 22 October 1850.
YORK*:	York. 22 July to 10 December 1850.

A

ABBOTT, ELIZA E., 24, F, None listed, -, Ireland, 466, 449, CHAS-.

ABBOTT, JOHN C., 30, M, Clerk, -, Ireland, 466, 449, CHAS-. In HH of Eliza E. Abbott f 24 born Ireland.

ABELS, NANCY, 60, F, None listed, -, Ireland, 213, 213, LAU. In HH of Robert S. Abels m 53 born VA.

ADAIR, MARY, 81, F, None listed, -, Ireland, 785, 823, PICK. In HH of Joseph Rother m 45 born SC.

ADAMS, ANN, 38, F, None listed, -, Ireland, 281, 287, RICH. In HH of Elizabeth Adams f 48 born Ireland.

ADAMS, CASSADY, 37, M, Laborer, -, Ireland, 1108, 1086, CHAS%.

ADAMS, ELIZABETH, 48, F, None listed, -, Ireland, 281, 287, RICH.

ADAMS, G., 55, F, None listed, -, Ireland, 10, 10, LANC. In HH of James Adams m 31, High Sheriff, born SC.

ADAMS, HANIE, 65, M, Farmer, -, Ireland, 44, 44, CHES.

ADAMS, JOHN, 7, M, None listed, -, Ireland, 1108, 1086, CHAS%. In HH of Cassady Adams m 37 born Ireland.

ADAMS, MARGARET, 31, F, None listed, -, Ireland, 1108, 1086, CHAS%. In HH of Cassady Adams m 37 born Ireland.

ADAMS, MARY, 27, F, None listed, -, Ireland, 474, 474, CHES. In HH of W.J. Adams m 25 born SC.

ADAMS, MARY, 58, F, None listed, -, Ireland, 44, 44, CHES. In HH of Hanie Adams m 65 born Ireland.

ADAMS, NANCY, 22, F, None listed, -, Ireland, 418, 418, CHES. In HH of J.A. Adams m 38 born SC.

ADDISON, ELIZABETH, 59, F, None listed, -, Ireland, 408, 406, CHAS%. In HH of John Addison m 34 born Ireland.

ADDISON, GEORGE, 50, M, Watch maker, -, Ireland, 91, 83, CHAS+.

ADDISON, JOHN, 34, M, Engineer, -, Ireland, 408, 406, CHAS%.

ADDISON, LOUISA, 30, F, None listed, -, Ireland, 408, 406, CHAS%. In HH of John Addison m 34 born Ireland.

ADDISON, MARY, 73, F, None listed, -, Ireland, 291, 297, Rick+.

ADDISON, MARY ANN, 12, F, None listed, -, Ireland, 408, 406, CHAS%. In HH of John Addison m 34 born Ireland.

ADGER, ELIZA, 23, F, None

listed, -, Ireland, 738, 739, FAIR. In HH of Joseph E. Adger m 25 born SC.

ADGER, JAMES, 73, M, Merchant, -, Ireland, 13, 13, CHAS%.

ADGER, SUSAN, 80, F, None listed, -, Ireland, 309, 315, RICH. In HH of William Law m 71 born Ireland.

AGNESS, MARY, 25, F, None listed, -, Ireland, 367, 340, CHAS*. In HH of Jose Stevens m 60 born Nassau N.P.

AGNEW, JOHN, 29, M, Merchant, -, Ireland, 689, 698, RICH.

AGNEW, LETITIA S., 36, F, None listed, -, Ireland, 1523, 1523, ABB. In HH of Enoch Agnew m 42 MD {A Dr.}, born SC.

AGNEW, ROBERT, 27, M, Student, -, Ireland, 445, 456, RICH.

AGNEW, SAMUEL T., 22, M, Clerk, -, Ireland, 389, 399, RICH. In HH of William Barkerloo m 23 born NY.

AIKEN, DAVID, 65, M, Planter, -, Ireland, 518, 518, FAIR.

AIKEN, HAMISH, 87, F, None listed, -, Ireland, 6, 6, CHES.

AIKEN, JANE, 40, F, None listed, -, Ireland, 429, 429, FAIR. In HH of John Aiken m 47 born SC.

AIKEN, MARGARET, 30, F, None listed, -, Ireland, 444, 444, FAIR. In HH of Hugh R. Aiken m 40 born SC.

AIKEN, NANCY, 55, F, None listed, -, Ireland, 846, 847, FAIR. In HH of Robert Aiken m 55 born Ireland.

AIKEN, NANCY, 57, F, None listed, -, Ireland, 518, 518, FAIR. In HH of David Aiken m 65 born Ireland.

AIKEN, ROBERT, 55, M, Planter, -, Ireland, 846, 847, FAIR.

AIRS, MARY, 25, F, None listed, -, Ireland, 474, 440, CHAS*. In HH of Eliza Flagg f 60 born SC.

ALEXANDER, WILLIAM, 21, M, Tailor, -, Ireland, 766, 766, ABB. In HH of James Shillito m 50 born SC.

ALGER, S., 22, M, Priv. U.S.A., -, Ireland, 47, 43, CHAS$. In HH of John Ewing m 50 born MA.

ALGUIRE, JOHN, 22, M, None listed, -, Ireland, 2231, 2231, ABB. In HH of Hugh M. Hardlan m 39 born SC.

ALLEN, GEORGE, 25, M, Laborer, -, Ireland, 322, 294, CHAS+. In HH of John Dowling m 34 born Ireland.

ALLEN, MARTHA, 30, F, None listed, -, Ireland, 1422, 1422, ABB. In HH of William Allen m 35 born Ireland.

2

ALLEN, WILLIAM, 26, M, Laborer, -, Ireland, 322, 294, CHAS+. In HH of John Dowling m 34 born Ireland.

ALLEN, WILLIAM, 35, M, Hireling, -, Ireland, 1422, 1422, ABB.

ALLISON, JOHN, 88, M, None listed, -, Ireland, 2334, 2334, SPART. In HH of James Allison m 26 born SC.

ALLWELL, GEORGE, 38, M, City Police, -, Ireland, 243, 228, CHAS+. In HH of John Conners m 30 born Ireland.

AMARN, ARCHEY, 8, M, None listed, -, Ireland, 537, 496, CHAS+. In HH of Ellen Kennedy f 36 born Ireland.

AMARN, ARTHUR, 38, M, Laborer, -, Ireland, 537, 496, CHAS+. In HH of Ellen Kennedy f 36 born Ireland.

AMARN, CATHERINE, 16, F, None listed, -, Ireland, 537, 496, CHAS+. In HH of Ellen Kennedy f 36 born Ireland.

AMARN, JOHN, 17, M, Laborer, -, Ireland, 537, 496, CHAS+. In HH of Ellen Kennedy f 36 born Ireland.

AMARN, MARGARET, 32, F, None listed, -, Ireland, 537, 496, CHAS+. In HH of Ellen Kennedy f 36 born Ireland.

AMARN, OHARA, 2, M, None listed, -, Ireland, 537, 496, CHAS+. In HH of Ellen Kennedy f 36 born Ireland.

AMARN, WILLIAM, 4, M, None listed, -, Ireland, 537, 496, CHAS+. In HH of Ellen Kennedy f 36 born Ireland.

ANDERSON, SUSANNA, 28, F, None listed, -, Ireland, 69, 69, NEWB. In HH of Mary Graham 52 f born SC

ANDERSON, WILLIAM, 78, M, None listed, -, Ireland, 885, 885, ABB.

ANDREWS, JANE, 30, F, None listed, -, Ireland, 1088, 1065, CHAS-. In HH of H.S. Hayden m 35 born CT.

ANDREWS, MATILDA, 19, F, None listed, -, Ireland, 154, 144, CHAS-. In HH of Catherine Gordon f 28 born MA.

ANGUS, BRIGET, 40, F, None listed, -, Ireland, 327, 301, CHAS*. In HH of John Angus m 46 born Ireland.

ANGUS, CAROLINE, 17, F, None listed, -, Ireland, 327, 301, CHAS*. In HH of John Angus m 46 born Ireland.

ANGUS, JOHN, 46, M, Bricklayer, -, Ireland, 327, 301, CHAS*.

ANGUS, MARY, 28, F, None listed, -, Ireland, 327, 301, CHAS*. In HH of John Angus m 46 born Ireland.

ANTHONY, JANE, 67, F, None listed, -, Ireland, 442, 439, CHAS%.

ANTONY, JANE, 80, F, None

listed, -, Ireland, 1644, 1644, EDGE. In HH of Lewis Clarke m 45 born NC.

APPLETON, WILLIAM, 22, M, Baker, -, Ireland, 269, 253, CHAS-. In HH of William Stratton m 44 born NY.

ARMSTRONG, JAMES, 33, M, Clerk, -, Ireland, 123, 114, CHAS+.

ARMSTRONG, JAMES B., 23, M, Clerk, -, Ireland, 540, 523, CHAS-. In Merchants Hotel.

ARMSTRONG, JANE, 36, F, None listed, -, Ireland, 1117, 1117, YORK. In HH of Jesse K. Armstrong m 54 born York Dist., SC.

ARMSTRONG, MAR-GARET, 40, F, None listed, -, Ireland, 852, 892, PICK.

ARMSTRONG, WILLIAM, 21, M, Clerk, -, Ireland, 540, 523, CHAS-. In Merchants Hotel.

ARNOLD, JOHN, 30, M, Stone cutter, -, Ireland, 20, 23, CHAS. In HH of Rachael Tunno f 70 black born SC.

ARNOLD, R., 35, M, Clerk, -, Ireland, 2276, 2276, SPART. In HH of Minor McConnly m 30 born SC.

ASHBY, ELLEN, 29, F, None listed, -, Ireland, 400, 411, RICH. In HH of Lewis P. Ashby m 29 born SC.

ATON, ANN, 8, F, None

listed, -, Ireland, 323, 294, CHAS+. In HH of Charles Aton m 65 born Ireland.

ATON, CHARLES, 65, M, Laborer, -, Ireland, 323, 294, CHAS+.

ATON, JAMES, 20, M, Stone cutter, -, Ireland, 323, 294, CHAS+. In HH of Charles Aton m 65 born Ireland.

ATON, JOHN, 23, M, None listed, -, Ireland, 323, 294, CHAS+. In HH of Charles Aton m 65 born Ireland.

ATON, MARGARET, 50, F, None listed, -, Ireland, 323, 294, CHAS+. In HH of Charles Aton m 65 born Ireland.

ATON, THOMAS, 18, M, Stone cutter, -, Ireland, 323, 294, CHAS+. In HH of Charles Aton m 65 born Ireland.

ATON, WILLIAM, 16, M, Stone cutter, -, Ireland, 323, 294, CHAS+. In HH of Charles Aton m 65 born Ireland.

AUSTIN, ALEXANDER, 57, M, Farmer, -, Ireland, 1495, 1495, ABB.

AUSTIN, ISABELLA, 31, F, None listed, -, Ireland, 1495, 1495, ABB. In HH of Alexander Austin m 57 born Ireland.

AUSTIN, JAMES SR., 60, M, Wagon Master, -, Ireland, 147, 147, LAU.

AUSTIN, R., 28, M, MD, -, Ireland, 61, 61, BARN.

AUSTIN, SAMUEL, 48, M, Farmer, -, Ireland, 1354, 1354, LAU.

AUSTIN, THOMAS, 48, M, Farmer, -, Ireland, 77, 77, LAU.

AUSTIN, WILLIAM, 49, M, Farmer, -, Ireland, 35, 35, LAU.

B

BAGLEY, WM. L., 27, M, Sadler, -, Ireland, 465, 422, CHAS. In HH of Leslie O'Wen m 47 born Ireland.

BAILEY, ANN, 70, F, None listed, -, Ireland, 12, 12, CHAS+. In HH of Caroline Douglas f 30 born GA.

BAILEY, JAMES, 28, M, House Carpenter, -, Ireland, 784, 784, EDGE.

BAILEY, RICHARD, 27, M, Carpenter, -, Ireland, 1309, 1309, EDGE.

BAILEY, ROBERT, 38, M, Shoemaker, -, Ireland, 1237, 1237, GREE.

BAILEY, WILLIAM, 39, M, Cabinetmaker, -, Ireland, 397, 397, EDGE.

BAKER, JANE, 11, F, None listed, -, Ireland, 1000, 977, CHAS%. In HH of Thos. Baker m 35 born Ireland.

BAKER, LYDIA, 5, F, None listed, -, Ireland, 1000, 977, CHAS%. In HH of Thos. Baker m 35 born Ireland.

BAKER, MARY ANN, 26, F, None listed, -, Ireland, 1000, 977, CHAS%. In HH of Thos. Baker m 35 born Ireland.

BAKER, RICHARD, 44, M, Cath. Minister, -, Ireland, 885, 865, CHAS-.

BAKER, THOS., 35, M, Plasterer, -, Ireland, 1000, 977, CHAS%.

BARBER, ANN, 74, F, None listed, -, Ireland, 468, 426, CHAS.

BARKLEY, MARY, 91, F, None listed, -, Ireland, 479, 479, FAIR. In HH of S.G. Barkley m 54 born SC.

BARNES, ANDREW, 36, M, Laborer, -, Ireland, 120, 111, CHAS+. In HH of Mary Hays f 50 born Ireland.

BARNES, ANN, 1, F, None listed, -, Ireland, 874, 851, CHAS%. In HH of Thomas Barnes m 40 born Ireland.

BARNES, ANN, 30, F, None listed, -, Ireland, 120, 111, CHAS+. In HH of Mary Hays f 50 born Ireland.

BARNES, JAMES, 2, F, None listed, -, Ireland, 874, 851, CHAS%. In HH of Thomas Barnes m 40 born Ireland.

BARNES, JULIA, 28, F, None listed, -, Ireland, 874, 851, CHAS%. In HH of Thomas Barnes m 40 born Ireland.

BARNES, THOMAS, 40, M,

Laborer, -, Ireland, 874, 851, CHAS%.

BARNETT, DAVID T., 32, M, Blacksmith, -, Ireland, 1197, 1197, YORK.

BARR, JAMES, 37, M, Farmer, -, Ireland, 478, 478, CHES.

BARR, SARAH, 9? , F, Farmer, -, Ireland, 478, 478, CHES. In HH of James Barr m 37 born Ireland. Sarah listed after James Barr most likely wife, as next age listed is age 9, the 1860 census should be

BARRY, JAMES, 50, M, Farmer, -, Ireland, 346, 308, CHAS+. In Boarding house.

BAXTER, JAS., 35, M, Teacher, -, Ireland, 600, 600, CHES. In HH of James Carlisle m 54 born Ireland.

BAXTER, WILLIAM, 60, M, Farmer, -, Ireland, 539, 539, LAU.

BEATTIE, ANN, 45, F, None listed, -, Ireland, 567, 550, CHAS-.

BEATY, ARCHIBALD, 70, M, Planter, -, Ireland, 983, 984, FAIR.

BEATY, JANE, 56, F, None listed, -, Ireland, 983, 984, FAIR. In HH of Archibald Beaty m 70 born Ireland.

BECK, JOHN, 28, M, Ordinance man, -, Ireland, 1005, 982, CHAS%.Under command of Major P. Hagnes,

Comg. Off. U.S. Arnsel.

BECKETT, MARGARET, 87, F, None listed, -, Ireland, 578, 595, RICH. In HH of Eliza B. Waddell f 50 born SC.

BEESNER, DANIEL, 36, M, Laborer, -, Ireland, 406, 370, CHAS. In HH of Thomas Sullivan m 40 born Ireland.

BEGGARD, JAS., 67, M, Farmer, -, Ireland, 352, 352, KERS.

BEHAN, THOMAS, 40, M, Gardener, -, Ireland, 1158, 1137, CHAS%.

BELL, ALEX., 33, M, Farmer, -, Ireland, 1326, 1326, LAU.

BELL, ELIZA, 47, F, None listed, -, Ireland, 67, 67, FAIR. In HH of Thomas R. Bell m 25 born SC.

BELL, JAMES, 22, M, Farmer, -, Ireland, 969, 969, LAU.

BELL, JAMES, 74, M, Farmer, -, Ireland, 703, 704, AND*.

BELL, JOHN, 32, M, None listed, -, Ireland, 1326, 1326, LAU. In HH of Alex Bell m 33 born Ireland.

BELL, MARGARET, 20, F, None listed, -, Ireland, 1326, 1326, LAU. In HH of Alex Bell m 33 born Ireland.

BELL, ROBERT, 84, M, Farmer, -, Ireland, 1327, 1327, LAU.

BELL, SARAH, 77, F, None listed, -, Ireland, 1326, 1326, LAU. In HH of Alex Bell m 33 born Ireland.

BELL, WILLIAM, 21, M, Mason, -, Ireland, 185, 168, CHAS. In HH of S. Morrison m 30 born Ireland.

BELL, WM. C., 20, M, Acct., -, Ireland, 55, 55, KERS. In Hotel.

BELMAIN, HONORIA, 24, F, None listed, -, Ireland, 269, 253, CHAS-. In HH of William Stratton m 44 born NY.

BELMAIN, HONORIE, 24, F, None listed, -, Ireland, 6, 6, CHAS$. In HH of William Belmain m 36 born Scotland.

BERNARD, MARY, 40, F, None listed, -, Ireland, 1195, 1174, CHAS%. In HH of Catherine LeBruce f 52 born SC.

BERRY, BRIDGET, 14, F, None listed, -, Ireland, 805, 788, CHAS%. In HH of John Berry m 50 born Ireland.

BERRY, DAN, 9, M, None listed, -, Ireland, 805, 788, CHAS%. In HH of John Berry m 50 born Ireland.

BERRY, JOHN, 6, M, None listed, -, Ireland, 804, 787, CHAS%. In HH of John Berry m 35 born Ireland.

BERRY, JOHN, 35, M, Laborer, -, Ireland, 804, 787, CHAS%.

BERRY, JOHN, 50, M, Drayman, -, Ireland, 805, 788, CHAS%.

BERRY, MARGARET, 32, F, None listed, -, Ireland, 804, 787, CHAS%. In HH of John Berry m 35 born Ireland.

BERRY, MARY, 18, F, None listed, -, Ireland, 805, 788, CHAS%. In HH of John Berry m 50 born Ireland.

BERRY, REDMOND, 7, M, None listed, -, Ireland, 805, 788, CHAS%. In HH of John Berry m 50 born Ireland.

BERRY, ROBERT, 8, M, None listed, -, Ireland, 804, 787, CHAS%. In HH of John Berry m 35 born Ireland.

BIGLEY, WILLIAM, 22, M, Clerk, -, Ireland, 170, 153, CHAS. In HH of John Young m 23 born SC.

BILFORD, ARCHD.F., 23, M, Carpenter, -, Ireland, 390, 354, CHAS. In HH of Hugh ONeile m 30 born Ireland.

BINLY, A.B., 28, M, Priv. U.S.A., -, Ireland, 47, 43, CHAS$. In HH of John Ewing m 50 born MA.

BLACK, ANN, 14, F, None listed, -, Ireland, 524, 524, FAIR. In HH of William Carley m 38 born Ireland.

BLACK, FANNY, 15, F, None listed, -, Ireland, 524, 524, FAIR. In HH of William Carley m 38 born Ireland.

BLACK, GEORGE, 37, M, Bricklayer, -, Ireland, 476, 459, CHAS-.

BLACK, MARY, 59, F, None listed, -, Ireland, 1239, 1239, UNION.

BLACK, NANCY, 88, F, None listed, -, Ireland, 87, 87, CHES. In HH of Joseph Black m 46 born SC.

BLAIN, HENRIETTA, 21, F, None listed, -, Ireland, 52, 48, CHAS-. In HH of S.E.F. Blain f 35 born Ireland.

BLAIN, JOSEPH, 18, M, None listed, -, Ireland, 52, 48, CHAS-. In HH of S.E.F. Blain f 35 born Ireland.

BLAIN, LOUISA, 14, F, None listed, -, Ireland, 52, 48, CHAS-. In HH of S.E.F. Blain f 35 born Ireland.

BLAIN, S.E.L., 35, F, None listed, -, Ireland, 52, 48, CHAS-.

BLAIR, ANDREW, 14, M, None listed, -, Ireland, 1261, 1261, YORK. In HH of James Blair m 45 born Ireland.

BLAIR, ELIZABETH, 31, F, None listed, -, Ireland, 432, 432, FAIR. In HH of William Blair m 40 born SC.

BLAIR, JAMES, 10, M, None listed, -, Ireland, 1261, 1261, YORK. In HH of James Blair m 45 born Ireland.

BLAIR, JAMES, 45, M, Farmer, -, Ireland, 1261, 1261,

YORK.

BLAIR, JOHN, 16, M, None listed, -, Ireland, 1261, 1261, YORK. In HH of James Blair m 45 born Ireland.

BLAIR, LATTICIA, 35, F, None listed, -, Ireland, 1261, 1261, YORK. In HH of James Blair m 45 born Ireland.

BLAIR, NANCEY, 68, F, None listed, -, Ireland, 62, 62, YORK+.

BLAIR, SAMUEL, 13, M, None listed, -, Ireland, 1261, 1261, YORK. In HH of James Blair m 45 born Ireland.

BLAKE, JOHN, 33, M, Carpenter, -, Ireland, 189, 189, CHAS%.

BLAKE, JUDY, 25, F, None listed, -, Ireland, 189, 189, CHAS%. In HH of John Blake m 33 born Ireland.

BLAKE, MARY, 17, F, None listed, -, Ireland, 189, 189, CHAS%. In HH of John Blake m 33 born Ireland.

BLAKE, MARY, 21, F, None listed, -, Ireland, 863, 821, CHAS+. In HH of E. Pringle f 51 born SC.

BLAKE, NANCY, 50, F, None listed, -, Ireland, 189, 189, CHAS%. In HH of John Blake m 33 born Ireland.

BLAKE, PETER, 18, M, None listed, -, Ireland, 189, 189, CHAS%. In HH of John Blake m 33 born Ireland.

8

BLAKELY, HUGHEY, 29, M, Laborer, -, Ireland, 1138, 1138, UNION. In HH of Esther Stewart f 56 born Ireland.

BLAKELY, MARY, 21, F, None listed, -, Ireland, 1138, 1138, UNION. In HH of Esther Stewart f 56 born Ireland.

BLAKLEY, M.J., 24, F, None listed, -, Ireland, 535, 535, CHES. In HH of J.L. Houerton m 35 born VA.

BLANCHFIELD, JOANA, 34, F, None listed, -, Ireland, 841, 821, CHAS-. In HH of Samuel Dykes m 40 born England.

BLUNTEL, ROSANA, 15, F, None listed, -, Ireland, 846, 826, CHAS-. In HH of William Ashton m 38 born England.

BLYTHE, BRIDGET, 40, F, None listed, -, Ireland, 148, 148, CHAS%. In HH of Patrick Blythe m 19 born Ireland.

BLYTHE, CATHERINE, 20, F, None listed, -, Ireland, 148, 148, CHAS%. In HH of Patrick Blythe m 19 born Ireland.

BLYTHE, JOHN, 6, M, None listed, -, Ireland, 148, 148, CHAS%. In HH of Patrick Blythe m 19 born Ireland.

BLYTHE, PATRICK, 19, M, Laborer, -, Ireland, 148, 148, CHAS%.

BODIFORD, ISABELLA, 77, F, None listed, -, Ireland, 562, 562, NEWB. In HH of J.W. McLeod m 32 Born SC.

BOLAND, GEORGE, 33, M, Mechanic, -, Ireland, 471, 486, RICH.

BOLGER, CAROLINE, 50, F, None listed, -, Ireland, 358, 330, CHAS. In HH of Tho. W. Bolger m 60 born Ireland.

BOLGER, HENRY H., 31, M, Cabinet maker, -, Ireland, 140, 140, CHAS%.

BOLGER, MARY, 33, F, None listed, -, Ireland, 140, 140, CHAS%. In HH of Henry H. Bolger m 31 born Ireland.

BOLGER, MICHAEL, 29, M, Sadler, -, Ireland, 94, 106, CHAS.

BOLGER, SARAH, 50, F, None listed, -, Ireland, 480, 446, CHAS*. In HH of Rt. Revd. Jgn. A. Reynolds m 51 born KY.

BOLGER, THO. W., 60, M, Sadler, -, Ireland, 358, 330, CHAS.

BONNEFACE, CATHER-INE, 30, F, None listed, -, Ireland, 76, 68, CHAS+. In HH of D.L. McCarthy m 30 born Ireland.

BOSWELL, MARY, 80, F, None listed, -, Ireland, 1479, 1479, YORK.

BOUCHER, ELLEN, 25, F, None listed, -, Ireland, 373, 346, CHAS*. In HH of G.G.

Blackwood m 24 born SC.

BOWEN, ELLEN, 25, F, None listed, -, Ireland, 292, 292, CHAS%. In HH of Henry McGuire m 35 born Ireland.

BOWEN, JOHN, 27, M, Laborer, -, Ireland, 292, 292, CHAS%. In HH of Henry McGuire m 35 born Ireland.

BOWEN, SUSAN, 59, F, None listed, -, Ireland, 774, 774, YORK.

BOYCE, JEROME, 30, M, Laborer, -, Ireland, 471, 429, CHAS+.

BOYCE, JOHN, 26, M, Drayman, -, Ireland, 341, 341, CHAS%.

BOYCE, MARIA, 28, F, None listed, -, Ireland, 471, 429, CHAS+. In HH of Jerome Boyce m 30 born Ireland.

BOYCE, MARY, 27, F, None listed, -, Ireland, 341, 341, CHAS%. In HH of John Boyce m 26 born Ireland.

BOYD, CHARLES, 65, M, Farmer, -, Ireland, 1070, 1070, CHES.

BOYD, DANIEL, 73, M, Farmer, -, Ireland, 944, 944, ABB.

BOYD, JAMES, 25, M, Mason, -, Ireland, 185, 168, CHAS. In HH of S. Morrison m 30 born Ireland.

BOYD, JOHN, 40, M, None listed, -, Ireland, 345, 345, FAIR. In HH of Margaret

Boyd f 76 born Ireland.

BOYD, MARGARET, 76, F, None listed, -, Ireland, 345, 345, FAIR.

BOYD, MARY, 40, F, None listed, -, Ireland, 345, 345, FAIR. In HH of Margaret Boyd f 76 born Ireland.

BOYD, MARY, 53, F, None listed, -, Ireland, 109, 109, YORK. In HH of Thomas Boyd m 52 born Ireland.

BOYD, MARY A., 60, F, None listed, -, Ireland, 1100, 1100, CHES.

BOYD, ROBERT, 46, M, Farmer, -, Ireland, 946, 946, ABB.

BOYD, THOMAS, 52, M, Farmer, -, Ireland, 109, 109, YORK.

BOYD, WILLIAM, 24, M, Planter, -, Ireland, 343, 343, FAIR.

BOYD, WILLIAM, 25, M, Farmer, -, Ireland, 944, 944, ABB. In HH of Daniel Boyd m 73 born Ireland.

BOYLAN, PHILIP, 29, M, Clerk, -, Ireland, 270, 254, CHAS-. In HH of Thomas E. Baker m 50 born VA.

BOYLE, EDWARD, 23, M, Waiter, -, Ireland, 326, 301, CHAS. On Steam Ship Southerner.

BOYLE, MICHAEL, 31, M, Priv. U.S.A., -, Ireland, 47, 43, CHAS$. In HH of John Ewing m 50 born MA.

BOYS, ELIZABETH, 68, F, None listed, -, Ireland, 2066, 2066, GREE. In HH of John Boys m 70 born Ireland.

BOYS, JOHN, 70, M, Farmer, -, Ireland, 2066, 2066, GREE.

BRACKENRIDGE, ROBERT, 69, M, Farmer, -, Ireland, 347, 348, AND*.

BRADFORD, WM., 30, M, Farmer, -, Ireland, 22, 22, CHES.

BRADLEY, JOHN W., 48, M, Merchant, -, Ireland, 624, 642, RICH.

BRADLEY, PATRICK, 26, M, Painter, -, Ireland, 346, 308, CHAS+. In Boarding house.

BRADSHAW, JAMES, 17, M, Student, -, Ireland, 2338, 2338, GREE. In HH of William Erwin m 32 born Ireland.

BRADY, ANN, 35, F, None listed, -, Ireland, 269, 250, CHAS+. In HH of John Brady m 50 born Ireland.

BRADY, CATHERINE, 40, F, None listed, -, Ireland, 401, 361, CHAS+.

BRADY, ELLEN, 39, F, None listed, -, Ireland, 165, 155, CHAS-.

BRADY, JOHN, 50, M, Wharfinger, -, Ireland, 269, 250, CHAS+.

BRADY, MARY, 30, F, None listed, -, Ireland, 207, 189, CHAS*. In HH of Patrick Brady m 49 born Ireland.

BRADY, PATRICK, 22, M, Driver, -, Ireland, 124, 115, CHAS+. In Boarding house.

BRADY, PATRICK, 49, M, Shop keeper, -, Ireland, 207, 189, CHAS*.

BRADY, PATRICK, 56, M, Lumber Merchant, -, Ireland, 269, 250, CHAS+. In HH of John Brady m 50 born Ireland.

BRALTRO, ELLEN, 21, F, Servant, -, Ireland, 882, 840, CHAS+. In Charleston Hotel.

BRALTRO, LATTAH, 24, F, Servant, -, Ireland, 882, 840, CHAS+. In Charleston Hotel.

BRALTRO, MARY, 28, F, Servant, -, Ireland, 882, 840, CHAS+. In Charleston Hotel.

BRAMAN, BERNARD, 30, M, Stone Mason, -, Ireland, 1404, 1404, CHES.

BRANYON, JOHN M., 58, M, Planter, -, Ireland, 542, 557, RICH. Date 1849 by name. In Lunatic Asylum.

BRASSELL, JOHN, 20, M, Laborer, -, Ireland, 748, 706, CHAS+. In HH of H.A. Mayer m 45 born Ireland.

BREMAR, ANN, 22, F, None listed, -, Ireland, 183, 167, CHAS*. In HH of John Bremar m 34 born Germany.

BREMAR, CATHERINE, 22, F, None listed, -, Ireland, 553, 519, CHAS*. In Catholic

Seminary.

BRENAN, LUKE, 26, M, Laborer, -, Ireland, 137, 125, CHAS*.

BRENAN, M., 25, M, Priv. U.S.A., -, Ireland, 47, 43, CHAS$. In HH of John Ewing m 50 born MA.

BRENAN, MARY, 20, F, None listed, -, Ireland, 137, 125, CHAS*. In HH of Luke Brenan m 26 born Ireland.

BRENAN, MARY, 27, F, None listed, -, Ireland, 241, 227, CHAS+. In HH of James Kennedy m 30 born Ireland.

BRENNAN, PATRICK, 58, M, Merchant, -, Ireland, 686, 705, RICH. Date of 1849 by name.

BRENNET, CATHERINE, 18, F, None listed, -, Ireland, 257, 257, CHAS%. In HH of Michael Moran m 40 born Ireland.

BRENNET, THOMAS, 30, M, Laborer, -, Ireland, 257, 257, CHAS%. In HH of Michael Moran m 40 born Ireland.

BRENNOCK, WM. M., 24, M, Shop keeper, -, Ireland, 978, 958, CHAS-.

BRENNON, PATRICK, 25, M, Student, -, Ireland, 300, 300, FAIR. In HH of Charles Martin m 43 born SC.

BRICE, ELIZABETH, 25, F, None listed, -, Ireland, 671,

672, FAIR. In HH of John Brice m 48 born Ireland.

BRICE, GRACE, 9, F, None listed, -, Ireland, 671, 672, FAIR. In HH of John Brice m 48 born Ireland.

BRICE, HANNAH, 26, F, None listed, -, Ireland, 671, 672, FAIR. In HH of John Brice m 48 born Ireland.

BRICE, JOHN, 48, M, Planter, -, Ireland, 671, 672, FAIR.

BRICE, MARY, 35, F, None listed, -, Ireland, 671, 672, FAIR. In HH of John Brice m 48 born Ireland.

BRICE, MARY J., 39, F, None listed, -, Ireland, 1009, 1054, PICK. In HH of Allexnader Brice m 47 born SC.

BRICE, WILLIAM, 20, M, None listed, -, Ireland, 671, 672, FAIR. In HH of John Brice m 48 born Ireland.

BRIDE, CATHERINE, 28, F, None listed, -, Ireland, 119, 110, CHAS+. In HH of William Condell m 34 born Ireland.

BRIDE, MICHAEL, 30, M, Laborer, -, Ireland, 119, 110, CHAS+. In HH of William Condell m 34 born Ireland.

BRODIE, ALEXANDER, 66, M, Planter, -, Ireland, 833, 843, RICH+.

BRODIE, CHARLOTTE, 55, F, None listed, -, Ireland, 833, 843, RICH+. In HH of Alexander Brodie m 66 born Ireland.

BRODIE, JR., ALEXANDER, 39, M, Merchant, -, Ireland, 327, 333, RICH.

BROTHEY, ANN, 29, F, Servant, -, Ireland, 285, 262, CHAS. In Planters Hotel.

BROWN, ABRAM, 38, M, Farmer, -, Ireland, 1002, 1002, CHES.

BROWN, ALFRED L., 28, M, Merchant, -, Ireland, 836, 816, CHAS-. In Boarding house.

BROWN, EDWARD, 32, M, Ordinance man, -, Ireland, 1005, 982, CHAS%.Under command of Major P. Hagnes, Comg. Off. U.S. Arnsel.

BROWN, ELISZ, 58, F, None listed, -, Ireland, 83, 83, CHES. In HH of Eliza Brown m 67 born VA.

BROWN, ELIZA, 10, F, None listed, -, Ireland, 1002, 1002, CHES. In HH of Abram Brown m 38 born Ireland.

BROWN, ELLEN, 36, F, None listed, -, Ireland, 1002, 1002, CHES. In HH of Abram Brown m 38 born Ireland.

BROWN, HANNAH, 30, F, None listed, -, Ireland, 249, 234, CHAS+. In HH of John Brown m 36 born Ireland.

BROWN, JAMES, 14, M, Stone cutter, -, Ireland, 249, 234, CHAS+. In HH of John Brown m 36 born Ireland.

BROWN, JOHN, 36, M, Stone cutter, -, Ireland, 249, 234, CHAS+.

BROWN, MARGARET, 12, F, None listed, -, Ireland, 249, 234, CHAS+. In HH of John Brown m 36 born Ireland.

BROWN, MARTHA, 30, F, None listed, -, Ireland, 1005, 982, CHAS%.Under command of Major P. Hagnes, Comg. Off. U.S. Arnsel.

BROWN, MARY, 50, F, None listed, -, Ireland, 280, 286, RICH. In HH of Alexander Brown m 58 born Scotland.

BROWN, ROBT., 55, M, Shoemaker, -, Ireland, 596, 596, CHES. In HH of James Boyd m 38 born SC.

BROWN, SARAH, 50, F, None listed, -, Ireland, 596, 596, CHES. In HH of James Boyd m 38 born SC.

BROWNING, ELIZA, 40, F, None listed, -, Ireland, 1025, 1002, CHAS-. In HH of Charles Seyle m 32 born SC.

BRUAN, BRIDGET, 70, F, None listed, -, Ireland, 743, 744, FAIR. In HH of Alfred Clark m 33 born Ct.

BRUAN, IRSTUM, 29, M,

Planter, -, Ireland, 743, 744, FAIR. In HH of Alfred Clark m 33 born CT.

BRUAN, MARTHA, 30, F, None listed, -, Ireland, 743, 744, FAIR. In HH of Alfred Clark m 33 born Ct.

BRUCE, HUGH, 51, M, Farmer, -, Ireland, 598, 598, CHES.

BRUEN, MARY, 21, F, None listed, -, Ireland, 877, 856, CHAS-. In HH of Rufus Fairchild m 40 born PA.

BRYAN, ANDREW, 25, M, Shoe maker, -, Ireland, 388, 350, CHAS+.

BRYAN, CATHERINE, 23, F, None listed, -, Ireland, 388, 350, CHAS+. In HH of Andrew Bryan m 25 born Ireland.

BRYAN, LUKE, 19, M, Laborer, -, Ireland, 388, 350, CHAS+. In HH of Andrew Bryan m 25 born Ireland.

BUCKLEY, CATHERINE, 40, F, None listed, -, Ireland, 415, 374, CHAS+. In HH of Caroline Segee f 30 born Ireland.

BUCKLEY, D., 35, M, Carter, -, Ireland, 24, 22, CHAS$.

BUCKLEY, MARY, 28, F, None listed, -, Ireland, 24, 22, CHAS$. In HH of D. Buckley m 35 born Ireland.

BULKLEY, JAMES, 32, M, Shop keeper, -, Ireland, 397,

381, CHAS-. In HH of Edward Cassady m 30 born Ireland.

BULL, SARAH, 56, F, None listed, -, Ireland, 314, 314, ABB. In HH of John B. Bull m 58 born SC.

BUNCKARD, JANE A., 30, F, None listed, -, Ireland, 67, 66, CHAS*. In HH of William Bunckard m 40 born Ireland.

BUNCKARD, WILLIAM, 40, M, Bricklayer, -, Ireland, 67, 66, CHAS*.

BURDEN, BRIDGET, 40, F, None listed, -, Ireland, 407, 371, CHAS. In HH of Thomas Burden m 45 born Ireland.

BURDEN, THOMAS, 45, M, Shoemaker, -, Ireland, 407, 371, CHAS.

BURDIN, EDWARD, 26, M, Laborer, -, Ireland, 405, 369, CHAS. In HH of William Doran m 36 born MA.

BURGESS, THOS., 67, M, Planter, -, Ireland, 349, 349, SUMT.

BURK, ANDREW, 34, M, Laborer, -, Ireland, 166, 148, CHAS. In HH of John Jenkins m 25 born England.

BURK, JAMES, 20, M, Laborer, -, Ireland, 166, 148, CHAS. In HH of John Jenkins m 25 born England.

BURK, JOHN, 25, M, Laborer, -, Ireland, 166, 148, CHAS. In HH of John Jenkins m 25 born England.

BURKE, CATHERINA, 30, F, None listed, -, Ireland, 486, 443, CHAS. In HH of John Burke m 35 born Ireland.

BURKE, EDWARD, 30, M, Laborer, -, Ireland, 464, 461, CHAS%. In HH of Thomas Cantwell m 45 born Ireland.

BURKE, ELLEN, 22, F, None listed, -, Ireland, 474, 432, CHAS. In HH of William Ryan m 56 born Ireland.

BURKE, JAMES, 21, M, Shop keeper, -, Ireland, 978, 958, CHAS-. In HH of Wm. M. Brennock m 24 born Ireland.

BURKE, JOHN, 35, M, Clerk, -, Ireland, 486, 443, CHAS.

BURKE, JOHN, 35, M, Laborer, -, Ireland, 409, 368, CHAS+. In HH of Thomas Herbert m 27 born Ireland.

BURKE, JOHN, 35, M, Laborer, -, Ireland, 463, 446, CHAS-. In HH of James Ryan m 30 born Ireland.

BURKE, JOHN, 38, M, Laborer, -, Ireland, 464, 461, CHAS%. In HH of Thomas Cantwell m 45 born Ireland.

BURKE, L., 30, M, Store keeper, -, Ireland, 850, 830, CHAS-.

BURKE, MARY, 20, F, None listed, -, Ireland, 399, 382, CHAS-. In HH of Richard Smith m 60 born MD.

BURKE, MICHAEL, 27, M, Clerk, -, Ireland, 474, 432, CHAS. In HH of William Ryan m 56 born Ireland.

BURKE, ORMSLEY, 52, M, Shop keeper., -, Ireland, 328, 311, CHAS-.

BURKE, PETER, 9, M, None listed, -, Ireland, 16, 19, CHAS. In HH of Catherine Murphy 28 f born Ireland.

BURKE, THOMAS, 24, M, Store keeper, -, Ireland, 850, 830, CHAS-. In HH of L. Burke m 30 born Ireland.

BURKE, WILLIAM, 8, M, None listed, -, Ireland, 16, 19, CHAS. In HH of Catherine Murphy 28 f born Ireland.

BURNES, MARY, 18, F, None listed, -, Ireland, 925, 902, CHAS%. In HH of Emeline Taylor f 45 born SC.

BURNES, WILLIAM, 11, M, None listed, -, Ireland, 1415, 1415, ABB. In HH of David Moore m 37 born Ireland.

BURNET, ROBERT, 22, M, None listed, -, Ireland, 436, 436, ABB. In HH of Robert Belcher 39 born SC.

BURNS, ANN, 20, F, None listed, -, Ireland, 127, 118, CHAS+. In Boarding house.

BURNS, ANN, 24, F, None listed, -, Ireland, 714, 704, CHAS%. In HH of John Burns m 28 born Ireland.

BURNS, ANN, 60, F, None

listed, -, Ireland, 429, 398, CHAS*. In HH of Garret Burns m 23 born Ireland.

BURNS, ELIZABETH, 27, F, None listed, -, Ireland, 542, 557, RICH. Date 1850 by name. In Lunatic Asylum.

BURNS, ELLEN, 24, F, None listed, -, Ireland, 438, 421, CHAS-. In Pavillion Hotel.

BURNS, GARRET, 23, M, Shoemaker, -, Ireland, 429, 398, CHAS*.

BURNS, GARRET, 34, M, Shop keeper, -, Ireland, 166, 157, CHAS+.

BURNS, JAMES, 30, M, Shoemaker, -, Ireland, 429, 398, CHAS*. In HH of Garret Burns m 23 born Ireland.

BURNS, JOHN, 28, M, Laborer, -, Ireland, 714, 704, CHAS%.

BURNS, PATRICK, 35, M, Cooper, -, Ireland, 1990, 1996, EDGE.

BURRELL, ELIZABETH, 50, F, None listed, -, Ireland, 141, 129, CHAS*. In HH of William Jennings m 30 born SC.

BUSBY?, ROBERT, 67, M, Farmer, -, Ireland, 889, 889, GREE.

BUTLER, ANDREW, 40, M, Laborer, -, Ireland, 338, 303, CHAS+. In HH of Bernard Sweeney m 37 born Ireland.

BUTLER, JOHN, 37, M, Tailor, -, Ireland, 490, 485, CHAS%.

BUTLER, MARÝ, 30, F, None listed, -, Ireland, 490, 485, CHAS%. In HH of John Butler m 37 born Ireland.

BUTLER, MORRIS, 35, M, Laborer, -, Ireland, 144, 135, CHAS+. In HH of Daniel Larry m 30 born Ireland.

BUTTER, EDWARD, 63, M, Planter, -, Ireland, 155, 155, BEAU.

BUTTER, ELISA, 60, F, None listed, -, Ireland, 155, 155, BEAU. In HH of Edward Butter m 63 born Ireland.

BYERS, JANE, 22, F, None listed, -, Ireland, 845, 825, CHAS-. In HH of B. Lynap m 33 born Ireland.

BYERS, JOHN, 28, M, Mariner, -, Ireland, 845, 825, CHAS-. In HH of B. Lynap m 33 born Ireland.

BYRN, JOHN, 28, M, Carpenter, -, Ireland, 38, 33, CHAS+. In Boarding house.

BYRNE, JOHN K., 38, M, Teacher, -, Ireland, 1099, 1104, MAR. In HH of Joseph Bird.

BYRNES, MARY, 23, F, Servant, -, Ireland, 882, 840, CHAS+. In Charleston Hotel.

C

CABEEN, JAMES, 17, M, None listed, -, Ireland, 672,

673, FAIR. In HH of Sarah Cabeen f 46 born Ireland.

CABEEN, NANCY, 19, F, None listed, -, Ireland, 672, 673, FAIR. In HH of Sarah Cabeen f 46 born Ireland.

CABEEN, RICHARD, 37, M, Planter, -, Ireland, 686, 687, FAIR. In HH of Lamuel Bryce m 41 born SC.

CABEEN, SARAH, 46, F, None listed, -, Ireland, 672, 673, FAIR.

CABEEN, WALTER B., 21, M, None listed, -, Ireland, 672, 673, FAIR. In HH of Sarah Cabeen f 46 born Ireland.

CAFFRY, ANN, 8, F, None listed, -, Ireland, 307, 284, CHAS. In HH of Dennis O Caffry m 45 born Ireland.

CAFFRY, DENNIS, 18, M, None listed, -, Ireland, 307, 284, CHAS. In HH of Dennis O Caffry m 45 born Ireland.

CAFFRY, DENNIS O., 45, M, Laborer, -, Ireland, 307, 284, CHAS.

CAFFRY, MIKE, 28, M, Laborer, -, Ireland, 307, 284, CHAS. In HH of Dennis O Caffry m 45 born Ireland.

CAFFRY, PATRICK, 14, M, None listed, -, Ireland, 307, 284, CHAS. In HH of Dennis O Caffry m 45 born Ireland.

CAFFRY, PATSEY, 38, F, None listed, -, Ireland, 307, 284, CHAS. In HH of Dennis

O Caffry m 45 born Ireland.

CAFFRY, RACHEL, 26, F, None listed, -, Ireland, 307, 284, CHAS. In HH of Dennis O Caffry m 45 born Ireland.

CAGNEY, CHARLOTTE, 49, F, None listed, -, Ireland, 743, 731, CHAS%. In HH of John Cagney m 53 born Ireland.

CAGNEY, ELIZABETH, 21, F, None listed, -, Ireland, 743, 731, CHAS%. In HH of John Cagney m 53 born Ireland.

CAGNEY, JOHN, 53, M, Teacher, -, Ireland, 743, 731, CHAS%.

CAHAL, JAMES, 35, M, None listed, -, Ireland, 33, 29, CHAS$.

CAHAL, THOMAS, 24, M, Carpenter, -, Ireland, 38, 34, CHAS$. In HH of Mary McKuon f 40 born Ireland.

CAHILL, ELLEN, 4, F, None listed, -, Ireland, 281, 261, CHAS+. In HH of John Cahill m 45 born Ireland.

CAHILL, ELLEN, 40, F, None listed, -, Ireland, 281, 261, CHAS+. In HH of John Cahill m 45 born Ireland.

CAHILL, JAMES, 16, M, None listed, -, Ireland, 281, 261, CHAS+. In HH of John Cahill m 45 born Ireland.

CAHILL, JOHN, 45, M, Laborer, -, Ireland, 281, 261, CHAS+.

CAHILL, STEPHEN, 50, M,

Laborer, -, Ireland, 282, 261, CHAS+.

CAIRN, JOHN, 34, M, R.R. Laborer, -, Ireland, 987, 964, CHAS%. In Boarding house.

CAIRNES, ELIZA, 35, F, None listed, -, Ireland, 1486, 1486, YORK. In HH of Robert Cairnes m 35 born Ireland.

CAIRNES, JOHN, 42, M, Farmer, -, Ireland, 1487, 1487, YORK.

CAIRNES, ROBERT, 35, M, Farmer, -, Ireland, 1486, 1486, YORK.

CAIRNES, SUSAN, 27, F, None listed, -, Ireland, 1486, 1486, YORK. In HH of Robert Cairnes m 35 born Ireland.

CALDWELL, ELIZABAETH {sic}, 35, F, None listed, -, Ireland, 975, 976, FAIR. In HH of John Caldwell m 40 born Ireland.

CALDWELL, GALBRAITH, 65, M, Farmer, -, Ireland, 1528, 1528, YORK.

CALDWELL, JAMES, 60, M, Farmer, -, Ireland, 990, 990, YORK.

CALDWELL, JAMES E., 49, M, Planter, -, Ireland, 226, 226, FAIR.

CALDWELL, JOHN, 8, M, None listed, -, Ireland, 975, 976, FAIR. In HH of John Caldwell m 40 born Ireland.

CALDWELL, JOHN, 40, M, Planter, -, Ireland, 975, 976,

FAIR.

CALDWELL, JOSEPH, 87, M, None listed, -, Ireland, 164, 166, AND.

CALDWELL, NANCY, 24, F, None listed, -, Ireland, 938, 939, FAIR. In HH of William Caldwell m 30 born Ireland.

CALDWELL, ROBERT, 63, M, Farmer, -, Ireland, 223, 223, YORK*.

CALDWELL, ROBERT, 65, M, Farmer, -, Ireland, 990, 990, YORK. In HH of James Caldwell m 60 born Ireland.

CALDWELL, THOMAS, 67, M, Farmer, -, Ireland, 489, 489, COLL.

CALDWELL, WILLIAM, 30, M, Planter, -, Ireland, 938, 939, FAIR.

CALHOUN, HUGH, 32, M, Carpenter, -, Ireland, 2379, 2379, ABB.

CALLAGHAN, BRIGET, 30, F, None listed, -, Ireland, 300, 277, CHAS+. In HH of Dennis Callaghan m 43 born Ireland.

CALLAGHAN, CHARLES, 35, M, Laborer, -, Ireland, 240, 226, CHAS+. In HH of William Farley m 38 born Ireland.

CALLAGHAN, DAN, 26, M, Laborer, -, Ireland, 300, 277, CHAS+. In HH of Dennis Callaghan m 43 born Ireland.

CALLAGHAN, DENNIS, 24, M, Drayman, -, Ireland, 507,

465, CHAS+. In HH of H. Bruns m 24 born Germany.

CALLAGHAN, DENNIS, 28, M, Laborer, -, Ireland, 202, 190, CHAS+. In Boarding house.

CALLAGHAN, DENNIS, 43, M, Laborer, -, Ireland, 300, 277, CHAS+.

CALLAGHAN, DIRMOT, 34, M, Laborer, -, Ireland, 300, 277, CHAS+. In HH of Dennis Callaghan m 43 born Ireland.

CALLAGHAN, DORR-ANCE, 7, M, None listed, -, Ireland, 304, 281, CHAS. In HH of John O Callaghan m 37 born Ireland.

CALLAGHAN, FANNY, 30, F, None listed, -, Ireland, 304, 281, CHAS. In HH of John O Callaghan m 37 born Ireland.

CALLAGHAN, JANE, 20, F, Servant, -, Ireland, 355, 327, CHAS. In HH of Col. W.S. King 48 m born CT.

CALLAGHAN, JOHN. O, 37, M, Laborer, -, Ireland, 304, 281, CHAS.

CALLAGHAN, LARRY, 8, M, None listed, -, Ireland, 300, 277, CHAS+. In HH of Dennis Callaghan m 43 born Ireland.

CALLAGHAN, MARGARET, 15, F, None listed, -, Ireland, 489, 445, CHAS. In HH of Wm. Callaghan m 45 born Ireland.

CALLAGHAN, MAR-GARET, 40, F, None listed, -, Ireland, 300, 277, CHAS+. In HH of Dennis Callaghan m 43 born Ireland.

CALLAGHAN, MARY, 34, F, None listed, -, Ireland, 240, 226, CHAS+. In HH of William Farley m 38 born Ireland.

CALLAGHAN, MARY, 48, F, None listed, -, Ireland, 28, 28, CHAS*. In HH of J.H. Stevens f 47 born SC.

CALLAGHAN, SARAH, 40, F, None listed, -, Ireland, 489, 445, CHAS. In HH of Wm. Callaghan m 45 born Ireland.

CALLAGHAN, SUE, 6, F, None listed, -, Ireland, 300, 277, CHAS+. In HH of Dennis Callaghan m 43 born Ireland.

CALLAGHAN, SUSAN, 22, F, None listed, -, Ireland, 300, 277, CHAS+. In HH of Dennis Callaghan m 43 born Ireland.

CALLAGHAN, THOS., 34, M, Laborer, -, Ireland, 337, 311, CHAS. In HH of William H. Fowler m 38 running Boarding house born England.

CALLAGHAN, WM., 45, M, Shop keeper, -, Ireland, 489, 445, CHAS.

CALLAGHER, PETER, 22, M, Stone mason, -, Ireland, 322, 297, CHAS. In Boarding house.

CAMBRIDGE, PETER, 35, M, Laborer, B, Ireland, 53, 48, CHAS-.

CAMBRIDGE, SOPHY, 30, F, None listed, B, Ireland, 53, 48, CHAS-. In HH of Peter Cambridge m 35 black born Ireland.

CAMERAND, JOSEPH, 82, M, Planter, -, Ireland, 804, 805, FAIR.

19

CAMERAND, NANCY, 84, F, None listed, -, Ireland, 804, 805, FAIR. In HH of Joseph Camerand m 82 born Ireland.

CAMICK, SAMUEL, 58, M, Planter, -, Ireland, 833, 834, FAIR.

CAMPBELL, ALEXANDER, 46, M, Planter, -, Ireland, 1220, 1220, UNION.

CAMPBELL, EDWARD, 17, M, Clerk, -, Ireland, 141, 132, CHAS+. In HH of John Hill m 47 born PA.

CAMPBELL, HENRY, 16, M, None listed, -, Ireland, 768, 748, CHAS-. In HH of Owen Campbell m 25 born Ireland.

CAMPBELL, JOHN, 30, M, Clothing Store, -, Ireland, 266, 251, CHAS-.

CAMPBELL, MARGARET, 45, F, None listed, -, Ireland, 1220, 1220, UNION. In HH of Alexander Campbell m 46 born Ireland.

CAMPBELL, MARGARET, 50, F, None listed, -, Ireland, 551, 551, FAIR.

CAMPBELL, MARY, 40, F, None listed, -, Ireland, 271, 252, CHAS+.

CAMPBELL, MARY, 50, F, None listed, -, Ireland, 849, 852, AND. In HH of George Campbell m 72 born SC.

CAMPBELL, OWEN, 25, M, Pavior, -, Ireland, 768, 748, CHAS-.

CAMPBELL, ROSANA, 30, F, None listed, -, Ireland, 768, 748, CHAS-. In HH of Owen Campbell m 25 born Ireland.

CAMPTON, ANN, 58, F, None listed, -, Ireland, 811, 811, YORK.

CANAN, CATHERINE, 20, F, None listed, -, Ireland, 119, 112, CHAS*. In HH of Dennis Canan m 35 born Ireland.

CANAN, DENNIS, 35, M, Laborer, -, Ireland, 119, 112, CHAS*.

CANARY, CORNELIUS, 28, M, Laborer, -, Ireland, 170, 160, CHAS+.

CANARY, ELIZABETH, 30, F, None listed, -, Ireland, 170, 160, CHAS+. In HH of Cornelius Canary m 28 born Ireland.

CANARY, TIMOTHY, 7, M, None listed, -, Ireland, 170, 160, CHAS+. In HH of Cornelius Canary m 28 born Ireland.

CANNON, BARNY, 45, M, Ditcher, -, Ireland, 86, 86, BARN. In HH of Thos. Simpson m 39 born Ireland.

CANNON, BRIDGET, 28, F, None listed, -, Ireland, 476, 442, CHAS*. In HH of William N. Hambleton m 30 born Ireland.

CANTWELL, MARGARET, 35, F, None listed, -, Ireland, 464, 461, CHAS%. In HH of Thomas Cantwell m 45 born

Ireland.

CANTWELL, THOMAS, 45, M, Clerk, -, Ireland, 464, 461, CHAS%.

CAPADY, DENNIS, 16, M, Bricklayer, -, Ireland, 426, 424, CHAS%. In HH of James Capady m 47 born Ireland.

CAPADY, FRANCES, 12, F, None listed, -, Ireland, 426, 424, CHAS%. In HH of James Capady m 47 born Ireland.

CAPADY, FRANCES, 43, F, None listed, -, Ireland, 426, 424, CHAS%. In HH of James Capady m 47 born Ireland.

CAPADY, JAMES, 47, M, Laborer, -, Ireland, 426, 424, CHAS%.

CAPADY, MARY E., 20, F, None listed, -, Ireland, 426, 424, CHAS%. In HH of James Capady m 47 born Ireland.

CAPADY, THOMAS, 9, M, None listed, -, Ireland, 426, 424, CHAS%. In HH of James Capady m 47 born Ireland.

CAR, JANE, 66, F, None listed, -, Ireland, 49, 49, CHES.

CARCY, BRIGET, 27, F, None listed, -, Ireland, 1027, 1005, CHAS%. In HH of Patrick Carcy m 47 born Ireland.

CARCY, DAN, 28, M, Pavior, -, Ireland, 1027, 1005, CHAS%. In HH of Patrick Carcy m 47 born Ireland.

CARCY, NANCY, 45, F, None listed, -, Ireland, 1027, 1005, CHAS%. In HH of Patrick Carcy m 47 born Ireland.

CARCY, PATRICK, 47, M, Laborer, -, Ireland, 1027, 1005, CHAS%.

CARDINE, SARAH, 30, F, None listed, -, Ireland, 472, 430, CHAS.

CARDWELL, A. S., 55, M, Ship Captain, -, Ireland, 137, 137, BEAU.

CARENER, JAS., 35, M, Laborer, -, Ireland, 2057, 2060, EDGE. In HH of Michael Corner m 27 born Ireland.

CAREY, E.M., 40, M, Druggest, -, Ireland, 230, 208, CHAS.

CAREY, JAMES, 21, M, Laborer, -, Ireland, 389, 351, CHAS+. In HH of Edward Collins m 40 born Ireland.

CARFIT, MARGARET, 18, F, None listed, -, Ireland, 296, 280, CHAS-. In HH of J. Moise f 45 born SC.

CARLEY, MARY A., 39, F, None listed, -, Ireland, 524, 524, FAIR. In HH of William Carley m 38 born Ireland.

CARLEY, WILLIAM, 38, M, Tailor, -, Ireland, 524, 524, FAIR.

CARLISLE, JAMES, 54, M, Farmer, -, Ireland, 600, 600, CHES.

CARLISLE, JAMES N., 32,

M, Printer, -, Ireland, 1976, 1982, EDGE. In HH of Edward Smith m 48 born SC.

CARLISLE, JOHN, 50, M, Farmer, -, Ireland, 886, 886, CHES.

CARLISLE, MARGARET, 80, F, None listed, -, Ireland, 718, 676, CHAS+.

CARLISLE, WM., 53, M, MD, -, Ireland, 258, 258, KERS.

CARMES, DORA, 32, F, None listed, -, Ireland, 709, 701, CHAS%. In HH of Simon Carmes m 38 born Ireland.

CARMES, JOSEPHINE, 10, F, None listed, -, Ireland, 709, 701, CHAS%. In HH of Simon Carmes m 38 born Ireland.

CARMES, SIMON, 38, M, Laborer, -, Ireland, 709, 701, CHAS%.

CARNES, ELLEN, 30, F, Servant, -, Ireland, 882, 840, CHAS+. In Charleston Hotel.

CARNEY, ADALINE, 35, F, None listed, -, Ireland, 1005, 982, CHAS%.Under command of Major P. Hagnes, Comg. Off. U.S. Arnsel.

CARNEY, PATRICK, 33, M, Ordinance man, -, Ireland, 1005, 982, CHAS%.Under command of Major P. Hagnes, Comg. Off. U.S. Arnsel.

CAROL, HAMETAR, 66, M, Farmer, -, Ireland, 770, 770, YORK.

CARPENTER, CATH-ERINE, 21, F, None listed, -, Ireland, 1136, 1115, CHAS%. In HH of Maria Carpenter f 52 born Ireland.

CARPENTER, MARIA, 52, F, None listed, -, Ireland, 1136, 1115, CHAS%.

CARR, JAMES, 29, M, Plant-er, -, Ireland, 163, 163, FAIR.

CARR, JOHN, 40, M, None listed, -, Ireland, 472, 438, CHAS*. In HH of Jane Davis f 55 born Ireland.

CARR, WILLIAM, 20, M, Planter, -, Ireland, 599, 600, FAIR. In HH of John Hare m 29 born Ireland.

CARREGAN, MARY, 28, F, None listed, -, Ireland, 19, 16, CHAS+. In HH of Thomas Carregan m 25 born Ireland.

CARREGAN, THOMAS, 25, M, Coachman, -, Ireland, 19, 16, CHAS+.

CARRIGAN, CATHERINE, 26, F, None listed, -, Ireland, 67, 67, CHAS^. In HH of Joshua Motte m 35 born SC.

CARRIGAN, MARY, 33, F, None listed, -, Ireland, 83, 81, CHAS*. In HH of John Burns m 30 born GA.

CARROL, ANN, 25, F, None listed, -, Ireland, 871, 829, CHAS+. In HH of John H. Margarat m 68 born SC.

CARROL, CATHERINE, 8, F, None listed, -, Ireland, 469,

427, CHAS+. In HH of James Carrol m 48 born Ireland.

CARROL, JAMES, 48, M, Shoe maker, -, Ireland, 469, 427, CHAS+.

CARROL, JOHN, 26, M, Laborer, -, Ireland, 388, 350, CHAS+. In HH of Andrew Bryan m 25 born Ireland.

CARROL, PATRICK, 27, M, Laborer, -, Ireland, 261, 244, CHAS+. In HH of Hugh McNamara m 28 born Ireland.

CARROL, PATRICK, 30, M, None listed, -, Ireland, 470, 428, CHAS+. In HH of Thomas Carroll m 44 born Ireland.

CARROL, PATRICK, 35, M, Plasterer, -, Ireland, 871, 829, CHAS+. In HH of John H. Margarat m 68 born SC.

CARROL, SARAH, 33, F, None listed, -, Ireland, 469, 427, CHAS+. In HH of James Carrol m 48 born Ireland.

CARROL, THOMAS, 27, M, Laborer, -, Ireland, 261, 244, CHAS+. In HH of Hugh McNamara m 28 born Ireland.

CARROL, THOMAS, 44, M, Shoemaker, -, Ireland, 470, 428, CHAS+.

CARROL, TIM, 20, M, None listed, -, Ireland, 281, 261, CHAS+. In HH of John Cahill m 45 born Ireland.

CARROLL, CATHERINE, 30, F, None listed, -, Ireland, 202, 181, CHAS. In HH of Patrick Carroll m 40 born Ireland.

CARROLL, DANIEL, 30, M, Taylor, -, Ireland, 782, 782, CHES.

CARROLL, JULIA ANN, 78, F, None listed, -, Ireland, 1132, 1132, EDGE.

CARROLL, MARY, 68, F, None listed, -, Ireland, 338, 338, EDGE.

CARROLL, PATRICK, 40, M, Laborer, -, Ireland, 202, 181, CHAS.

CART, JOHN, 25, M, Drayman, -, Ireland, 853, 811, CHAS+. In HH of Bernard Carrol m 45 born Ireland.

CARTER, M., 40, F, None listed, -, Ireland, 822, 822, LANC*. In HH of A. Carter m 35 born SC.

CARTER, MARY, 73, F, None listed, -, Ireland, 1069, `1069, SUMT. In HH of E.M. Gregg m 48 born SC.

CARTERS, JOHN, 28, M, Carpenter, -, Ireland, 397, 381, CHAS-. In HH of Edward Cassady m 30 born Ireland.

CARTHY, MARY, 16, F, None listed, -, Ireland, 814, 794, CHAS-. In HH of John G. Willis m 45 born NC.

CARTLEY, JOHN, 24, M, Laborer, -, Ireland, 326, 295, CHAS+. In HH of Edwd McLaughlin m 23 born Ireland.

CARTMAN, THOMAS, 20, M, Laborer, -, Ireland, 845, 825, CHAS-. In HH of B. Lynap m 33 born Ireland.

CASEY, ANN, 19, F, None listed, -, Ireland, 503, 496, CHAS%. In HH of William Ronan m 42 born NY.

CASEY, BRIDGED, 12, F, None listed, -, Ireland, 246, 224, CHAS. In HH of Michael Casey m 31 born Ireland.

CASEY, CATHERINE, 32, F, None listed, -, Ireland, 595, 604, RICH+. In HH of Henry Casey m 45 born Ireland.

CASEY, ELIZABETH, 6, F, None listed, -, Ireland, 595, 604, RICH+. In HH of Henry Casey m 45 born Ireland.

CASEY, EMMA, 27, F, None listed, -, Ireland, 246, 224, CHAS. In HH of Michael Casey m 31 born Ireland.

CASEY, FLORANCE, 18, F, None listed, -, Ireland, 246, 224, CHAS. In HH of Michael Casey m 31 born Ireland.

CASEY, HENRY, 45, M, Planter, -, Ireland, 595, 604, RICH+.

CASEY, ISABELLA, 4, F, None listed, -, Ireland, 595, 604, RICH+. In HH of Henry Casey m 45 born Ireland.

CASEY, KATEY, 16, F, None listed, -, Ireland, 246, 224, CHAS. In HH of Michael Casey m 31 born Ireland.

CASEY, MARGARET, 18, F, None listed, -, Ireland, 385, 347, CHAS+. In HH of Daniel Twohilt m 30 born Ireland.

CASEY, MARY, 38, F, None listed, -, Ireland, 423, 382, CHAS+.

CASEY, MICHAEL, 31, M, Laborer, -, Ireland, 246, 224, CHAS.

CASEY, MIKE, 9, M, None listed, -, Ireland, 246, 224, CHAS. In HH of Michael Casey m 31 born Ireland.

CASEY, PATRICK, 30, M, Store Keeper, -, Ireland, 215, 202, CHAS+. In HH of Peter Kelly m 35 born Ireland.

CASSADY, ALICE, 55, F, None listed, -, Ireland, 322, 297, CHAS. In Boarding house.

CASSADY, EDWARD, 30, M, Carpenter, -, Ireland, 397, 381, CHAS-.

CASSADY, ELIZABETH, 30, F, None listed, -, Ireland, 397, 381, CHAS-. In HH of Edward Cassady m 30 born Ireland.

CASSADY, FRANCIS, 50, M, Teacher/farmer, -, Ireland, 130, 130, BEAU*.

CASSEY, BAT., 23, M, Laborer, -, Ireland, 169, 159, CHAS+. In HH of John Sweeny m 79 born Ireland.

CASTLE, JAMES, 25, M, Merchant, -, Ireland, 25, 30, CHAS. In HH of Frances L. Broadfoot f 75 born England.

CASTLE, MARY, 20, F, None listed, -, Ireland, 25, 30, CHAS. In HH of Frances L. Broadfoot f 75 born England.

CATHCART, ANN E., 28, F, None listed, -, Ireland, 312, 318, RICH. In HH of James Cathcart m 55 born Ireland.

CATHCART, CHARLES, 40, M, Planter, -, Ireland, 928, 829, FAIR.

CATHCART, ELIZA J.R., 15, F, None listed, -, Ireland, 312, 318, RICH. In HH of James Cathcart m 55 born Ireland.

CATHCART, ELLEN, 23, F, None listed, -, Ireland, 711, 712, FAIR. In HH of Richard Cathcart m 55 born Ireland.

CATHCART, GEORGE H., 37, M, Clerk, -, Ireland, 320, 326, RICH.

CATHCART, JAMES, 10, M, None listed, -, Ireland, 312, 318, RICH. In HH of James Cathcart m 55 born Ireland.

CATHCART, JAMES, 55, M, Merchant, -, Ireland, 312, 318, RICH.

CATHCART, JAMES, 86, M, None listed, -, Ireland, 928, 829, FAIR. In HH of Charles Cathcart m 40 born Ireland.

CATHCART, JANE, 55, F, None listed, -, Ireland, 736, 737, FAIR.

CATHCART, MARIA L., 34, F, None listed, -, Ireland, 320,

326, RICH. In HH of George H. Cathcart m 37 born Ireland.

CATHCART, NANCY, 52, F, None listed, -, Ireland, 928, 829, FAIR. In HH of Charles Cathcart m 40 born Ireland.

CATHCART, RICHARD, 55, M, Planter, -, Ireland, 711, 712, FAIR.

CATHCART, ROBERT, 35, M, Merchant, -, Ireland, 313, 318, RICH.

CATHCART, ROBERT J., 18, M, Student, -, Ireland, 312, 318, RICH. In HH of James Cathcart m 55 born Ireland.

CATHCART, WILLIAM J., 5, M, None listed, -, Ireland, 312, 318, RICH. In HH of James Cathcart m 55 born Ireland.

CATHERWOOD, SAML., 25, M, Druggist, -, Ireland, 133, 133, BEAU.

CAUSSE, J., 22, M, Clerk, -, Ireland, 150, 141, CHAS+. In Boarding house.

CAVANAGH, MARA ?, 17, F, None listed, -, Ireland, 2007, 2013, EDGE. In HH of William Herbert m 37 born Ireland.

CAVE, BRIGET, 11, F, None listed, -, Ireland, 467, 434, CHAS*. In HH of Patrick Cave m 31 born Ireland.

CAVE, BRIGET, 28, F, None listed, -, Ireland, 467, 434, CHAS*. In HH of Patrick Cave

m 31 born Ireland.

CAVE, PATRICK, 31, M, Laborer, -, Ireland, 467, 434, CHAS*.

CAVE, PATRICK, 60, M, Laborer, -, Ireland, 467, 434, CHAS*. In HH of Patrick Cave m 31 born Ireland.

CAVERE, ELIZABAETH {SIC}, 34, F, None listed, -, Ireland, 766, 746, CHAS-. In HH of Patarick Hogan m 37 born Ireland.

CAVIN, WILLIAM, 45, M, Clerk, -, Ireland, 599, 616, RICH. In HH of James JW. Gaither m 29 born District of Columbia DC.

CAVINER, ANN, 20, F, None listed, -, Ireland, 2056, 2062, EDGE. In HH of Edward Caviner m 60 born Ireland.

CAVINER, ARTHUR, 8, M, None listed, -, Ireland, 2056, 2062, EDGE. In HH of Edward Caviner m 60 born Ireland.

CAVINER, CATHARINE, 56, F, None listed, -, Ireland, 2056, 2062, EDGE. In HH of Edward Caviner m 60 born Ireland.

CAVINER, EDWARD, 60, M, Laborer, -, Ireland, 2056, 2062, EDGE.

CAVINER, JOHN, 18, M, Ditcher, -, Ireland, 2056, 2062, EDGE. In HH of Edward Caviner m 60 born Ireland.

CAVINER, MARY, 12, F,

None listed, -, Ireland, 2056, 2062, EDGE. In HH of Edward Caviner m 60 born Ireland.

CHADES, JOHN, 36, M, Amer?, -, Ireland, 568, 568, CHES.

CHADES, ROSA, 57, F, None listed, -, Ireland, 568, 568, CHES. In HH of John Chades m 36 born Ireland.

CHAHILL, CATH., 50, F, None listed, -, Ireland, 1384, 1384, CHES. In HH of Santeer Chahill m 50 born Ireland

CHAHILL, JAS., 27, M, Farmer, -, Ireland, 1387, 1387, CHES.

CHAHILL, PERRY, 22, M, Farmer, -, Ireland, 1385, 1385, CHES.

CHAHILL, SANTEER, 50, M, Farmer, -, Ireland, 1384, 1384, CHES.

CHAHILL, TIMOTHY, 29, M, Farmer, -, Ireland, 1384, 1384, CHES. In HH of Santeer Chahill m 50 born Ireland

CHALMERS, JAMES, 66, M, Farmer, -, Ireland, 776, 776, NEWB.

CHAMBERS, AGNES, 41, F, None listed, -, Ireland, 74, 74, GEOR*.

CHAMBERS, JAMES, 24, M, Painter, -, Ireland, 337, 302, CHAS+. In HH of John Lindsay m 30 born England.

CHISOLM, MELVINA, 30, F, None listed, -, Ireland, 893, 873, CHAS-. In HH of O.

Chisolm m 33 born SC.

CHISOLM, RACHEL, 60, F, None listed, -, Ireland, 676, 677, FAIR. In HH of Thomas Chisolm m 55 born Ireland.

CHISOLM, THOMAS, 55, M, Planter, -, Ireland, 676, 677, FAIR.

CHNOTBURY, ELLEN, 60, F, None listed, -, Ireland, 44, 44, CHAS!. In HH of George Chnotbury m 60 born SC.

CHURCH, MARGARET, 70, F, None listed, -, Ireland, 230, 216, CHAS-.

CLARK, CATHERINE, 38, F, None listed, -, Ireland, 237, 222, CHAS-.Poor House.

CLARK, ELLEN, 20, F, None listed, -, Ireland, 312, 296, CHAS-. In HH of Bernard Connely m 26 born Ireland.

CLARK, JOHN, 28, M, Laborer, -, Ireland, 272, 252, CHAS+. In HH of John McCormick m 40 born Ireland.

CLARK, JULIAS, 16, M, Tinner, -, Ireland, 361, 332, CHAS. In HH of N.A. Roye m 28 born SC.

CLARK, MARY, 25, F, None listed, -, Ireland, 272, 252, CHAS+. In HH of John McCormick m 40 born Ireland.

CLARK, PATRICK, 24, M, Tailor, -, Ireland, 312, 296, CHAS-. In HH of Bernard Connely m 26 born Ireland.

CLARY, HANNAH, 63, F,

None listed, -, Ireland, 1358, 1358, CHES. In HH of Thos. Clary m 59 born SC.

CLARY, JOHN, 29, M, Laborer, -, Ireland, 2052, 2058, EDGE. In HH of Jas. Linch m 28 born Ireland.

CLARY, THOS., 20, M, Laborer, -, Ireland, 2057, 2060, EDGE. In HH of Michael Corner m 27 born Ireland.

CLATWORTHY, JAMES, 45, M, Carpenter, -, Ireland, 547, 547, ABB.

CLAXTON, WILLIAM, 35, M, Planter, -, Ireland, 299, 299, FAIR.

CLAYTON, JOHN, 70, M, None listed, -, Ireland, 1144, 1144, CHES. In HH of Francis Hardin 30 born SC. Note: Listed as in Poor House.

CLEAR, JOHN, 24, M, Policeman, -, Ireland, 497, 490, CHAS%. In HH of Barbary Smith f 50 born SC.

CLEARY, PATRICK, 24, M, Laborer, -, Ireland, 326, 295, CHAS+. In HH of Edwd McLaughlin m 23 born Ireland.

CLEARY, TOM, 26, M, Laborer, -, Ireland, 31, 27, CHAS$. In HH of E. Reynolds m 33 mulatto born Ireland.

CLEARY, WILLIAM, 25, M, Clerk, -, Ireland, 167, 158, CHAS+. In Boarding house.

CLIFFORD, FRANCES A., 70, F, None listed, -, Ireland,

692, 692, COLL. In HH of L.C. Clifford m 36 born Ireland.

CLIFFORD, JAMES, 29, M, Laborer, -, Ireland, 457, 415, CHAS+. In HH of James Karvin m 30 born Ireland.

CLIFFORD, JOHN, 32, M, Mariner, -, Ireland, 337, 311, CHAS. In HH of William H. Fowler m 38 running Boarding house born England.

CLIFFORD, L.C., 36, M, None listed, -, Ireland, 692, 692, COLL.

CLOSE, L.P.H., 32, M, Merchant, -, Ireland, 794, 774, CHAS-.

CLOTTER, SARAH, 8, F, None listed, -, Ireland, 553, 519, CHAS*. In Catholic Seminary.

CLOTTWORTHY, JAMES, 17, M, Upholsterer, -, Ireland, 811, 791, CHAS-. In HH of John Caldwell m 53 born Scotland.

CLOWNEY, JOHN, 17, M, Planter, -, Ireland, 471, 471, FAIR. In HH of Nancy Clowney f 48 born Ireland.

CLOWNEY, JOSEPH, 33, M, Planter, -, Ireland, 470, 470, FAIR.

CLOWNEY, MOSES, 28, M, Overseer, -, Ireland, 1, 1, UNN+. In HH of C.S. Sims m 52 born SC.

CLOWNEY, NANCY, 48, F,

None listed, -, Ireland, 471, 471, FAIR.

CLOWNEY, ROBERT C., 11, M, None listed, -, Ireland, 471, 471, FAIR. In HH of Nancy Clowney f 48 born Ireland.

CLOWNEY, SAMUEL C., 13, M, None listed, -, Ireland, 471, 471, FAIR. In HH of Nancy Clowney f 48 born Ireland.

CLOWNEY, WM. J., 15, M, None listed, -, Ireland, 471, 471, FAIR. In HH of Nancy Clowney f 48 born Ireland.

COALEY, MARY, 37, F, None listed, -, Ireland, 570, 570, LAU. In HH of Mark Coaley m 36 born Vermont.

COALMA, ROBERT, 58, M, Farmer, -, Ireland, 378, 378, LAU.

COBB, ELLENDER, 64, F, None listed, -, Ireland, 350, 363, PICK. In HH of Elijah Pitts m 25 born SC.

COBBLES, MARAGET, 25, F, None listed, -, Ireland, 1088, 1065, CHAS-. In HH of H.S. Hayden m 35 born CT.

COBURN, JAMES, 56, M, Mechanic, -, Ireland, 338, 338, BARN. In HH of William Moore m 50 born SC.

COCKLIN, PATRICK, 28, M, None listed, -, Ireland, 281, 261, CHAS+. In HH of John Cahill m 45 born Ireland.

COFFEE, ANNA, 15, F, None listed, -, Ireland, 24, 29, CHAS. In HH of Thomas Coffee m 38 born Ireland.

COFFEE, CATHERINE, 35, F, None listed, -, Ireland, 203, 182, CHAS. In HH of Jeremiah Coffee m 40 born Ireland.

COFFEE, DANIEL, 30, M, Laborer, -, Ireland, 184, 167, CHAS. In Boarding house.

COFFEE, JEREMIAH, 40, M, Laborer, -, Ireland, 203, 182, CHAS.

COFFEE, MARGARET, 13, F, None listed, -, Ireland, 24, 29, CHAS. In HH of Thomas Coffee m 38 born Ireland.

COFFEE, MARY, 34, F, None listed, -, Ireland, 24, 29, CHAS. In HH of Thomas Coffee m 38 born Ireland.

COFFEE, THOMAS, 38, M, Laborer, -, Ireland, 24, 29, CHAS.

COFFIN, JEREMIAH, 30, M, None listed, -, Ireland, 910, 887, CHAS%. In HH of Patrick Courtney m 27 born Ireland.

COFFRAM, JOHN, 35, M, Ordinance man, -, Ireland, 1005, 982, CHAS%.Under command of Major P. Hagnes, Comg. Off. U.S. Arnsel.

COGLE, PEGGY, 50, F, None listed, -, Ireland, 412, 395, CHAS-. In HH of H.N. Hart m 36 born Ireland.

COHN, D.J.M., 44, M, Planter, -, Ireland, 77, 77, BARN.

COLBRON, DENNIS, 25, M, Currier, -, Ireland, 116, 108, CHAS+. In HH of W.C. Ferguson m 25 born SC.

COLEMAN, BRIGET, 30, F, None listed, -, Ireland, 1146, 1125, CHAS%. In HH of Harris Simons m 43 born Ireland. Marie Ramsay Simons age 8/12 yr.

COLEMAN, JANE E., 29, F, None listed, -, Ireland, 139, 129, CHAS-. In HH of Hugh Stoop m 60 born Ireland.

COLEMAN, JOANA, 20, F, None listed, -, Ireland, 127, 118, CHAS+. In Boarding house.

COLEREGAN, P., 30, M, Shop keeper, -, Ireland, 456, 413, CHAS.

COLGAN, JOHN, 37, M, Merchant/taylor, -, Ireland, 39, 39, EDGE.

COLLER, MARY, 29, F, None listed, -, Ireland, 468, 426, CHAS. In HH ofAnn Barber f 74 born Ireland.

COLLINS, AGATHY, 36, F, None listed, -, Ireland, 218, 195, CHAS*. In HH of Daniel Collins m 44 born Ireland.

COLLINS, CATHERINE, 16, F, None listed, -, Ireland, 210, 198, CHAS+. In HH of Margaret Collins f 36 born Ireland.

COLLINS, CATHERINE, 25, F, None listed, -, Ireland, 270,

251, CHAS+. In HH of Richard M. Collins m 40 born Ireland.

COLLINS, CATHERINE, 44, F, None listed, -, Ireland, 609, 567, CHAS+. In HH of James Collins m 50 born Ireland.

COLLINS, CORNELIUS, 22, M, Laborer, -, Ireland, 397, 358, CHAS+. In HH of William Collins m 50 born Ireland.

COLLINS, DAN, 21, M, Laborer, -, Ireland, 218, 195, CHAS*. In HH of Daniel Collins m 44 born Ireland.

COLLINS, DANIEL, 44, M, Laborer, -, Ireland, 218, 195, CHAS*.

COLLINS, DENNIS, 15, M, None listed, -, Ireland, 218, 195, CHAS*. In HH of Daniel Collins m 44 born Ireland.

COLLINS, EDWARD, 40, M, Laborer, -, Ireland, 389, 351, CHAS+.

COLLINS, ELIZA, 9, F, None listed, -, Ireland, 210, 198, CHAS+. In HH of Margaret Collins f 36 born Ireland.

COLLINS, ELLEN, 11, F, None listed, -, Ireland, 210, 198, CHAS+. In HH of Margaret Collins f 36 born Ireland.

COLLINS, ELLEN, 25, F, None listed, -, Ireland, 416, 375, CHAS+. In HH of Elizabeth Sweeney f 40 born Ireland.

COLLINS, HONORA, 75, F, None listed, -, Ireland, 416, 375, CHAS+. In HH of Elizabeth Sweeney f 40 born Ireland.

COLLINS, HONORE, 9, F, None listed, -, Ireland, 397, 358, CHAS+. In HH of William Collins m 50 born Ireland.

COLLINS, HONORE, 43, F, None listed, -, Ireland, 397, 358, CHAS+. In HH of William Collins m 50 born Ireland.

COLLINS, JAMES, 50, M, Mason, -, Ireland, 609, 567, CHAS+.

COLLINS, JAMES N., 40, M, Teacher, -, Ireland, 472, 430, CHAS+.

COLLINS, JOANA, 6, F, None listed, -, Ireland, 270, 251, CHAS+. In HH of Richard M. Collins m 40 born Ireland.

COLLINS, JOANA, 20, F, None listed, -, Ireland, 397, 358, CHAS+. In HH of William Collins m 50 born Ireland.

COLLINS, JOHANA, 21, F, None listed, -, Ireland, 210, 198, CHAS+. In HH of Margaret Collins f 36 born Ireland.

COLLINS, JOHN, 14, M, None listed, -, Ireland, 332, 338, RICH. In HH of William McGuinnis m 45 born Ireland.

COLLINS, MARGARET, 18, F, None listed, -, Ireland, 210, 198, CHAS+. In HH of Margaret Collins f 36 born

Ireland.

COLLINS, MARGARET, 36, F, None listed, -, Ireland, 210, 198, CHAS+.

COLLINS, MARY, 18, F, None listed, -, Ireland, 218, 195, CHAS*. In HH of Daniel Collins m 44 born Ireland.

COLLINS, MARY, 20, F, None listed, -, Ireland, 210, 198, CHAS+. In HH of Margaret Collins f 36 born Ireland.

COLLINS, MARY, 21, F, None listed, -, Ireland, 177, 163, CHAS*. In HH of George Easterby m 30 born SC.

COLLINS, MARY, 30, F, None listed, -, Ireland, 609, 567, CHAS+. In HH of James Collins m 50 born Ireland.

COLLINS, MARY, 35, F, None listed, -, Ireland, 389, 351, CHAS+. In HH of Edward Collins m 40 born Ireland.

COLLINS, MICH., 28, M, Laborer, -, Ireland, 337, 311, CHAS. In HH of William H. Fowler m 38 running Boarding house born England.

COLLINS, NORA, 14, F, None listed, -, Ireland, 210, 198, CHAS+. In HH of Margaret Collins f 36 born Ireland.

COLLINS, PATRICK, 32, M, Engineer, -, Ireland, 609, 567, CHAS+. In HH of James Collins m 50 born Ireland.

COLLINS, PATRICK, 40, M, Plasterer, -, Ireland, 172, 162, CHAS+. In HH of John Haley m 40 born Ireland.

COLLINS, RICHARD M., 40, M, Teacher, -, Ireland, 270, 251, CHAS+.

COLLINS, ROSANA, 19, F, None listed, -, Ireland, 761, 741, CHAS-. In HH of H.F. Brandt m 40 born France.

COLLINS, TIMOTHY, 30, M, Clerk, -, Ireland, 416, 375, CHAS+. In HH of Elizabeth Sweeney f 40 born Ireland.

COLLINS, WILLIAM, 50, M, Laborer, -, Ireland, 397, 358, CHAS+.

COLLUM, JOHN, 29, M, Laborer, -, Ireland, 237, 222, CHAS-.Poor House.

COLO, NANCY, 28, F, None listed, -, Ireland, 46, 43, CHAS-. In HH of F.L. Roux m 38 born SC.

COMER, JAS., 60, M, None, -, Ireland, 876, 876, KERS.

COMERFORD, MICHAEL, 48, M, Merchant, -, Ireland, 263, 268, RICH.

CONALLY, MARIAH, 19, F, None listed, -, Ireland, 765, 765, EDGE. In HH of James P. Carrol m 41 born SC.

CONDELL, BRIGET, 33, F, None listed, -, Ireland, 118, 110, CHAS+. In HH of William Condell m 34 born Ireland.

31

CONDELL, WILLIAM, 34, M, Tailor, -, Ireland, 118, 110, CHAS+.

CONDOR, CATHERINE, 20, F, None listed, -, Ireland, 834, 814, CHAS-. In HH of T.W. Rogers m 30 born Ireland.

CONGREVE, JAMES, 21, M, Laborer, -, Ireland, 172, 162, CHAS+. In HH of John Haley m 40 born Ireland.

CONLEY, MARGARET, 20, F, None listed, -, Ireland, 252, 237, CHAS+. In HH of Michael Lines m 30 born Ireland.

CONLEY, MICHAEL, 30, M, Laborer, -, Ireland, 252, 237, CHAS+. In HH of Michael Lines m 30 born Ireland.

CONLEY, WINNIE, 25, F, None listed, -, Ireland, 252, 237, CHAS+. In HH of Michael Lines m 30 born Ireland.

CONNELEY, THOMAS, 28, M, Laborer, -, Ireland, 351, 324, CHAS. In Boarding house.

CONNELL, EMMA, 7, M, None listed, -, Ireland, 814, 797, CHAS%. In HH of Patrick Connell m 30 born Ireland.

CONNELL, LOUISA, 27, F, None listed, -, Ireland, 814, 797, CHAS%. In HH of Patrick Connell m 30 born Ireland.

CONNELL, PATRICK, 30, M, Laborer, -, Ireland, 814, 797, CHAS%.

CONNELLEY, JANE, 19, F, None listed, -, Ireland, 488, 444, CHAS. In HH of Frances Fahy m 24 born Ireland.

CONNELLY, H., 20, M, Fifer U.S.A., -, Ireland, 47, 43, CHAS$. In HH of John Ewing m 50 born MA.

CONNELY, BERNARD, 26, M, Laborer, -, Ireland, 312, 296, CHAS-.

CONNELY, MARY, 25, F, None listed, -, Ireland, 312, 296, CHAS-. In HH of Bernard Connely m 26 born Ireland.

CONNER, MARGARET, 19, F, Servant, -, Ireland, 355, 327, CHAS. In HH of Col. W.S. King 48 m born CT.

CONNER, MARY, 55, F, None listed, -, Ireland, 31, 31, CHAS%.

CONNERS, ELIZABETH, 23, F, None listed, -, Ireland, 243, 228, CHAS+. In HH of John Conners m 30 born Ireland.

CONNERS, JOHN, 30, M, Laborer, -, Ireland, 243, 228, CHAS+.

CONNOLEY, BRIGET, 25, F, None listed, -, Ireland, 94, 86, CHAS+. In HH of Bernard ONeill m 28 born Ireland.

CONNOLEY, CAROLINE, 28, F, None listed, -, Ireland, 94, 86, CHAS+. In HH of Bernard ONeill m 28 born Ireland.

CONNOLEY, CATHERINE, 24, F, None listed, -, Ireland, 658, 638, CHAS-. In HH of John Ervan m 60 born PA.

CONNOLEY, CATHERINE, 35, F, None listed, -, Ireland, 715, 706, CHAS%. In HH of Owen Connoley m 37 born Ireland.

CONNOLEY, OWEN, 37, M, Laborer, -, Ireland, 715, 706, CHAS%.

CONNOLEY, PETER, 12, M, None listed, -, Ireland, 715, 706, CHAS%. In HH of Owen Connoley m 37 born Ireland.

CONNOLEY, SARAH, 28, F, None listed, -, Ireland, 585, 543, CHAS+. In HH of Lewis Hatch m 40 born MA.

CONNOLEY, WILLIAM, 59, M, Laborer, -, Ireland, 88, 80, CHAS+. In HH of Michael Welch m 35 born Ireland.

CONNOLLEY, MARY, 25, F, None listed, -, Ireland, 556, 522, CHAS*. In HH of Edward Barnwell Jr. m 37 born SC.

CONNOLLY, ANN, 13, F, None listed, -, Ireland, 145, 145, BEAU. In HH of Michael O'Conner m 57 born Ireland.

CONNOR, JAMES, 32, M, Laborer, -, Ireland, 91, 92, RICH. Note: out of dwelling and Family order, Pg. 3.

CONWAY, JOHN, 30, M, Laborer, -, Ireland, 322, 297, CHAS. In Boarding house.

COOK, ANN, 20, F, None listed, -, Ireland, 112, 107, CHAS*. In HH of William Cook m 24 born Ireland.

COOK, JAMES, 34, M, Laborer, -, Ireland, 406, 370, CHAS. In HH of Thomas Sullivan m 40 born Ireland.

COOK, MARGARET, 22, F, None listed, -, Ireland, 439, 422, CHAS-. In HH of Truman Cook m 40 born NY.

COOK, WILLIAM, 24, M, Coachman, -, Ireland, 112, 107, CHAS*.

COOK, WILLIAM, 49, M, Farmer, -, Ireland, 516, 516, ABB.

COONER, SARAH, 62, F, None listed, -, Ireland, 773, 773, YORK. In HH of Martha Harrison f 60 born York Dist., SC.

COOPER, J.M., 28, M, Merchant, -, Ireland, 32, 32, KERS.

COPLAND, REBECCA, 95, F, None listed, -, Ireland, 1356, 1356, SPART. In HH of Charles Copeland m 61 born SC.

CORANEY, CHRISTOPHER, 42, M, None listed, -, Ireland, 237, 222, CHAS-.Poor House.

CORBET, BRIGET, 23, F, None listed, -, Ireland, 218, 205, CHAS+. In HH of John Corbet m 27 born Ireland.

CORBET, H.M. MRS., 30, F, None listed, -, Ireland, 185, 185, Beau+. In HH of Dr. D.H. Hamilton m 35 born SC.

CORBET, JOHN, 27, M, Laborer, -, Ireland, 218, 205, CHAS+.

CORBETT, JAMES, 45, M, Merchant, -, Ireland, 552, 535, CHAS-.

CORCAN, ALEXR., 21, M, Bricklayer, -, Ireland, 10,   9, CHAS-. In HH of James McCarrel m 25 born Ireland.

CORCON, ELLEN, 34, F, None listed, -, Ireland, 1114, 1092, CHAS%. In HH of Patrick Corcon m 38 born Ireland.

CORCON, JAMES, 10, M, None listed, -, Ireland, 1114, 1092, CHAS%. In HH of Patrick Corcon m 38 born Ireland.

CORCON, MARY, 8, F, None listed, -, Ireland, 1114, 1092, CHAS%. In HH of Patrick Corcon m 38 born Ireland.

CORCON, PATRICK, 38, M, Laborer, -, Ireland, 1114, 1092, CHAS%.

CORCON, THOMAS, 5, M, None listed, -, Ireland, 1114, 1092, CHAS%. In HH of Patrick Corcon m 38 born Ireland.

CORCON, WILLIAM, 12, M, None listed, -, Ireland, 1114, 1092, CHAS%. In HH of Patrick Corcon m 38 born Ireland.

CORCORAN, DELIA, 34, F, None listed, -, Ireland, 1057, 1035, CHAS%. In HH of James Corcoran m 38 born Ireland.

CORCORAN, JAMES, 18, M, Laborer, -, Ireland, 32, 32, CHAS!. In HH of Thos. Corcoran m 40 born Ireland.

CORCORAN, JAMES, 38, M, Laborer, -, Ireland, 1057, 1035, CHAS%.

CORCORAN, JOHN, 13, M, None listed, -, Ireland, 1057, 1035, CHAS%. In HH of James Corcoran m 38 born Ireland.

CORCORAN, MARGARET, 32, F, None listed, -, Ireland, 32, 32, CHAS!. In HH of Thos. Corcoran m 40 born Ireland.

CORCORAN, MARY, 32, F, None listed, -, Ireland, 1057, 1035, CHAS%. In HH of James Corcoran m 38 born Ireland.

CORCORAN, MARY, 76, F, None listed, -, Ireland, 32, 32, CHAS!. In HH of Thos. Corcoran m 40 born Ireland.

CORCORAN, THOMAS, 11, M, None listed, -, Ireland, 1057, 1035, CHAS%. In HH of James Corcoran m 38 born Ireland.

CORCORAN, THOS., 40, M, Accountant, -, Ireland, 32, 32, CHAS!.

CORCORAN, WILLIAM, 30, M, Laborer, -, Ireland, 32, 32, CHAS!. In HH of Thos. Corcoran m 40 born Ireland.

CORCORAY, JOHN, 37, M, None listed, -, Ireland, 237, 222, CHAS-.Poor House.

CORCOSAN, ANN, 44, F, None listed, -, Ireland, 1135, 1114, CHAS%. In HH of Thomas Corcosan m 48 born Ireland.

CORCOSAN, CATHERINE, 4, F, None listed, -, Ireland, 1135, 1114, CHAS%. In HH of Thomas Corcosan m 48 born Ireland.

CORCOSAN, ELISHA, 12, M, None listed, -, Ireland, 1135, 1114, CHAS%. In HH of Thomas Corcosan m 48 born Ireland.

CORCOSAN, ELIZA, 16, F, None listed, -, Ireland, 1135, 1114, CHAS%. In HH of Thomas Corcosan m 48 born Ireland.

CORCOSAN, LUCY, 6, F, None listed, -, Ireland, 1135, 1114, CHAS%. In HH of Thomas Corcosan m 48 born

Ireland.

CORCOSAN, THOMAS, 8, M, None listed, -, Ireland, 1135, 1114, CHAS%. In HH of Thomas Corcosan m 48 born Ireland.

CORCOSAN, THOMAS, 48, M, Carter, -, Ireland, 1135, 1114, CHAS%.

CORCOSAN, WILLIAM, 14, M, None listed, -, Ireland, 1135, 1114, CHAS%. In HH of Thomas Corcosan m 48 born Ireland.

CORDES, ANN, 25, F, None listed, -, Ireland, 40, 36, CHAS$. In HH of M. Fitz-simmons f 54 born SC.

CORK, JANE, 42, F, None listed, -, Ireland, 354, 354, FAIR.

CORKIN, MARY, 31, F, None listed, -, Ireland, 1620, 1620, EDGE. In HH of Robt Corkin m 40 born Ireland. Family No. out of order following 1628.

CORKIN, ROBT, 40, M, Superintendent, -, Ireland, 1620, 1620,EDGE. Occupation: "Superintending weaving machine" Family No. out of order following 1628.

CORMICK, BRIGET, 50, M, None listed, -, Ireland, 422, 381, CHAS+. In HH of Patrick Cormick m 56 born Ireland.

CORMICK, CHARLES, 24, M, Laborer, -, Ireland, 422, 381,

CHAS+. In HH of Patrick Cormick m 56 born Ireland.

CORMICK, COLLINE, 7, F, None listed, -, Ireland, 422, 381, CHAS+. In HH of Patrick Cormick m 56 born Ireland.

CORMICK, DERMOT, 32, M, Laborer, -, Ireland, 422, 381, CHAS+. In HH of Patrick Cormick m 56 born Ireland.

CORMICK, ELLEN, 9, F, None listed, -, Ireland, 422, 381, CHAS+. In HH of Patrick Cormick m 56 born Ireland.

CORMICK, MICHAEL, 18, M, None listed, -, Ireland, 422, 381, CHAS+. In HH of Patrick Cormick m 56 born Ireland.

CORMICK, PATRICK, 56, M, Laborer, -, Ireland, 422, 381, CHAS+.

CORMICK, SUSAN, 29, F, None listed, -, Ireland, 422, 381, CHAS+. In HH of Patrick Cormick m 56 born Ireland.

CORMWAY, ELLEN, 27, F, Servant, -, Ireland, 273, 250, CHAS. In HH of Bridget Moore m 25 born Ireland.

CORNAN, BERNARD, 3, M, None listed, -, Ireland, 63, 56, CHAS+. In HH of Patrick Cornan m 28 born Ireland.

CORNAN, MARY, 26, F, None listed, -, Ireland, 63, 56, CHAS+. In HH of Patrick Cornan m 28 born Ireland.

CORNAN, PATRICK, 28, M, Laborer, -, Ireland, 63, 56,

CHAS+.

CORNER, MICHAEL, 27, M, Laborer, -, Ireland, 2057, 2060, EDGE.

COTTRELL, BRIGET, 42, F, None listed, -, Ireland, 191, 179, CHAS-. In HH of Patrick OConnel m 35 born Ireland.

COTTRELL, CATHERINE, 31, F, None listed, -, Ireland, 191, 179, CHAS-. In HH of Patrick OConnel m 35 born Ireland.

COUGHAY, HUGH, 20, M, Laborer, -, Ireland, 629, 587, CHAS+. In HH of Pat. Powers m 50 born Ireland.

COUGHAY, JANE, 19, F, None listed, -, Ireland, 629, 587, CHAS+. In HH of Pat. Powers m 50 born Ireland.

COULEY, BARNEY, 26, M, Fireman, -, Ireland, 326, 301, CHAS. In HH of William Rollins m 40 born {-}.

COULEY, MAURICE, 40, M, Laborer, -, Ireland, 322, 297, CHAS. In Boarding house.

COURAY, ELIZABETH, 27, F, None listed, -, Ireland, 319, 293, CHAS+. In HH of Michael Couray m 27 born Ireland.

COURAY, MICHAEL, 27, M, Laborer, -, Ireland, 319, 293, CHAS+.

COURTNEY, HANNAH, 25, F, None listed, -, Ireland, 910, 887, CHAS%. In HH of Patrick

Courtney m 27 born Ireland.

COURTNEY, JOHN, 5, M, None listed, -, Ireland, 910, 887, CHAS%. In HH of Patrick Courtney m 27 born Ireland.

COURTNEY, PATRICK, 27, M, Laborer, -, Ireland, 910, 887, CHAS%.

COURTNEY, WILLIAM, 40, M, Ditcher, -, Ireland, 94, 94, Beau+.

COUTHNEY, ANDRIE, 28, M, Seaman, -, Ireland, 326, 301, CHAS. On Steam Ship Southerner.

COWAN, ISABELLA, 80, F, None listed, -, Ireland, 2222, 2222, ABB. In HH of Samuel Irwin m 70 born Ireland

COWAN, JOHN, 33, M, Laborer, -, Ireland, 839, 839, UNION. In HH of Albert Means m 32 born SC.

COWAN, WILLIAM, 60, M, Blacksmith, -, Ireland, 225, 225, ABB.

COWAN, WILLIAM, 84, M, None, -, Ireland, 405, 405, UNION. In HH of George West m 29 born SC.

COWELL, THOMAS, 19, M, Blacksmith, -, Ireland, 52, 52, CHAS^. In HH of John Amiel m 54 born England.

CRAGAN, PETER, 28, M, Fireman, -, Ireland, 326, 301, CHAS. In HH of William Rollins m 40 born {-}.

CRAIG, JANE, 51, F, None listed, -, Ireland, 455, 455, CHES. In HH of John Craig m 53 born Ireland.

CRAIG, JOHN, 53, M, Farmer, -, Ireland, 455, 455, CHES.

CRANFORD, CHARLES M., 25, M, Hotel Keeper, -, Ireland, 513, 513, FAIR. Hotel Keeper of the Fairfield Hotel. In HH of J.M. Cranford m 27 born Ireland.

CRANFORD, J.M., 27, M, Hotel Keeper, -, Ireland, 513, 513, FAIR. Hotel Keeper of the Fairfield Hotel.

CRANFORD, JOSEPH H., 21, M, Coach Maker, -, Ireland, 513, 513, FAIR. In HH of J.M. Cranford m 27 born Ireland. At the Fairfield Hotel.

CRANFORD, JUDA, 20, F, None listed, -, Ireland, 1365, 1365, CHES. In HH of Meredith Cranford m 25 born SC.

CRAWFORD, DANIEL, 38, M, Merchant, -, Ireland, 288, 294, RICH.

CRAWFORD, HELEN, 28, F, None listed, -, Ireland, 305, 311, RICH. In HH of Andrew Crawford m 46 born SC.

CRAWFORD, ISABELLA, 32, F, None listed, -, Ireland, 288, 294, RICH. In HH of Daniel Crawford m 38 born Ireland.

CRAWFORD, JAMES, 50, M, Famer, -, Ireland, 792, 796, AND.

CRAWFORD, JAMES, 60, M, Farmer, -, Ireland, 1571, 1571, YORK.

CRAWFORD, JANE, 50, M, None listed, -, Ireland, 305, 311, RICH. In HH of Andrew Crawford m 46 born SC.

CRAWFORD, JANE, 50, F, None listed, -, Ireland, 482, 497, RICH. In HH of Isaac Walker m 57 born Ireland.

CRAWFORD, JOHN A., 53, M, Pres. Coml.Bank, -, Ireland, 359, 368, RICH.

CRAWFORD, JOHN D., 52, M, Shoemaker, -, Ireland, 901, 901, CHES.

CRAWFORD, MAR-GARET, 55, F, None listed, -, Ireland, 530, 530, FAIR. In HH of Malcolm Frazier m 38 born NC.

CRAWFORD, MATTHEW, 50, M, Merchant, -, Ireland, 324, 330, RICH.

CRAWFORD, NANCY, 48, F, None listed, -, Ireland, 1540, 1540, ABB. In HH of Robert Crawford m 54 born SC.

CRAWFORD, SAMUEL, 22, M, Planter, -, Ireland, 321, 321, FAIR.

CRAWFORD, SARAH, 72, F, None listed, -, Ireland, 790, 794, AND.

CRAWFORD, THOMAS, 45, M, Stone mason, -, Ireland, 709, 710, FAIR.

CRAWFORD, WILLIAM, 84, M, None, -, Ireland, 1559, 1559, ABB. In HH of Thomas Crawford m 44 born SC.

CREEDON, JAMES, 37, M, Laborer, -, Ireland, 322, 297, CHAS. In Boarding house.

CREGAN, PATRICK, 27, M, Laborer, -, Ireland, 237, 222, CHAS-.Poor House.

CREGAN, PETER, 30, M, Laborer, -, Ireland, 340, 304, CHAS+. In HH of Patrick Murray m 30 born Ireland.

CREGAN, ROSE, 5, F, None listed, -, Ireland, 340, 304, CHAS+. In HH of Patrick Murray m 30 born Ireland.

CREGAN, ROXANA, 21, F, None listed, -, Ireland, 237, 222, CHAS-.Poor House.

CREIGG, THOMAS, 38, M, School teacher, -, Ireland, 17, 17, BEAU-. In HH of Thomas B. Davis m 38 born SC.

CREIGHAN, BRIDGET, 18, F, None listed, -, Ireland, 459, 442, CHAS-.

CREIGHTON, CON., 24, M, Laborer, -, Ireland, 322, 297, CHAS. In Boarding house.

CREIGHTON, FRANCIS, 5, M, None listed, -, Ireland, 348, 322, CHAS. In HH of Stephen Croughton m 35 born Ireland.

CREIGHTON, JOHN, 10, M, None listed, -, Ireland, 348, 322, CHAS. In HH of Stephen Croughton m 35 born Ireland.

CREIGHTON, MARY, 7, F, None listed, -, Ireland, 348, 322, CHAS. In HH of Stephen Croughton m 35 born Ireland.

CREIGHTON, PATRICK, 40, M, Porter, -, Ireland, 322, 297, CHAS. In Boarding house.

CREYON, ELIZABEATH, 31, F, None listed, -, Ireland, 873, 874, FAIR. In HH of James Creyon m 95 born Ireland.

CREYON, JAMES, 95, M, Planter, -, Ireland, 873, 874, FAIR.

CREYON, MARY, 32, F, None listed, -, Ireland, 873, 874, FAIR. In HH of James Creyon m 95 born Ireland.

CREYON, MARY, 60, F, None listed, -, Ireland, 873, 874, FAIR. In HH of James Creyon m 95 born Ireland.

CREYON, MICHAEL, 40, M, None listed, -, Ireland, 873, 874, FAIR. In HH of James Creyon m 95 born Ireland.

CRGAN, HUBBART, 30, M, Blacksmith, -, Ireland, 1896, 1896, SUMT.

CRGAN, MARY, 29, F, None listed, -, Ireland, 1896, 1896, SUMT. In HH of Hubbart Crgan m 30 born Ireland.

CRIBBAGE, SARAH, 22, F, None listed, -, Ireland, 111, 111, SUMT. In HH of David Cribbage m 38 born SC.

CROCKER, HONERE, 63, F, None listed, -, Ireland, 16, 19, CHAS. In HH of Catherine Murphy 28 f born Ireland.

CROCKER, OWEN, 76, M, Laborer, -, Ireland, 16, 19, CHAS. In HH of Catherine Murphy 28 f born Ireland.

CROGAN, CATHERINE, 24, F, None listed, -, Ireland, 193, 181, CHAS+. In HH of Peter Crogan m 30 born Ireland.

CROGAN, ELIZABETH, 45, F, None listed, -, Ireland, 523, 516, CHAS%. In HH of Michael Crogan m 45 born Ireland.

CROGAN, JAMES, 34, M, Laborer, -, Ireland, 468, 434, CHAS*.

CROGAN, MICHAEL, 45, M, Drayman, -, Ireland, 523, 516, CHAS%.

CROGAN, PETER, 30, M, City Police, -, Ireland, 193, 181, CHAS+.

CROMLAY, CATHERINE, 48, F, None listed, -, Ireland, 122, 113, CHAS+. In HH of Daniel Cromlay m 50 born Ireland.

CROMLAY, DANIEL, 50, M, Bootmaker, -, Ireland, 122, 113, CHAS+.

CROMLAY, JAMES, 48, M, Bootmaker, -, Ireland, 122, 113,

CHAS+. In HH of Daniel Cromlay m 50 born Ireland.

CROOK, JAMES, 13, M, None listed, -, Ireland, 1326, 1326, LAU. In HH of Alex Bell m 33 born Ireland.

CROOKS, WILLIAM, 84, M, Farmer, -, Ireland, 1018, 1063, PICK.

CROOKS, WILLIAM, 85, M, Farmer, -, Ireland, 1018, 1063, PICK.

CROUGHTON, ELLEN, 30, F, None listed, -, Ireland, 348, 322, CHAS. In HH of Stephen Croughton m 35 born Ireland.

CROUGHTON, STEPHEN, 35, M, Laborer, -, Ireland, 348, 322, CHAS.

CULBERT, JAMES, 32, M, Shoe dealer, -, Ireland, 483, 479, CHAS%.

CULBERT, JOHN, 33, M, Merchant, -, Ireland, 879, 856, CHAS%.

CULBERT, MARY ANN, 21, F, None listed, -, Ireland, 483, 479, CHAS%. In HH of James Culbert m 32 born Ireland.

CULENDER, LAURENS, 60, M, Farmer, -, Ireland, 420, 420, YORK*.

CULLEN, BRIDGET, 48, F, None listed, -, Ireland, 536, 551, RICH. In HH of Thomas Cullen m 50 born Ireland.

CULLEN, THOMAS, 50, M, Tailor, -, Ireland, 536, 551, RICH.

CULLENDER, JOHN, 45, M, None listed, -, Ireland, 420, 420, YORK*. In HH of Laurens Culender m 60 born Ireland.

CULLENDER, SARAH, 35, F, None listed, -, Ireland, 420, 420, YORK*. In HH of Laurens Culender m 60 born Ireland.

CULLEY, MARGARET, 35, M, None listed, -, Ireland, 346, 308, CHAS+. In Boarding house.

CULLEY, PETER, 40, \, Stone cutter, -, Ireland, 346, 308, CHAS+. In Boarding house.

CULLIN, THOMAS, 55, M, Attendant, -, Ireland, 542, 557, RICH.At Lunatic Asylum.

CUMMINS, JOHN, 29, M, Shoe dealer, -, Ireland, 826, 806, CHAS-.

CUMMINS, MICHAEL, 21, M, Clerk, -, Ireland, 826, 806, CHAS-. In HH of John Cummins m 29 born Ireland.

CUNNINGHAM, A.M., 30, M, Planter, -, Ireland, 132, 132, BEAU.

CUNNINGHAM, ALEXDR., 49, M, Ditcher, -, Ireland, 794, 794, SUMT.

CUNNINGHAM, ELIZABETH, 85, F, None listed, -, Ireland, 2224, 2224, ABB. In HH of James Cunningham m 40 born SC.

CUNNINGHAM, JOHN, 85,

M, None, -, Ireland, 1433, 1433, CHES.

CURBERRY, JOHN, 22, M, Clerk, -, Ireland, 277, 277, CHAS%. In HH of William McClure m 60 born Ireland.

CURLEY, MARCELLA, 28, F, None listed, -, Ireland, 197, 185, CHAS+. In HH of Stephen Curley m 32 born Ireland.

CURLEY, STEPHEN, 32, M, Shoemaker, -, Ireland, 197, 185, CHAS+.

CURRAN, JAMES, 26, M, None listed, -, Ireland, 215, 202, CHAS+. In HH of Peter Kelly m 35 born Ireland.

CURRY, ANNA, 15, F, None listed, -, Ireland, 984, 963, CHAS-. In HH of Charles McElleron m 30 born Ireland.

CURRY, PATRICK, 23, M, Laborer, -, Ireland, 166, 148, CHAS. In HH of John Jenkins m 25 born England.

CURTIN, CATHERINE, 36, F, None listed, -, Ireland, 744, 731, CHAS%.

D

DACOSTA, HENRY, 10, M, None listed, M, Ireland, 56, 51, CHAS-. In HH of W.P. DaCosta m 40 mulatto born Ireland.

DACOSTA, JAMES, 17, M, Shoemaker, M, Ireland, 56, 51, CHAS-. In HH of W.P. DaCosta m 40 mulatto born Ireland.

DACOSTA, JOSEPH, 8, M, None listed, M, Ireland, 56, 51, CHAS-. In HH of W.P. DaCosta m 40 mulatto born Ireland.

DACOSTA, LOUISA R., 35, F, None listed, M, Ireland, 56, 51, CHAS-. In HH of W.P. DaCosta m 40 mulatto born Ireland.

DACOSTA, LOUISA V., 6, F, None listed, M, Ireland, 56, 51, CHAS-. In HH of W.P. DaCosta m 40 mulatto born Ireland.

DACOSTA, THOMAS, 14, M, None listed, M, Ireland, 56, 51, CHAS-. In HH of W.P. DaCosta m 40 mulatto born Ireland.

DACOSTA, W.P., 40, M, Cotton gin maker, M, Ireland, 56, 51, CHAS-.

DACOSTA, WILLIAM, 12, M, None listed, M, Ireland, 56, 51, CHAS-. In HH of W.P. DaCosta m 40 mulatto born Ireland.

DAGMAN, FRANCIS, 40, M, Laborer, -, Ireland, 624, 582, CHAS+. In HH of Wash-ington Gascoin m 56 born Ireland.

DAILEY, THOS., 40, M, None listed, -, Ireland, 5, 5, BEAU+. In HH of William F. Jackson m 28, jailor, born SC.

Thos. Dailey in jail (stealing negro).

DAJAL, S(?), 35, M, Farmer, -, Ireland, 491, 491, LAU. In HH of J. Crews. m 27 born NC.

DALEY, ELLEN, 20, F, Servant, -, Ireland, 224, 202, CHAS. In HH of Helena Fryer f 40 born England.

DALEY, FRANCES, 23, M, Baker, -, Ireland, 132, 124, CHAS+. In HH of John McCrale {McCrate} m 30 born Canada.

DALEY, JEREMIAH, 47, M, None listed, -, Ireland, 280, 260, CHAS+. In HH of Edward Finn m 28 born Ireland.

DALEY, MOSES, 25, M, Clerk, -, Ireland, 804, 784, CHAS-. In HH of John Daly m 30 born Ireland.

DALEY, PATRICK, 28, M, Laborer, -, Ireland, 337, 311, CHAS. In HH of William H. Fowler m 38 running Boarding house born England.

DALY, JOHN, 30, M, Shoe dealer, -, Ireland, 804, 784, CHAS-.

DANCER, JEREMIAH, 24, M, Laborer, -, Ireland, 169, 159, CHAS+. In HH of John Sweeny m 79 born Ireland.

DANDURTY, BRIDGET, 2, F, None listed, -, Ireland, 912, 889, CHAS%. In HH of Ellen Dandurty f 30 born Ireland.

DANDURTY, ELLEN, 30, F, None listed, -, Ireland, 912, 889, CHAS%.

DANDURTY, THOMAS, 4, M, None listed, -, Ireland, 912, 889, CHAS%. In HH of Ellen Dandurty f 30 born Ireland.

DANIELS, JOHN, 38, M, Laborer, -, Ireland, 1045, 1023, CHAS%.

DANIELS, SARAH, 15, F, None listed, -, Ireland, 1045, 1023, CHAS%. In HH of John Daniels m 38 born Ireland.

DANIELS, SARAH, 37, F, None listed, -, Ireland, 1045, 1023, CHAS%. In HH of John Daniels m 38 born Ireland.

DARCEY, ELIZA, 12, F, None listed, -, Ireland, 1071, 1049, CHAS%. In HH of Thomas Darcey m 40 born Ireland.

DARCEY, ELLEN, 35, F, None listed, -, Ireland, 1071, 1049, CHAS%. In HH of Thomas Darcey m 40 born Ireland.

DARCEY, THOMAS, 40, M, Laborer, -, Ireland, 1071, 1049, CHAS%.

DARCEY, TONEY, 8, M, None listed, -, Ireland, 1071, 1049, CHAS%. In HH of Thomas Darcey m 40 born Ireland.

DARCEY, WILLIAM, 10, M, None listed, -, Ireland, 1071, 1049, CHAS%. In HH of Thomas Darcey m 40 born

Ireland.

DAREN, ELLEN, 40, F, None listed, -, Ireland, 745, 725, CHAS-. In HH of Frederick Wittpen m 43 born Germany.

DARGAN, SIDNEY, 45, M, Minister, -, Ireland, 542, 557, RICH. Date 1845 by name. In Lunatic Asylum.

DARSEY, TIMOTHY, 26, M, Painter, -, Ireland, 346, 308, CHAS+. In Boarding house.

DARWIN, MARY, 19, F, None listed, -, Ireland, 1086, 1064, CHAS%. In HH of A.G. Rose m 57 born SC.

DAVIDSON, JAMES, 21, M, None, -, Ireland, 5, 5, CHAS*. In HH of Thomas Davidson m 45 born Ireland.

DAVIDSON, MARY J., 38, F, None listed, -, Ireland, 5, 5, CHAS*. In HH of Thomas Davidson m 45 born Ireland.

DAVIDSON, THOMAS, 45, M, Lumber Measurer, -, Ireland, 5, 5, CHAS*.

DAVIS, ALEXANDER, 28, M, Musician, -, Ireland, 237, 222, CHAS-.Poor House.

DAVIS, JANE, 55, F, Boarding house, -, Ireland, 472, 438, CHAS*.

DAVIS, M. MRS., 95, F, None listed, -, Ireland, 201, 201, LANC*. In HH of Wm. Read m 55 born SC.

DAWSON, ANN, 24, F, None listed, -, Ireland, 518, 477, CHAS+. In HH of Mary Dawson f 50 born Ireland.

DAWSON, ANN, 34, F, Seamstress, -, Ireland, 237, 222, CHAS-.Works in Poor House.

DAWSON, FRANK, 30, M, Clerk, -, Ireland, 518, 477, CHAS+. In HH of Mary Dawson f 50 born Ireland.

DAWSON, JAMES, 35, M, Laborer, -, Ireland, 217, 204, CHAS+.

DAWSON, JOB, 26, M, Clerk, -, Ireland, 518, 477, CHAS+. In HH of Mary Dawson f 50 born Ireland.

DAWSON, JOSEPH, 28, M, Druggist, -, Ireland, 518, 477, CHAS+. In HH of Mary Dawson f 50 born Ireland.

DAWSON, MARY, 28, F, None listed, -, Ireland, 217, 204, CHAS+. In HH of James Dawson m 35 born Ireland.

DAWSON, MARY, 50, F, None listed, -, Ireland, 518, 477, CHAS+.

DELAMA ?, CHARLES G., 52, M, Drover, -, Ireland, 33, 33, COLL+.

DELANEY, JANE, 30, F, None listed, -, Ireland, 202, 190, CHAS+. In Boarding house.

DELANEY, JOHN, 26, M, Laborer, -, Ireland, 337, 311, CHAS. In HH of William H. Fowler m 38 running Boarding House born England.

DELANY, MARTIN, 44, M, Farmer, -, Ireland, 1992, 1992, ABB.

DEMPSEY, ANN, 50, F, None listed, -, Ireland, 237, 222, CHAS-. In Poor House.

DENNIE, WM. P., 51, M, Taylor, -, Ireland, 874, 874, PICK+.

DENNINGTON, WILLIAM, 80, M, Farmer, -, Ireland, 1146, 1197, PICK.

DENNISON, ANNA, 14, F, None listed, -, Ireland, 466, 449, CHAS-. In HH of Eliza E. Abbott f 24 born Ireland.

DENNY, ANN, 50, F, None listed, -, Ireland, 170, 153, CHAS. In HH of John Young m 23 born SC.

DENNY, WILLIAM, 70, M, Printer, -, Ireland, 247, 222, CHAS*.

DERMOND, MARY, 38, F, None listed, -, Ireland, 657, 637, CHAS-. In HH of Michael Dermond m 47 born Ireland.

DERMOND, MICHAEL, 47, M, Laborer, -, Ireland, 657, 637, CHAS-.

DERMOND, PATRICK, 12, M, None listed, -, Ireland, 657, 637, CHAS-. In HH of Michael Dermond m 47 born Ireland.

DESMOND, CORNELIUS, 50, M, Tanner, -, Ireland, 1206, 1185, CHAS%.

DESMOND, PATRICK, 56,

M, Laborer, -, Ireland, 1206, 1185, CHAS%. In HH of Cornelius Desmond m 50 born Ireland.

DEVERAUX, ANN, 16, F, None listed, -, Ireland, 867, 825, CHAS+. In HH of Nicholas Deveraux m 55 born Ireland.

DEVERAUX, DORA, 8, F, None listed, -, Ireland, 867, 825, CHAS+. In HH of Nicholas Deveraux m 55 born Ireland.

DEVERAUX, DORA, 46, F, None listed, -, Ireland, 867, 825, CHAS+. In HH of Nicholas Deveraux m 55 born Ireland.

DEVERAUX, ELLEN, 22, F, None listed, -, Ireland, 867, 825, CHAS+. In HH of Nicholas Deveraux m 55 born Ireland.

DEVERAUX, JAMES, 14, M, None listed, -, Ireland, 867, 825, CHAS+. In HH of Nicholas Deveraux m 55 born Ireland.

DEVERAUX, JOHN, 12, M, None listed, -, Ireland, 867, 825, CHAS+. In HH of Nicholas Deveraux m 55 born Ireland.

DEVERAUX, MARY, 27, F, None listed, -, Ireland, 867, 825, CHAS+. In HH of Nicholas Deveraux m 55 born Ireland.

DEVERAUX, NICHOLAS, 4, M, None listed, -, Ireland, 867, 825, CHAS+. In HH of Nicholas Deveraux m 55 born Ireland.

DEVERAUX, NICHOLAS, 55, M, Cooper, -, Ireland, 867,

825, CHAS+.

DEVERAUX, PATRICK, 24, M, Cooper, -, Ireland, 867, 825, CHAS+. In HH of Nicholas Deveraux m 55 born Ireland.

DEVERAUX, WILLIAM, 18, M, Cooper, -, Ireland, 867, 825, CHAS+. In HH of Nicholas Deveraux m 55 born Ireland.

DEWLEY, BRIDGET, 35, F, None listed, -, Ireland, 921, 898, CHAS%. In HH of John Dewley m 32 born Ireland.

DEWLEY, JOHN, 32, M, Laborer, -, Ireland, 921, 898, CHAS%.

DEXTER, JOHN, 30, M, Laborer, -, Ireland, 144, 135, CHAS+. In HH of Daniel Larry m 30 born Ireland.

DICK, JAMES, 35, M, Shoemaker, -, Ireland, 1486, 1486, ABB.

DICK, JANE, 34, F, None listed, -, Ireland, 1486, 1486, ABB. In HH of James Dick m 35 born Ireland.

DICK, JOHN, 11, M, None listed, -, Ireland, 1486, 1486, ABB. In HH of James Dick m 35 born Ireland.

DICKSON, JAMES, 75, M, Weaver, -, Ireland, 300, 301, AND*.

DICKSON, JAMES K., 35, M, School master, -, Ireland, 878, 878, GREE.

DICKSON, WILLIAM, 37, M, Farmer, -, Ireland, 882, 882, GREE.

DICKY, JOHN, 44, M, Farmer, -, Ireland, 1050, 1050, CHES.

DILE, JOHN, 33, M, Laborer, -, Ireland, 166, 148, CHAS. In HH of John Jenkins m 25 born England.

DILLON, CATHERINE, 16, F, None listed, -, Ireland, 992, 971, CHAS-. In HH of S.B. Bernard m 38 born France.

DILLON, JAMES, 34, M, Laborer, -, Ireland, 222, 209, CHAS+. In HH of John Donnahugh m 22 born Ireland.

DILLON, MICHAEL, 29, M, Carpenter, -, Ireland, 35, 36, RICH.

DILLON, THOMAS, 32, M, Clerk, -, Ireland, 375, 358, CHAS-.

DINYER?, THOMAS, 40, M, None listed, -, Ireland, 1948, 1948, BARN. In HH of Wm. Bowers m 48 born SC.

DIVINE, PATRICK, 25, M, None, -, Ireland, 40, 37, CHAS-. Listed as prisoner.

DIXON, ELENOR, 82, F, None listed, -, Ireland, 1390, 1391, SPART. In HH of William Dixon m 80 born Ireland.

DIXON, REBECCA, 65, F, None listed, -, Ireland, 500, 500, SPART. In HH of Robert Dixon m 76 born Ireland.

DIXON, RICHARD, 27, M, Clerk, -, Ireland, 246, 251, RICH. In HH of James N. Stein m 30 born England.

DIXON, ROBERT, 76, M, Farmer, -, Ireland, 500, 500, SPART.

DIXON, W.P., 42, M, Farmer, -, Ireland, 320, 320, SPART.

DIXON, WILLIAM, 86, M, Farmer, -, Ireland, 1390, 1391, SPART.

DOGAN, PATRICK D., 40, M, Mason, -, Ireland, 542, 557, RICH. Date 1850 by name. In Lunatic Asylum.

DOGHERTY, CON., 80, M, Gass fitter, -, Ireland, 447, 405, CHAS. In HH of John Thompson m 35 born Ireland.

DOGHERTY, FRANCES, 84, F, None listed, -, Ireland, 447, 405, CHAS. In HH of John Thompson m 35 born Ireland.

DOGHERTY, JOHN, 28, M, Laborer, -, Ireland, 447, 405, CHAS. In HH of John Thompson m 35 born Ireland.

DOGHERTY, JOHN, 40, M, Carpenter, -, Ireland, 403, 386, CHAS-.

DOGHERTY, MARGARET, 30, F, None listed, -, Ireland, 403, 386, CHAS-. In HH of John Dogherty m 40 born Ireland.

DOGHERTY, MARY, 25, F, None listed, -, Ireland, 447,

405, CHAS. In HH of John Thompson m 35 born Ireland.

DOLAN, BARNEY, 30, M, Ditcher, -, Ireland, 1031, 1031, EDGE. In HH of William Dorn m 50 born SC.

DOLAND, JAMES, 20, M, Laborer, -, Ireland, 202, 181, CHAS. In HH of Patrick Carroll m 40 born Ireland.

DOLAND, JOHN, 18, M, Laborer, -, Ireland, 202, 181, CHAS. In HH of Patrick Carroll m 40 born Ireland.

DONAHOE, ANN, 40, F, None listed, -, Ireland, 50, 46, CHAS-. In HH of Michael Downey m 30 born Ireland.

DONAHOE, JAMES, 45, M, Laborer, -, Ireland, 50, 46, CHAS-. In HH of Michael Downey m 30 born Ireland.

DONAHOO, CATHARINE, 38, F, None listed, -, Ireland, 324, 324, CHAS%. In HH of James M. Caldwell m 42 born SC.

DONALDSON, ANN, 21, F, None listed, -, Ireland, 1078, 1055, CHAS-. In HH of J.F. Blacklock m 45 born SC.

DONALDSON, WILLIAM, 35, M, Clerk, -, Ireland, 837, 847, RICH+.

DONNAHO, MICHAEL, 40, M, Laborer, -, Ireland, 261, 244, CHAS+. In HH of Hugh McNamara m 28 born Ireland.

DONNAHOE, BRIGET, 35, F, None listed, -, Ireland, 1078, 1100, CHAS%. In HH of John Donnahoe m 39 born Ireland.

DONNAHOE, CHARLES, 30, M, Mariner, -, Ireland, 40, 37, CHAS-.Listed as prisioner, date 1850.

DONNAHOE, JAMES, 11, M, None listed, -, Ireland, 1078, 1100, CHAS%. In HH of John Donnahoe m 39 born Ireland.

DONNAHOE, JOHN, 39, M, Laborer, -, Ireland, 1078, 1100, CHAS%.

DONNAHOE, PATRICK, 15, M, Clerk, -, Ireland, 1078, 1100, CHAS%. In HH of John Donnahoe m 39 born Ireland.

DONNAHOE, PATRICK, 20, M, Laborer, -, Ireland, 144, 135, CHAS+. In HH of Daniel Larry m 30 born Ireland.

DONNAHUGH, JOHN, 22, M, Laborer, -, Ireland, 222, 209, CHAS+.

DONNALIAM, DENNIS, 32, M, Broker, -, Ireland, 86, 84, CHAS*.

DONNALIAM, ELIZABETH, 30, F, None listed, -, Ireland, 86, 84, CHAS*. In HH of Dennis Donnaliam m 32 born Ireland.

DONNELLY, ALICE, 18, F, None listed, -, Ireland, 9, 9, CHAS%. In HH of John Donnelly m 39 born Ireland.

DONNELLY, BRIGET, 17, F, None listed, -, Ireland, 39, 34, CHAS+. In HH of Dennis Connelly m 44 born Ireland.

DONNELLY, BRIGET, 36, F, None listed, -, Ireland, 9, 9, CHAS%. In HH of John Donnelly m 39 born Ireland.

DONNELLY, BRIGET, 40, F, None listed, -, Ireland, 39, 34, CHAS+. In HH of Dennis Connelly m 44 born Ireland.

DONNELLY, BRIGET, 46, F, None listed, -, Ireland, 632, 613, CHAS-. In HH of Patrick Donnelly m 50 born Ireland.

DONNELLY, CATHERINE, 16, F, None listed, -, Ireland, 632, 613, CHAS-. In HH of Patrick Donnelly m 50 born Ireland.

DONNELLY, CONSTANCE, 28, F, None listed, -, Ireland, 289, 263, CHAS*. In HH of Patrick Donnelly m 38 born Ireland.

DONNELLY, DANIEL, 20, M, Gas Fitter, -, Ireland, 289, 263, CHAS*. In HH of Patrick Donnelly m 38 born Ireland.

DONNELLY, DENNIS, 23, M, Plasterer, -, Ireland, 39, 34, CHAS+. In HH of Dennis Connelly m 44 born Ireland.

DONNELLY, DENNIS, 44, M, Builder, -, Ireland, 39, 34, CHAS+.

DONNELLY, JANE, 21, F, None listed, -, Ireland, 403, 363, CHAS+. In HH of William Elliott m 28 born Ireland.

DONNELLY, JANE, 32, F, None listed, -, Ireland, 289, 263, CHAS*. In HH of Patrick Donnelly m 38 born Ireland.

DONNELLY, JOHN, 39, M, Laborer, -, Ireland, 9, 9, CHAS%.

DONNELLY, MARY, 19, F, None listed, -, Ireland, 39, 34, CHAS+. In HH of Dennis Connelly m 44 born Ireland.

DONNELLY, MICHAEL, 28, M, Laborer, -, Ireland, 1135, 1114, CHAS%. In HH of Thomas Corcosan m 48 born Ireland.

DONNELLY, PATRICK, 14, M, None listed, -, Ireland, 9, 9, CHAS%. In HH of John Donnelly m 39 born Ireland.

DONNELLY, PATRICK, 38, M, Laborer, -, Ireland, 289, 263, CHAS*.

DONNELLY, PATRICK, 50, M, Laborer, -, Ireland, 632, 613, CHAS-.

DONNELLY, ROB. B., 28, M, Painter, -, Ireland, 391, 355, CHAS. In HH of F.W. Theus m 28 born Germany.

DONNELLY, TERESE, 26, F, None listed, -, Ireland, 1135, 1114, CHAS%. In HH of Thomas Corcosan m 48 born

Ireland.

DONNELLY, THOMAS, 19, M, Bricklayer, -, Ireland, 632, 613, CHAS-. In HH of Patrick Donnelly m 50 born Ireland.

DONNELLY, THOMAS, 25, M, Laborer, -, Ireland, 108, 103, CHAS*. In HH of Patrick Keefe m 40 born Ireland.

DONNELLY, WILLIAM, 13, M, None listed, -, Ireland, 289, 263, CHAS*. In HH of Patrick Donnelly m 38 born Ireland.

DONNOVAN, CLARISSA, 40, F, None listed, -, Ireland, 477, 435, CHAS+. In HH of Patrick O. Donnovan m 44 born Ireland.

DONNOVAN, DAN, 26, M, Plasterer, -, Ireland, 477, 435, CHAS+. In HH of Patrick O. Donnovan m 44 born Ireland.

DONNOVAN, JULIA, 28, F, None listed, -, Ireland, 477, 435, CHAS+. In HH of Patrick O. Donnovan m 44 born Ireland.

DONNOVAN, KATHLEEN, 24, F, None listed, -, Ireland, 477, 435, CHAS+. In HH of Patrick O. Donnovan m 44 born Ireland.

DONNOVAN, PATRICK O., 44, M, Builder, -, Ireland, 477, 435, CHAS+.

DONOHOE, MARY, 25, F, None listed, -, Ireland, 234, 209, CHAS*. In HH of Michael Donohoe m 35 born Ireland.

DONOHOE, MICHAEL, 35, M, Gardner, -, Ireland, 234, 209, CHAS*.

DONOHOUGH, A., 32, M, Laborer, -, Ireland, 405, 369, CHAS. In HH of William Doran m 36 born MA.

DONOVAN, BRIGET, 25, F, None listed, -, Ireland, 862, 820, CHAS+. In HH of W.H. Gainbow m 35 born France.

DONOVAN, JAMES, 24, M, Clerk, -, Ireland, 794, 774, CHAS-. In HH of L.P.H. Close m 32 born Ireland.

DONOVAN, THOMAS, 30, M, Laborer, -, Ireland, 322, 297, CHAS. In Boarding house.

DONSHAN, ROSE, 20, F, None listed, -, Ireland, 1062, 1040, CHAS%. In HH of Joseph Beach m 37 born NY.

DOOL, EASTER, 30, F, None listed, -, Ireland, 717, 718, FAIR. In HH of Mary Dool f 85 born Ireland.

DOOL, MARY, 85, F, None listed, -, Ireland, 717, 718, FAIR.

DOOLY, THOMAS, 77, M, Laborer, -, Ireland, 911, 888, CHAS%. In HH of Patrick Lanagan m 33 born Ireland.

DORAN, ANN, 25, F, None listed, -, Ireland, 766, 746, CHAS-. In HH of Patarick Hogan m 37 born Ireland.

DORAN, JAMES, 13, M, None listed, -, Ireland, 813, 796, CHAS%. In HH of Patrick Doran m 37 born Ireland.

DORAN, MAGDELINE, 8, F, None listed, -, Ireland, 813, 796, CHAS%. In HH of Patrick Doran m 37 born Ireland.

DORAN, MARY, 22, F, Laborer, -, Ireland, 405, 369, CHAS. In HH of William Doran m 36 born MA.

DORAN, MARY, 35, F, None listed, -, Ireland, 813, 796, CHAS%. In HH of Patrick Doran m 37 born Ireland.

DORAN, PATRICK, 37, M, Laborer, -, Ireland, 813, 796, CHAS%.

DORAN, THOMAS, 22, M, Laborer, -, Ireland, 166, 148, CHAS. In HH of John Jenkins m 25 born England.

DORAN, TIMOTHY, 11, M, None listed, -, Ireland, 813, 796, CHAS%. In HH of Patrick Doran m 37 born Ireland.

DORRELL, GEO., 42, M, Laborer, -, Ireland, 282, 261, CHAS+. In HH of Stephen Cahill m 50 born Ireland.

DORROH, SARAH, 64, F, None listed, -, Ireland, 1774, 1774, LAU.

DORSEY, ANN, 13, F, None listed, -, Ireland, 29, 36, CHAS. In HH of Michael Dorsey m 35 born Ireland.

DORSEY, CATHERINE, 6, F, None listed, -, Ireland, 29, 36, CHAS. In HH of Michael Dorsey m 35 born Ireland.

DORSEY, GEORGE, 18, M, Bar Keeper, -, Ireland, 322, 297, CHAS. In Boarding house.

DORSEY, JOHN, 11, M, None listed, -, Ireland, 29, 36, CHAS. In HH of Michael Dorsey m 35 born Ireland.

DORSEY, MARGARET, 7, F, None listed, -, Ireland, 29, 36, CHAS. In HH of Michael Dorsey m 35 born Ireland.

DORSEY, MARGARET, 18, F, None listed, -, Ireland, 984, 963, CHAS-. In HH of Charles McElleron m 30 born Ireland.

DORSEY, MARY, 9, F, None listed, -, Ireland, 29, 36, CHAS. In HH of Michael Dorsey m 35 born Ireland.

DORSEY, MARY, 30, F, None listed, -, Ireland, 29, 36, CHAS. In HH of Michael Dorsey m 35 born Ireland.

DORSEY, MICHAEL, 35, M, None listed, -, Ireland, 29, 36, CHAS.

DORSEY, PETER, 28, M, Laborer, -, Ireland, 415, 374, CHAS+. In HH of Caroline Segee f 30 born Ireland.

DOUGHERTY, ELLEN, 36, F, None listed, -, Ireland, 524, 490, CHAS*. In HH of George Robertson m 44 born SC.

DOUGHERTY, JOHN, 40, M, Facter, -, Ireland, 8, 8, CHAS*. In HH of Jos. Dougherty m 70 born Ireland.

DOUGHERTY, JOS., 70, M, Grocer, -, Ireland, 8, 8, CHAS*.

DOUGHERTY, JOSEPH, 34, M, Ship wright, -, Ireland, 8, 8, CHAS*. In HH of Jos. Dougherty m 70 born Ireland.

DOUGHERTY, MARGARET, 38, F, None listed, -, Ireland, 8, 8, CHAS*. In HH of Jos. Dougherty m 70 born Ireland.

DOUGHERTY, MARY, 36, F, None listed, -, Ireland, 8, 8, CHAS*. In HH of Jos. Dougherty m 70 born Ireland.

DOUGHTERY, LUKE, 37, M, Clerk, -, Ireland, 269, 269, COLL*. In HH of P. Burns m 32 born Scotland.

DOUGHTY, CATHARINE, 16, F, None listed, -, Ireland, 1095, 1073, CHAS%. In HH of John Doughty m 41 born Ireland.

DOUGHTY, JOHN, 13, M, None listed, -, Ireland, 1095, 1073, CHAS%. In HH of John Doughty m 41 born Ireland.

DOUGHTY, JOHN, 41, M, Bricklayer, -, Ireland, 1095, 1073, CHAS%.

DOUGHTY, JULIA, 10, F, None listed, -, Ireland, 1095, 1073, CHAS%. In HH of John

Doughty m 41 born Ireland.

DOUGHTY, MARGARET, 37, F, None listed, -, Ireland, 1095, 1073, CHAS%. In HH of John Doughty m 41 born Ireland.

DOUGLAS, JOHN, 60, M, Planter, -, Ireland, 976, 977, FAIR.

DOUNAN, CATHERINE, 30, F, None listed, -, Ireland, 47, 43, CHAS$. In HH of John Ewing m 50 born MA.

DOUNAN, HENRY, 36, M, Capt. U.S.A., -, Ireland, 47, 43, CHAS$. In HH of John Ewing m 50 born MA.

DOUNELL, CATHERINE, 21, F, None listed, -, Ireland, 648, 628, CHAS-. In HH of Mary Corbett f 59 born SC.

DOUONAHOUGH, MARGARET, 40, F, Servant, -, Ireland, 234, 212, CHAS. In HH of Geo. Brown m 45 born Scotland.

DOW, A.J., 45, M, Laborer, -, Ireland, 1819, 1825, EDGE.

DOWD, ALICE, 30, F, None listed, -, Ireland, 553, 519, CHAS*. In Catholic Seminary.

DOWD, HANNAH, 50, F, None listed, -, Ireland, 431, 390, CHAS+. In HH of Martin Dowd m 53 born Ireland.

DOWD, MARTIN, 53, M, Porter dealer, -, Ireland, 431, 390, CHAS+.

DOWD, W.O., 32, M, Planter, -, Ireland, 326, 327, ORNG+.

DOWLING, CATHERINE, 18, F, None listed, -, Ireland, 167, 158, CHAS+. In Boarding house.

DOWLING, ELIZA, 42, F, None listed, -, Ireland, 322, 294, CHAS+. In HH of John Dowling m 34 born Ireland.

DOWLING, EMMELINE, 67, F, None listed, -, Ireland, 427, 396, CHAS*. In HH of Elizabeth Hood f 45 born NY.

DOWLING, JOHANNES, 24, M, Merchant, -, Ireland, 1894, 1894, SUMT.

DOWLING, JOHN, 34, M, Store keeper, -, Ireland, 322, 294, CHAS+.

DOWLING, MICHAEL, 24, M, Laborer, -, Ireland, 471, 468, CHAS%. In HH of Herman Meyer m 33 born Germany.

DOWLING, MICHAEL, 25, M, None listed, -, Ireland, 167, 158, CHAS+. In Boarding house.

DOWNEY, CATHERINE, 30, F, None listed, -, Ireland, 493, 451, CHAS+. In HH of Patrick Downey m 41 born Ireland.

DOWNEY, DOROTHY, 38, F, None listed, -, Ireland, 493, 451, CHAS+. In HH of Patrick Downey m 41 born Ireland.

DOWNEY, ELIZA., 17, F, None listed, -, Ireland, 1620, 1620, LAU. In HH of Samuel

Downey m 50 born Ireland.

DOWNEY, MARY, 16, F, None listed, -, Ireland, 493, 451, CHAS+. In HH of Patrick Downey m 41 born Ireland.

DOWNEY, MARY, 33, F, None listed, -, Ireland, 50, 46, CHAS-. In HH of Michael Downey m 30 born Ireland.

DOWNEY, MARY, 45, F, None listed, -, Ireland, 1620, 1620, LAU. In HH of Samuel Downey m 50 born Ireland.

DOWNEY, MICHAEL, 10, M, None listed, -, Ireland, 493, 451, CHAS+. In HH of Patrick Downey m 41 born Ireland.

DOWNEY, MICHAEL, 30, M, Laborer, -, Ireland, 50, 46, CHAS-.

DOWNEY, PATRICK, 34, M, Laborer, -, Ireland, 222, 209, CHAS+. In HH of John Donnahugh m 22 born Ireland.

DOWNEY, PATRICK, 41, M, Laborer, -, Ireland, 493, 451, CHAS+.

DOWNEY, SAMUEL, 50, M, Farmer, -, Ireland, 1620, 1620, LAU.

DOYLE, ANN, 43, F, None listed, -, Ireland, 1691, 1691, GREE. In HH of John Doyle m 37 born Ireland.

DOYLE, CATHERINE, 35, F, None listed, -, Ireland, 111, 106, CHAS*. In Boarding house.

DOYLE, ELIZABETH, 26, F, None listed, -, Ireland, 27, 24, CHAS$. In HH of Philip Doyle m 30 born Ireland.

DOYLE, JAMES, 32, M, Laborer, -, Ireland, 501, 453, CHAS.

DOYLE, JOHN, 1, M, None listed, -, Ireland, 1691, 1691, GREE. In HH of John Doyle m 37 born Ireland.

DOYLE, JOHN, 30, M, Laborer, -, Ireland, 240, 226, CHAS+. In HH of William Farley m 38 born Ireland.

DOYLE, JOHN, 35, M, Carpenter, -, Ireland, 111, 106, CHAS*. In Boarding house.

DOYLE, JOHN, 37, M, Laborer, -, Ireland, 1691, 1691, GREE.

DOYLE, MARGARET, 39, F, None listed, -, Ireland, 500, 515, RICH.

DOYLE, MARY, 15, F, None listed, -, Ireland, 1691, 1691, GREE. In HH of John Doyle m 37 born Ireland.

DOYLE, MARY, 24, F, None listed, -, Ireland, 501, 453, CHAS. In HH of James Doyle m 32 born Ireland.

DOYLE; MARY, 55, F, None listed, -, Ireland, 500, 515, RICH. In HH of Hugh McElrone m 42 born Ireland.

DOYLE, MICHAEL, 30, M, Coach maker, -, Ireland, 128, 128, BEAU+.

DOYLE, PATRICK, 16, M, None listed, -, Ireland, 522, 515, CHAS%. In HH of James Power m 35 born Ireland.

DOYLE, PHILIP, 30, M, Laborer, -, Ireland, 27, 24, CHAS$.

DOYLEY, MARGARET, 22, F, None listed, -, Ireland, 277, 261, CHAS-. In HH of Alexander Hamilton m 52 born SC.

DRAKE, ANNA, 28, F, None listed, -, Ireland, 785, 765, CHAS-. In HH of Miles Drake m 42 born Ireland.

DRAKE, COLLIN, 18, M, Laborer, -, Ireland, 350, 312, CHAS+. In HH of Mike Drake m 48 born Ireland.

DRAKE, DANIEL, 12, M, None listed, -, Ireland, 350, 312, CHAS+. In HH of Mike Drake m 48 born Ireland.

DRAKE, EDWARD, 16, M, Laborer, -, Ireland, 350, 312, CHAS+. In HH of Mike Drake m 48 born Ireland.

DRAKE, ELLEN, 21, F, None listed, -, Ireland, 350, 312, CHAS+. In HH of Mike Drake m 48 born Ireland.

DRAKE, FRANK, 14, M, None listed, -, Ireland, 350, 312, CHAS+. In HH of Mike Drake m 48 born Ireland.

DRAKE, MARY, 8, F, None listed, -, Ireland, 350, 312, CHAS+. In HH of Mike Drake

m 48 born Ireland.

DRAKE, MIKE, 30, M, Mason, -, Ireland, 350, 312, CHAS+. In HH of Mike Drake m 48 born Ireland.

DRAKE, MIKE, 48, M, Laborer, -, Ireland, 350, 312, CHAS+.

DRAKE, MILES, 42, M, Merchant, -, Ireland, 785, 765, CHAS-.

DRAKE, NANCY, 64, F, None listed, -, Ireland, 318, 319, AND*. In HH of James Drake Senr. m 66 born SC.

DRAKE, NORA, 46, F, None listed, -, Ireland, 350, 312, CHAS+. In HH of Mike Drake m 48 born Ireland.

DRAKE, SUSAN, 26, F, None listed, -, Ireland, 350, 312, CHAS+. In HH of Mike Drake m 48 born Ireland.

DREW, EDWARD, 25, M, Laborer, -, Ireland, 110, 102, CHAS+. In HH of John May m 30 born Ireland.

DUBOIS, ELEANOR, 60, F, None listed, -, Ireland, 84, 78, CHAS-.

DUFFY, JOHN, 30, M, Cooper, -, Ireland, 1990, 1996, EDGE. In HH of Patrick Burns m 35 born Ireland.

DUFFY, MARGARET, 32, F, None listed, -, Ireland, 332, 315, CHAS-. In HH of Samuel Duffy m 40 born Ireland.

DUFFY, SAMUEL, 40, M, Carpenter, -, Ireland, 332, 315, CHAS-.

DUGAN, MARY, 20, F, Servant, -, Ireland, 300, 277, CHAS. In HH of Michael Hogan m 30 born Ireland.

DUGAN, PATRICK, 37, M, Stone Mason, -, Ireland, 542, 557, RICH. Date 1849 by name. In Lunatic Asylum.

DUGGAN, BRIGET, 28, F, None listed, -, Ireland, 237, 224, CHAS+. In HH of John Duggan m 32 born Ireland.

DUGGAN, BRIGET, 40, F, None listed, -, Ireland, 353, 315, CHAS+. In HH of Dennis Duggan m 44 born Ireland.

DUGGAN, DENNIS, 18, M, Laborer, -, Ireland, 353, 315, CHAS+. In HH of Dennis Duggan m 44 born Ireland.

DUGGAN, DENNIS, 44, M, Laborer, -, Ireland, 353, 315, CHAS+.

DUGGAN, JAMES, 8, M, None listed, -, Ireland, 198, 186, CHAS+. In HH of Martin Duggan m 40 born Ireland.

DUGGAN, JOHN, 17, M, None listed, -, Ireland, 198, 186, CHAS+. In HH of Martin Duggan m 40 born Ireland.

DUGGAN, JOHN, 32, M, Laborer, -, Ireland, 237, 224, CHAS+.

DUGGAN, MARGARET, 35, F, None listed, -, Ireland, 444, 411, CHAS*. In HH of James Ruth m 32 born Ireland.

DUGGAN, MARTIN, 5, M, None listed, -, Ireland, 198, 186, CHAS+. In HH of Martin Duggan m 40 born Ireland.

DUGGAN, MARTIN, 40, M, Laborer, -, Ireland, 198, 186, CHAS+.

DUGGAN, MARY, 12, F, None listed, -, Ireland, 198, 186, CHAS+. In HH of Martin Duggan m 40 born Ireland.

DUGGAN, MARY, 27, F, None listed, -, Ireland, 353, 315, CHAS+. In HH of Dennis Duggan m 44 born Ireland.

DUGGAN, MARY, 34, F, None listed, -, Ireland, 117, 109, CHAS+. In HH of Patrick Duggan m 35 born Ireland.

DUGGAN, MARY, 35, F, None listed, -, Ireland, 198, 186, CHAS+. In HH of Martin Duggan m 40 born Ireland.

DUGGAN, MICHAEL, 10, M, None listed, -, Ireland, 198, 186, CHAS+. In HH of Martin Duggan m 40 born Ireland.

DUGGAN, PATRICK, 25, M, Laborer, -, Ireland, 353, 315, CHAS+. In HH of Dennis Duggan m 44 born Ireland.

DUGGAN, PATRICK, 35, M, Mason, -, Ireland, 117, 109, CHAS+.

DUGGAN, PETER, 40, M, Bricklayer, -, Ireland, 466, 433, CHAS*.

DUGGAN, ROSANA, 36, F, None listed, -, Ireland, 466, 433, CHAS*. In HH of Peter Duggan m 40 born Ireland.

DUGGAN, TIMOTHY, 14, M, None listed, -, Ireland, 198, 186, CHAS+. In HH of Martin Duggan m 40 born Ireland.

DULFIN, WALTER, 35, M, None listed, -, Ireland, 921, 898, CHAS%. In HH of John Dewley m 32 born Ireland.

DUMFREY, THOMAS, 36, M, R.R. Laborer, -, Ireland, 987, 964, CHAS%. In Boarding house.

DUNBAR, ADAM, 56, F, None listed, -, Ireland, 759, 760, FAIR. In HH of John L. Youngue m 63 born SC.

DUNBAR, JAMES, 50, M, Farmer, -, Ireland, 1693, 1693, GREE.

DUNFIELD, THOMAS, 34, M, Laborer, -, Ireland, 463, 446, CHAS-. In HH of James Ryan m 30 born Ireland.

DUNLAP, JAMES, 60, M, Laborer, -, Ireland, 656, 636, CHAS-.

DUNLAP, JENNET, 65, F, None listed, -, Ireland, 909, 909, CHES. In HH of Robt. Dunlap m 25 born SC.

DUNLAP, WM. C., 42, M, Driver, -, Ireland, 540, 523, CHAS-. In Merchants Hotel. Occupation: Omnibus Driver.

DUNN, ANN, 30, F, None listed, -, Ireland, 253, 238, CHAS+. In HH of John Dunn m 32 born Ireland.

DUNN, CASPARETTA, 30, F, None listed, -, Ireland, 184, 167, CHAS. In HH of Joseph Dunn m 30 born Ireland.

DUNN, CATHERINE, 30, F, Servant, -, Ireland, 78, 88, CHAS. In HH of Otis Mills m 53 born MA.

DUNN, CHARLES, 30, M, Clerk, -, Ireland, 1097, 1074, CHAS-. In HH of William Dunn m 37 born Ireland.

DUNN, IVARIA, 28, F, Servant, -, Ireland, 55, 65, CHAS. In HH of John Ravenel m 53 born SC.

DUNN, J., 25, M, Blacksmith, -, Ireland, 465, 422, CHAS. In HH of Leslie O'Wen m 47 born Ireland.

DUNN, JAMES, 8, M, None listed, -, Ireland, 429, 398, CHAS*. In HH of Garret Burns m 23 born Ireland.

DUNN, JAMES, 45, M, Laborer, -, Ireland, 237, 222, CHAS-.Poor House.

DUNN, JOHN, 12, M, None listed, -, Ireland, 429, 398, CHAS*. In HH of Garret Burns m 23 born Ireland.

DUNN, JOHN, 32, M, State Constable, -, Ireland, 253, 238, CHAS+.

DUNN, JOSEPH, 30, M, Tavern keeper, -, Ireland, 184, 167, CHAS.

DUNN, MARGARET, 25, F, None listed, -, Ireland, 1097, 1074, CHAS-. In HH of William Dunn m 37 born Ireland.

DUNN, MORRIS, 25, M, Laborer, -, Ireland, 292, 292, CHAS%. In HH of Henry McGuire m 35 born Ireland.

DUNN, WILLIAM, 37, M, Shop keeper, -, Ireland, 1097, 1074, CHAS-.

DUNN, WILLIAM C., 41, M, Tailor, -, Ireland, 466, 466, LAU.

DUNNOVAN, FLORANCE, 24, F, None listed, -, Ireland, 184, 167, CHAS. In Boarding house.

DUNNOVEN, KATEY, 29, F, None listed, -, Ireland, 569, 552, CHAS-. In HH of Patrick Dunnoven m 34 born Ireland.

DUNNOVEN, PATRICK, 34, M, Laborer, -, Ireland, 569, 552, CHAS-.

DURKIN, ELLEN, 28, F, None listed, -, Ireland, 498, 452, CHAS. In HH of John Durkin m 30 born Ireland.

DURKIN, JOHN, 30, M, Laborer, -, Ireland, 498, 452, CHAS.

DWYER, ANN A., 34, F, Nurse Maniac De, -, Ireland, 237, 222, CHAS-.Occupation: Nurse Maaniac Dept. Works in Poor House.

DWYRE, THOMAS, 39, M, Ditcher, -, Ireland, 29, 29, BEAU*. In HH of Miles J. Gray m 26 born SC.

E

EARLEY, CATHERINE, 25, F, None listed, -, Ireland, 346, 308, CHAS+. In HH of James Earley m 40 born Ireland.

EARLEY, JAMES, 40, M, Boarding house, -, Ireland, 346, 308, CHAS+.

EATON, JAMES, 22, M, Stone cutter, -, Ireland, 63, 63, FAIR. In HH of Adna Johnson m 53 born CT.

EDMONDS, JOHN, 25, M, Laborer, -, Ireland, 271, 252, CHAS+. In HH of Mary Campbell f 49 born Ireland.

EGAN, JOHN, 25, M, Clerk, -, Ireland, 194, 178, CHAS*.

EGAN, PATRICK, 16, M, Laborer, -, Ireland, 457, 415, CHAS+. In HH of James Karvin m 30 born Ireland.

EGEAN, JAMES, 60, M, Farmer, -, Ireland, 941, 941, LEX.

EHRLICH, REBECCA, 33, F, None listed, -, Ireland, 349, 355, RICH. In HH of Michael Ehrlich m 42 born Germany.

EISNAGHAM, THOMAS F., 52, M, Merchant, -, Ireland,

2008, 2010, EDGE.

ELDER, JANE, 75, F, None listed, -, Ireland, 595, 595, CHES. In HH of Robert Elder m 32 born SC.

ELLARD, THOMAS, 19, M, Engineer, -, Ireland, 259, 243, CHAS+. In HH of T.L. Quackenbush m 35 born NY.

ELLIOT, MARTIN, 35, M, Laborer, -, Ireland, 538, 497, CHAS+. In HH of John Sharley m 30 born Ireland.

ELLIOTT, JANE, 88, F, None listed, -, Ireland, 766, 767, FAIR.

ELLIOTT, MARY, 28, F, None listed, -, Ireland, 403, 363, CHAS+. In HH of William Elliott m 28 born Ireland.

ELLIOTT, WILLIAM, 30, M, Clerk, -, Ireland, 403, 363, CHAS+.

ELLISON, MARGARET, 58, F, None listed, -, Ireland, 309, 315, RICH. In HH of William Law m 71 born Ireland.

ENGLAND, ELIZABETH, 60, F, None listed, -, Ireland, 274, 251, CHAS.

ENGLISH, ARCHY, 30, M, Farmer, -, Ireland, 461, 461, CHES. In HH of M. English f 66 born Ireland.

ENGLISH, JAMES, 50, M, Ship wright, -, Ireland, 7, 7, CHAS*.

ENGLISH, JAS., 26, M,

Farmer, -, Ireland, 461, 461, CHES. In HH of M. English f 66 born Ireland.

ENGLISH, M., 66, F, None listed, -, Ireland, 461, 461, CHES.

ENGLISH, MARY, 32, F, None listed, -, Ireland, 461, 461, CHES. In HH of M. English f 66 born Ireland.

ENGLISH, SAM, 28, M, Farmer, -, Ireland, 461, 461, CHES. In HH of M. English f 66 born Ireland.

ENGLISH, WM., 34, M, Farmer, -, Ireland, 461, 461, CHES. In HH of M. English f 66 born Ireland.

ENNESS, MILES, 25, M, Coalpasser, -, Ireland, 326, 301, CHAS. In HH of William Rollins m 40 born {-}. In crew of the Steam Ship Isabel.

ENNIS, MARY, 23, F, None listed, -, Ireland, 88, 81, CHAS-. In HH of Patrick Ennis m 22 born Ireland.

ENNIS, PATRICK, 22, M, Laborer, -, Ireland, 88, 81, CHAS-.

ERVAN, BERRY M., 35, M, Merchant, -, Ireland, 658, 638, CHAS-. In HH of John Ervan m 60 born PA.

ERVIN, MARY J., 28, F, None listed, -, Ireland, 1038, 1038, ABB. In HH of Frances Witherspoon f 60 born SC.

ERWIN, WILLIAM, 32, M,

School master, -, Ireland, 2338, 2338, GREE.

EVANS, MARY, 35, F, None listed, -, Ireland, 254, 239, CHAS-. In HH of Robert Evans m 35 born Ireland.

EVANS, ROBERT, 35, M, Turner, -, Ireland, 254, 239, CHAS-.

EVENS, CHARLES, 28, M, Stonemason, -, Ireland, 696, 696, ABB.

EVENS, ELIZABETH, 14, F, None listed, -, Ireland, 698, 698, ABB. In HH of Mary Cobb 42 born SC.

EVENS, ELIZABETH, 26, F, None listed, -, Ireland, 696, 696, ABB. In HH of Charles Evens 28 born Ireland.

EVENS, ISABELLA, 37, F, None listed, -, Ireland, 695, 695, ABB.

EVENS, JAMES, 7, M, None listed, -, Ireland, 695, 695, ABB. In HH of Isaabella Evens f 37 born Ireland.

EVENS, SARAH, 12, F, None listed, -, Ireland, 695, 695, ABB. In HH of Isaabella Evens f 37 born Ireland.

EWART, DAVID, 65, M, Merchant, -, Ireland, 567, 584, RICH.

EWART, JOHN, 58, M, Merchant, -, Ireland, 260, 265, RICH.

EWART, MARY A., 22, F, None listed, -, Ireland, 445,

458, RICH. In HH of James B. Ewart m 22 born SC.

F

FACEY, MARGARET, 19, F, Servant, -, Ireland, 279, 256, CHAS.

FAGAN, ANDREW, 23, M, Laborer, -, Ireland, 172, 162, CHAS+. In HH of John Haley m 40 born Ireland.

FAGAN, BELENA, 10, F, None listed, -, Ireland, 556, 515, CHAS+. In HH of William H. Fagan m 37 born Ireland.

FAGAN, DENNIS, 48, M, Laborer, -, Ireland, 486, 444, CHAS+.

FAGAN, JANE, 31, F, None listed, -, Ireland, 556, 515, CHAS+. In HH of William H. Fagan m 37 born Ireland.

FAGAN, KATEY, 44, F, None listed, -, Ireland, 486, 444, CHAS+. In HH of Dennis Fagan m 48 born Ireland.

FAGAN, MCHUGH, 8, F, None listed, -, Ireland, 556, 515, CHAS+. In HH of William H. Fagan m 37 born Ireland.

FAGAN, NANCY, 26, F, None listed, -, Ireland, 486, 444, CHAS+. In HH of Dennis Fagan m 48 born Ireland.

FAGAN, PATRICK, 28, M, Slater, -, Ireland, 486, 444,

CHAS+. In HH of Dennis Fagan m 48 born Ireland.

FAGAN, RICHARD, 26, M, Laborer, -, Ireland, 172, 162, CHAS+. In HH of John Haley m 40 born Ireland.

FAGAN, WILLIAM H., 37, M, Laborer, -, Ireland, 556, 515, CHAS+.

FAGEN, LUKE, 25, M, Laborer, -, Ireland, 337, 311, CHAS. In HH of William H. Fowler m 38 running Boarding house born England.

FAHY, FRANCES, 24, M, Merchant, -, Ireland, 488, 444, CHAS.

FAHY, MARY, 19, F, None listed, -, Ireland, 488, 444, CHAS. In HH of Frances Fahy m 24 born Ireland.

FAHY, PATRICK, 22, M, Merchant, -, Ireland, 488, 444, CHAS. In HH of Frances Fahy m 24 born Ireland.

FAHY, THOMAS, 16, M, Merchant, -, Ireland, 488, 444, CHAS. In HH of Frances Fahy m 24 born Ireland.

FALKNER, JOHN, 47, M, Farmer, -, Ireland, 533, 533, ABB.

FANNING, JOHN, 26, M, Clerk, -, Ireland, 188, 192, RICH. In Hotel.

FARE, WILLIAM, 28, M, Ditcher, -, Ireland, 1997, 2003, EDGE.Note; out of order after fam. No. 2000. In HH of James

Gearty m 44 born Ireland.

FARHEIS, JAMES, 29, M, Laborer, -, Ireland, 292, 269, CHAS+. In HH of Michael McMurray m 50 born Ireland.

FARHEIT, MARGARET, 37, F, None listed, -, Ireland, 292, 269, CHAS+. In HH of Michael McMurray m 50 born Ireland.

FARIS, JANE, 48, F, None listed, -, Ireland, 839, 839, YORK. In HH of William A. Faris m 37 born Ireland.

FARIS, MARGARET, 56, F, None listed, -, Ireland, 839, 839, YORK. In HH of William A. Faris m 37 born Ireland.

FARIS, NANCY, 32, F, None listed, -, Ireland, 839, 839, YORK. In HH of William A. Faris m 37 born Ireland.

FARIS, WILLIAM A., 37, M, Farmer, -, Ireland, 839, 839, YORK.

FARLEY, BETSY, 16, F, None listed, -, Ireland, 677, 669, CHAS%. In HH of Henry Seevers m 35 born Germany.

FARLEY, CHARLES, 40, M, Stevedore, -, Ireland, 16, 19, CHAS. In HH of Catherine Murphy 28 f born Ireland.

FARLEY, J., 78, F, None listed, -, Ireland, 1219, 1219, CHES.

FARLEY, JOHN, 25, M, Laborer, -, Ireland, 2052, 2058,

EDGE. In HH of Jas. Linch m 28 born Ireland.

FARLEY, JOHN, 28, M, Laborer, -, Ireland, 2007, 2013, EDGE. In HH of William Herbert m 37 born Ireland.

FARLEY, MARGARET, 27, F, None listed, -, Ireland, 17, 20, CHAS.

FARLEY, MARGARET, 30, F, None listed, -, Ireland, 240, 226, CHAS+. In HH of William Farley m 38 born Ireland.

FARLEY, MARY, 37, F, None listed, -, Ireland, 17, 20, CHAS. In HH of Margaret Farley f 27 born Ireland.

FARLEY, MICHAEL, 32, M, Laborer, -, Ireland, 2052, 2058, EDGE. In HH of Jas. Linch m 28 born Ireland.

FARLEY, WILLIAM, 38, M, Stevedore, -, Ireland, 240, 226, CHAS+.

FARLIN, BRIGET, 8, F, None listed, -, Ireland, 400, 383, CHAS-. In Boarding house.

FARLIN, CATHERINE, 6, F, None listed, -, Ireland, 400, 383, CHAS-. In Boarding house.

FARLIN, MARY, 10, F, None listed, -, Ireland, 400, 383, CHAS-. In Boarding house.

FARLIN, PATRICK, 4, M, None listed, -, Ireland, 400,

383, CHAS-. In Boarding house.

FARLIN, PATRICK, 35, M, Laborer, -, Ireland, 400, 383, CHAS-. In Boarding house.

FARLIN, PETER, 11, M, None listed, -, Ireland, 400, 383, CHAS-. In Boarding house.

FARMER, ELLEN, 30, F, None listed, -, Ireland, 49, 46, CHAS-. In HH of Richard Farmer m 40 born Ireland.

FARMER, RICHARD, 40, M, Laborer, -, Ireland, 49, 46, CHAS-.

FARREL, MARIA, 17, F, None listed, -, Ireland, 228, 214, CHAS-. In HH of Mary Roddy f 60 born Ireland.

FARRELL, ELLEN, 29, F, None listed, -, Ireland, 733, 724, CHAS%.

FARRELL, JAMES, 11, M, None listed, -, Ireland, 733, 724, CHAS%. In HH of Ellen Farrell f 29 born Ireland.

FARRIS, PATRICK, 7, M, None listed, -, Ireland, 2106, 2106, BARN. In HH of Patrick Quinn m 30 born Ireland.

FAUGHNOL, ANDREW, 30, M, Laborer, -, Ireland, 2028, 2029, EDGE. In HH of Stephen Faughnol m 26 born Ireland.

FAUGHNOL, ANN, 20, F, None listed, -, Ireland, 2028, 2029, EDGE. In HH of Stephen Faughnol m 26 born Ireland.

FAUGHNOL, MICHEAL,
28, M, Boot & Shoemaker, -,
Ireland, 2028, 2029, EDGE. In
HH of Stephen Faughnol m 26
born Ireland.

FAUGHNOL, MILES, 27, M,
Boot & Shoemaker, -, Ireland,
2028, 2029, EDGE. In HH of
Stephen Faughnol m 26 born
Ireland.

FAUGHNOL, STEPHEN,
26, M, Shoe/boot maker, -,
Ireland, 2028, 2029, EDGE.

FEIRRIS, THOMAS, 24, M,
Laborer, -, Ireland, 63, 63,
FAIR. In HH of Adna Johnson
m 53 born CT.

FERAN, J., 25, M, Ditcher, -,
Ireland, 909, 910, ORNG+. In
HH of W. Jefcoat m 30 born
SC.

FERAN, J., 25, M, Ditcher, -,
Ireland, 909, 910, ORNG+. In
HH of U. Jefcoat m 30 born
SC.

FERGUSON, BRIGET, 28,
F, None listed, -, Ireland, 440,
423, CHAS-. In HH of John
Ferguson m 54 born Ireland.

FERGUSON, CATHERINE,
47, F, None listed, -, Ireland,
440, 423, CHAS-. In HH of
John Ferguson m 54 born
Ireland.

FERGUSON, CHARLES, 14,
M, None listed, -, Ireland, 333,
299, CHAS+. In HH of Susan
Ferguson f 35 born Ireland.

FERGUSON, DENNIS, 17,
M, Laborer, -, Ireland, 440, 423,
CHAS-. In HH of John
Ferguson m 54 born Ireland.

FERGUSON, DENNIS, 31,
M, Laborer, -, Ireland, 440, 423,
CHAS-. In HH of John
Ferguson m 54 born Ireland.

FERGUSON, FRANCIS, 8,
M, None listed, -, Ireland, 333,
299, CHAS+. In HH of Susan
Ferguson f 35 born Ireland.

FERGUSON, GEORGE D.,
28, M, Watchmaker, -, Ireland,
405, 416, RICH.

FERGUSON, HUGH, 16, M,
Carpenter, -, Ireland, 333, 299,
CHAS+. In HH of Susan
Ferguson f 35 born Ireland.

FERGUSON, JOHN, 12, M,
None listed, -, Ireland, 333, 299,
CHAS+. In HH of Susan
Ferguson f 35 born Ireland.

FERGUSON, JOHN, 54, M,
Laborer, -, Ireland, 440, 423,
CHAS-.

FERGUSON, KATEY, 15, F,
None listed, -, Ireland, 440, 423,
CHAS-. In HH of John
Ferguson m 54 born Ireland.

FERGUSON, PAT., 37, M,
Pavior, -, Ireland, 322, 297,
CHAS. In Boarding house.

FERGUSON, PATRICK, 36,
M, Attendant, -, Ireland, 542,
557, RICH. At Lunatic Asylum.

FERGUSON, SUSAN, 35, F,
None listed, -, Ireland, 333, 299,
CHAS+.

FIEHAN, ANASTACIA, 30, F, None listed, -, Ireland, 441, 438, CHAS%. In HH of Josh. Fiehan m 35 born Ireland.

FIEHAN, JOHN, 13, M, None listed, -, Ireland, 441, 438, CHAS%. In HH of Josh. Fiehan m 35 born Ireland.

FIEHAN, JOSH., 35, M, Clerk, -, Ireland, 441, 438, CHAS%.

FIEHAN, PATRICK, 10, M, None listed, -, Ireland, 441, 438, CHAS%. In HH of Josh. Fiehan m 35 born Ireland.

FIELDING, JOHN, 55, M, Teacher, -, Ireland, 147, 147, BEAU.

FIELDS, JAMES, 55, M, Ditcher, -, Ireland, 664, 664, UNION.

FIFE, ALEXANDER, 52, M, Planter, -, Ireland, 1159, 1160, FAIR.

FIFE, ELIZABETH, 74, F, None listed, -, Ireland, 1076, 1076, CHES. In HH of Samuel Fife m 75 born Ireland.

FIFE, JOSEPH, 35, M, Farmer, -, Ireland, 1084, 1084, CHES.

FIFE, SAMUEL, 75, M, Farmer, -, Ireland, 1076, 1076, CHES.

FINN, CATHERINE, 40, F, None listed, -, Ireland, 40, 40, CHAS!. In HH of Patrick Finn m 40 born Ireland.

FINN, EDWARD, 28, M, Laborer, -, Ireland, 280, 260, CHAS+.

FINN, HANNAH, 35, F, None listed, -, Ireland, 280, 260, CHAS+. In HH of Edward Finn m 28 born Ireland.

FINN, JOHN, 2, M, None listed, -, Ireland, 40, 40, CHAS!. In HH of Patrick Finn m 40 born Ireland.

FINN, MARY, 6, F, None listed, -, Ireland, 40, 40, CHAS!. In HH of Patrick Finn m 40 born Ireland.

FINN, PATRICK, 3, M, None listed, -, Ireland, 40, 40, CHAS!. In HH of Patrick Finn m 40 born Ireland.

FINN, PATRICK, 50, M, Mason, -, Ireland, 40, 40, CHAS!.

FINNEGAN, BRIGET, 15, F, None listed, -, Ireland, 216, 203, CHAS+. In HH of Edward Garrity m 25 born Ireland.

FINNEGAN, ELLEN, 30, F, None listed, -, Ireland, 339, 304, CHAS+. In HH of George Finnegan m 36 born Ireland.

FINNEGAN, GEORGE, 36, M, Mariner, -, Ireland, 339, 304, CHAS+.

FINNEGAN, LETITIA, 22, F, None listed, -, Ireland, 339, 304, CHAS+. In HH of George Finnegan m 36 born Ireland.

FINNEY, ALICE, 30, F, None listed, -, Ireland, 406, 404, CHAS%. In HH of Patrick

Finney m 36 born Ireland.

FINNEY, HUGH, 9, M, None listed, -, Ireland, 406, 404, CHAS%. In HH of Patrick Finney m 36 born Ireland.

FINNEY, MARY, 7, F, None listed, -, Ireland, 406, 404, CHAS%. In HH of Patrick Finney m 36 born Ireland.

FINNEY, PATRICK, 36, M, Laborer, -, Ireland, 406, 404, CHAS%.

FITSJERALD?, JOHN, 45, M, Boot maker, -, Ireland, 1998, 2001, EDGE. In HH of M.L. Georty m 46 born Ireland.

FITZERALD, MARY, 55, F, None listed, -, Ireland, 412, 372, CHAS. In HH of Christopher King m 23 born Ireland.

FITZGERALD, MAR-GARET, 32, F, None listed, -, Ireland, 410, 372, CHAS. In HH of George Redmond m 26 born Ireland.

FITZGERALD, MARY, 35, F, None listed, -, Ireland, 1107, 1084, CHAS-. In HH of W.J. Bennett m 42 born SC.

FITZGERALD, MICHAEL, 30, M, Laborer, -, Ireland, 410, 372, CHAS. In HH of George Redmond m 26 born Ireland.

FITZGERALD, STEPHEN, 18, M, Cabinet maker, -, Ireland, 75, 69, CHAS-. In HH of Daniel H. Silcore m 36 born England.

FITZGIBBON, MARY, 19, F, None listed, -, Ireland, 1003, 980, CHAS%. In HH of Timothy McNetty m 35 born Ireland.

FITZGIBON, DAVID, 30, M, None listed, -, Ireland, 1106, 1083, CHAS-. In Charleston Orphan House.

FITZGIBON, MARY ANN, 27, F, None listed, -, Ireland, 1106, 1083, CHAS-. In Charleston Orphan House.

FITZPATRICK, ANN, 40, F, None listed, -, Ireland, 988, 965, CHAS%. In HH of James Fitzpatrick m 40 born Ireland.

FITZPATRICK, BRIDGET, 23, F, None listed, -, Ireland, 636, 628, CHAS%. In HH of Nicholas Bunger m 36 born Germany.

FITZPATRICK, CATH-ERINE, 12, F, None listed, -, Ireland, 555, 514, CHAS+. In HH of John Fitzpatrick m 40 born Ireland.

FITZPATRICK, DOROTHY, 8, F, None listed, -, Ireland, 555, 514, CHAS+. In HH of John Fitzpatrick m 40 born Ireland.

FITZPATRICK, JAMES, 40, M, Farmer, -, Ireland, 988, 965, CHAS%.

FITZPATRICK, JOHN, 40, M, Laborer, -, Ireland, 555, 514, CHAS+.

FITZPATRICK, MAGDELINE, 37, F, None listed, -, Ireland, 555, 514, CHAS+. In HH of John Fitzpatrick m 40 born Ireland.

FITZPATRICK, PATRICK, 10, M, None listed, -, Ireland, 555, 514, CHAS+. In HH of John Fitzpatrick m 40 born Ireland.

FITZSIMONS, ANN, 26, F, None listed, -, Ireland, 335, 309, CHAS*. In HH of O.H. Middleton m 45 born SC.

FITZSIMONS, B., 31, M, Sadler, -, Ireland, 823, 803, CHAS-.

FITZSIMONS, MARY ANN, 27, F, None listed, -, Ireland, 823, 803, CHAS-. In HH of B. Fitzsimons m 31 born Ireland.

FITZSIMONS, ROBERT, 22, M, Sadler, -, Ireland, 823, 803, CHAS-. In HH of B. Fitzsimons m 31 born Ireland.

FLAGG, CAROLINE, 15, F, None listed, -, Ireland, 420, 379, CHAS+. In HH of Patrick Flagg m 40 born Ireland

FLAGG, DAVID, 21, M, Laborer, -, Ireland, 420, 379, CHAS+. In HH of Patrick Flagg m 40 born Ireland.

FLAGG, DOROTHEA, 38, F, None listed, -, Ireland, 420, 379, CHAS+. In HH of Patrick Flagg m 40 born Ireland.

FLAGG, PATRICK, 28, M, Laborer, -, Ireland, 420, 379,
CHAS+. In HH of Patrick Flagg m 40 born Ireland.

FLAGG, PATRICK, 40, M, Gass fitter, -, Ireland, 420, 379, CHAS+.

FLAGG, PATTY, 18, F, None listed, -, Ireland, 420, 379, CHAS+. In HH of Patrick Flagg m 40 born Ireland.

FLAGHERTY, COLINE, 26, F, None listed, -, Ireland, 638, 596, CHAS+. In HH of Dennis Flagherty m 44 born Ireland.

FLAGHERTY, DAN, 24, M, Bricklayer, -, Ireland, 638, 596, CHAS+. In HH of Dennis Flagherty m 44 born Ireland.

FLAGHERTY, DENNIS, 44, M, Laborer, -, Ireland, 638, 596, CHAS+.

FLAGHERTY, EMMA, 7, F, None listed, -, Ireland, 638, 596, CHAS+. In HH of Dennis Flagherty m 44 born Ireland.

FLAGHERTY, MARY, 38, F, None listed, -, Ireland, 638, 596, CHAS+. In HH of Dennis Flagherty m 44 born Ireland.

FLAGHERTY, SUSAN, 22, F, None listed, -, Ireland, 638, 596, CHAS+. In HH of Dennis Flagherty m 44 born Ireland.

FLAHARATY, EDWARD, 33, 0, Laborer, M, Ireland, 1197, 1176, CHAS%. In Boarding house.

FLAHARTEY, DENNIS, 35, M, Laborer, -, Ireland, 308, 284, CHAS.

FLAHARTEY, HANNAH,
58, F, Laborer, -, Ireland, 308,
284, CHAS. In HH of Dennis
Flahartey m 35 born Ireland.
FLAHARTEY, JOHN, 63,
M, Laborer, -, Ireland, 308,
284, CHAS. In HH of Dennis
Flahartey m 35 born Ireland.
FLAHARTEY, PEGGY, 31,
F, None listed, -, Ireland, 308,
284, CHAS. In HH of Dennis
Flahartey m 35 born Ireland.
FLAHERTY, JOHN, 50, M,
Planter, -, Ireland, 1870, 1870,
BARN.
FLANNAGAN, BRIGET, 28,
F, None listed, -, Ireland, 518,
484, CHAS*.
FLANNAGAN, P.A., 50, M,
Brick mason, -, Ireland, 36, 36,
LANC. In HH of David
Billings m 48 born NC.
FLANNIGAN, JOHN, 25, M,
Boot maker, -, Ireland, 556,
556, UNION. In Hotel.
FLANNIGAN, PATRICK,
33, M, Shoemaker, -, Ireland,
381, 391, RICH.
FLANNIGAN, RICHARD
F., 23, M, Merchant, -, Ireland,
382, 392, RICH.
FLANNIGAN, THOMAS,
18, M, Clerk, -, Ireland, 381,
391, RICH. In HH of Patrick
Flannigan m 33 born Ireland.
FLATHERTY, PATRICK
O., 28, M, Merchant, -, Ireland,
882, 840, CHAS+. In
Charleston Hotel.

FLEMING, ELIZA, 50, F,
None listed, -, Ireland, 159, 163,
RICH.
FLEMING, J., 29, M, Priv.
U.S.A., -, Ireland, 47, 43,
CHAS$. In HH of John Ewing
m 50 born MA.
FLEMMING, CHRISTIN,
13, F, Servant, -, Ireland, 462,
419, CHAS. In HH of The Hon.
T.L. Hutchenson m 38, Mayor
of Charleston, born SC.
FLEMMING, J., 35, M,
Laborer, -, Ireland, 405, 369,
CHAS. In HH of William
Doran m 36 born MA.
FLICK, JAMES, 37, M,
Painter, -, Ireland, 31, 31,
NEWB.
FLICK, JANE, 37, F, None
listed, -, Ireland, 31, 31, NEWB.
In HH of James Flick 37 m
Painter b. Ireland.
FLICK, MARY, 8, F, None
listed, -, Ireland, 31, 31, NEWB.
In HH of James Flick 37 m
Painter b. Ireland.
FLICK, MARY, 12, F, None
listed, -, Ireland, 31, 31, NEWB.
In HH of James Flick 37 m
Painter b. Ireland.
FLINN, BRIDGET, 27, F,
None listed, -, Ireland, 2, 2,
CHAS*. In HH of James
McAndrew m 29 born Ireland.
FLINN, JOHN, 50, M,
Laborer, -, Ireland, 202, 190,
CHAS+. In Boarding house.
FLINN, PAT, 30, M, Laborer,

-, Ireland, 447, 405, CHAS. In HH of John Thompson m 35 born Ireland.

FLINN, PATRICK, 24, M, Laborer, -, Ireland,   2,   2, CHAS*. In HH of James McAndrew m 29 born Ireland.

FLINN, THOS. J. MD, 53, M, Physician, -, Ireland, 1063, 1063, DARL.

FLINTON, PATRICK, 30, M, Planter, -, Ireland, 819, 819, BARN.

FLOOD, CAROLINE, 30, F, None listed, -, Ireland, 257, 257, CHAS%. In HH of Michael Moran m 40 born Ireland.

FLOOD, JAMES, 24, M, Clerk, -, Ireland, 124, 115, CHAS+. In Boarding house.

FLOOD, JOHN, 18, M, Joiner, -, Ireland, 124, 115, CHAS+. In Boarding house.

FLOURNY, J., 40, M, Ditcher, -, Ireland, 909, 910, ORNG+. In HH of U. Jefcoat m 30 born SC.

FLOURNY, J., 40, M, Ditcher, -, Ireland, 909, 910, ORNG+. In HH of W. Jefcoat m 30 born SC.

FLUD, AGNES, 33, F, None listed, -, Ireland, 19, 19, CHAS^. In HH of William Becket m 57 born SC.

FLYNN, ESTHER, 41, F, None listed, -, Ireland, 483, 498, RICH. In HH of Patrick

Flynn m 42 born Ireland.

FLYNN, MARTIN, 30, M, Laborer, -, Ireland, 883, 860, CHAS%. In HH of George H. Winges m 21 born SC.

FLYNN, MARY, 27, F, None listed, -, Ireland, 883, 860, CHAS%. In HH of George H. Winges m 21 born SC.

FLYNN, MARY, 28, F, None listed, -, Ireland, 1109, 1086, CHAS-. In HH of Patrick Flynn m 34 born Ireland.

FLYNN, MARY ANN, 23, F, None listed, -, Ireland, 264, 264, CHAS%.

FLYNN, P., 31, M, Priv. U.S.A., -, Ireland, 47, 43, CHAS$. In HH of John Ewing m 50 born MA.

FLYNN, PATRICK, 5, M, None listed, -, Ireland, 1109, 1086, CHAS-. In HH of Patrick Flynn m 34 born Ireland.

FLYNN, PATRICK, 34, M, Laborer, -, Ireland, 1109, 1086, CHAS-.

FLYNN, PATRICK, 40, M, Laborer, -, Ireland, 1197, 1176, CHAS%. In Boarding house.

FLYNN, PATRICK, 42, M, Conductor RR, -, Ireland, 483, 498, RICH.

FLYNN, THOMAS, 30, M, Merchant, -, Ireland, 882, 840, CHAS+. In Charleston Hotel.

FOLEY, BAT., 40, M, Laborer, -, Ireland, 169, 159, CHAS+. In HH of John

Sweeny m 79 born Ireland.

FOLEY, JULIA, 22, F, None listed, -, Ireland, 169, 159, CHAS+. In HH of John Sweeny m 79 born Ireland.

FOLEY, MARY, 25, F, None listed, -, Ireland, 169, 159, CHAS+. In HH of John Sweeny m 79 born Ireland.

FOLEY, PATRICK, 24, M, Laborer, -, Ireland, 169, 159, CHAS+. In HH of John Sweeny m 79 born Ireland.

FOLLY, MARY, 24, F, Servant, -, Ireland, 52, 62, CHAS. In HH of James Wilsman m 65 born England.

FOOLEY, MARTHA, 40, F, None listed, -, Ireland, 139, 130, CHAS+. In HH of Joseph Fry m 40 born Germany.

FORAN, J.J., 36, M, Clerk, -, Ireland, 162, 153, CHAS+. In HH of John H. Schriner m 56 born Germany.

FORD, JANE, 48, F, None listed, -, Ireland, 460, 460, CHES. In HH of Wm. Ford m 49 born Ireland.

FORD, JOSHUA, 31, M, Tailor, -, Ireland, 29, 29, RICH.

FORD, SUSAN A., 25, F, None listed, -, Ireland, 29, 29, RICH. In HH of Joshua Ford m 31 born Ireland. Date 1849 by name.

FORD, WM., 49, M, Farmer, -, Ireland, 460, 460, CHES.

FORLERY, JAMES, 40, M, Laborer, -, Ireland, 144, 135, CHAS+. In HH of Daniel Larry m 30 born Ireland.

FORSYTH, ALEXANDER, 37, M, Merchant, -, Ireland, 571, 588, RICH.

FORSYTH, WM. C., 25, M, Clerk, -, Ireland, 788, 768, CHAS-. In HH of John Harbeson m 48 born Ireland.

FORT, MARY, 28, F, None listed, -, Ireland, 667, 647, CHAS-. In Boarding house.

FOSE, MARTHA, 37, F, None listed, -, Ireland, 646, 605, CHAS+.

FOSE, MARY, 18, F, None listed, -, Ireland, 646, 605, CHAS+. In HH of Martha Fose f 37 born Ireland.

FOSE, WILLIAM, 20, M, Wharfinger, -, Ireland, 646, 605, CHAS+. In HH of Martha Fose f 37 born Ireland.

FOX, ANN, 58, F, None listed, -, Ireland, 426, 409, CHAS-. In HH of John M. Corcoran m 31 born SC.

FRAILED ?, SAMUEL, 55, M, Stone cutter, -, Ireland, 63, 63, FAIR. In HH of Adna Johnson m 53 born CT.

FREAN, THOMAS, 47, M, Dept. Treasurer, -, Ireland, 179, 183, RICH. Page out of order, follows HH 135/139.

FREEMAN, JOHN, 38, M, Laborer, -, Ireland, 241, 227, CHAS+. In HH of James

Kennedy m 30 born Ireland.

FROSE ?, JOHN F., 26, M, Cotton Buyer, -, Ireland, 2002, 2008, EDGE. In HH of William B. Cates m 41 born SC.

FULLERTON, DANIEL, 50, M, Farmer, -, Ireland, 659, 694, PICK.

FULLERTON, ROBERT, 46, M, Carpenter, -, Ireland, 659, 694, PICK. In HH of Daniel Fullerton m 50 born Ireland.

G

GAFFNEY, PETER, 38, M, Planter, -, Ireland, 393, 400, Rick+.

GAGE, JAS., 35, M, Stone Mason, -, Ireland, 1500, 1500, CHES.

GAILLARD, GEORGE, 66, M, Farmer, -, Ireland, 520, 520, SPART.

GALAPAR, EDWARD, 30, M, Merchant, -, Ireland, 2008, 2014, EDGE. In HH of Micheal OKeeffe m 37 born Ireland.

GALLAGEN, ANN, 4, F, None listed, -, Ireland, 232, 232, FAIR. In HH of Patrick Gallagen m 26 born SC.

GALLAGEN, JOHN, 1, M, None listed, -, Ireland, 232, 232, FAIR. In HH of Patrick Gallagen m 26 born SC.

GALLAGEN, JOSEPH, 3, M, None listed, -, Ireland, 232, 232, FAIR. In HH of Patrick Gallagen m 26 born SC.

GALLAGEN, MARGARET, 23, F, None listed, -, Ireland, 232, 232, FAIR. In HH of Patrick Gallagen m 26 born SC.

GALLAGHER, ANTHONY, 23, M, Fireman, -, Ireland, 326, 301, CHAS. In HH of William Rollins m 40 born {-}.

GALLAGHER, ANTHONY, 24, M, Laborer, -, Ireland, 241, 227, CHAS+. In HH of James Kennedy m 30 born Ireland.

GALLAGHER, BRIGET, 6, F, None listed, -, Ireland, 553, 519, CHAS*. In Catholic Seminary.

GALLAGHER, ELLEN, 14, F, None listed, -, Ireland, 992, 971, CHAS-. In HH of S.B. Bernard m 38 born France.

GALLAGHER, MARY, 8, F, None listed, -, Ireland, 553, 519, CHAS*. In Catholic Seminary.

GALLAGHER, PATRICK, 21, M, Laborer, -, Ireland, 241, 227, CHAS+. In HH of James Kennedy m 30 born Ireland.

GALLAHAN, ANTHONY, 30, M, Carpenter, -, Ireland, 184, 188, RICH.

GALLAHAN, BRIDGET, 26, F, None listed, -, Ireland, 184, 188, RICH. In HH of Anthony

Gallahan m 30 born Ireland.

GALLETY, PETER, 27, M, Laborer, -, Ireland, 322, 297, CHAS. In Boarding house.

GALLON, JAMES, 45, M, Farmer, -, Ireland, 1237, 1237, GREE. In HH of Robert Bailey m 38 born Ireland.

GAMBLE, JAMES, 50, F, Jeweller, -, Ireland, 682, 662, CHAS-.

GAMBLE, MARIA, 21, F, None listed, -, Ireland, 682, 662, CHAS-. In HH of James Gamble f 50 born Ireland.

GAMBLE, R.J., 22, M, Jeweller, -, Ireland, 682, 662, CHAS-. In HH of James Gamble f 50 born Ireland.

GAMEL, SAMUEL, 30, M, Turner, -, Ireland, 54, 49, CHAS-. In HH of Robert Leckia m 28 born Ireland.

GAMMER, SAMUEL S., 30, M, Stick maker, -, Ireland, 678, 658, CHAS-.

GANAN, FRANCES, 36, F, None listed, -, Ireland, 149, 149, CHAS%. In HH of John Gordon m 40 born NY.

GANAN, JAMES, 5, M, None listed, -, Ireland, 149, 149, CHAS%. In HH of John Gordon m 40 born NY.

GANAN, JAMES, 36, M, Wheelwright, -, Ireland, 149, 149, CHAS%. In HH of John Gordon m 40 born NY.

GANAN, MARY ANN, 8, F, None listed, -, Ireland, 149, 149, CHAS%. In HH of John Gordon m 40 born NY.

GANAN, WILLIAM, 13, M, None listed, -, Ireland, 149, 149, CHAS%. In HH of John Gordon m 40 born NY.

GANNON, BRIGET, 30, F, None listed, -, Ireland, 274, 254, CHAS+. In HH of Roger Gannon m 30 born Ireland.

GANNON, ROGER, 30, M, Shop keeper, -, Ireland, 274, 254, CHAS+.

GARATHY, THOMAS, 25, M, Clerk, -, Ireland, 380, 345, CHAS. In HH of Patrick Meran m 26 born Ireland.

GARATY, THOMAS, 40, M, Merchant, -, Ireland, 246, 231, CHAS+.

GARDNER, MARY, 46, F, None listed, -, Ireland, 1615, 1615, EDGE. In HH of James Jones m 45 born SC.

GARETY, EDWARD, 21, M, Fireman, -, Ireland, 326, 301, CHAS. In HH of William Rollins m 40 born {-}.

GARMARY, MARY, 75, F, None listed, -, Ireland, 285, 285, NEWB. In HH of John Germany 42 m Farmer born SC.

GARREN, JOHN CAIN, 30, M, Carpenter, -, Ireland, 202, 190, CHAS+. In HH of Michael Garren m 32 born Ireland.

GARREN, MARY, 26, F, None listed, -, Ireland, 202, 190, CHAS+. In HH of Michael Garren m 32 born Ireland.

GARREN, MICHAEL, 32, M, Stone cutter, -, Ireland, 202, 190, CHAS+.

GARRETY, ANN, 26, F, None listed, -, Ireland, 21, 21, CHAS*. In HH of Christopher Garrety m 35 born Ireland.

GARRETY, CHRISTOPHER, 35, M, Grocer, -, Ireland, 21, 21, CHAS*.

GARRITY, BRIGET, 45, F, None listed, -, Ireland, 216, 203, CHAS+. In HH of Edward Garrity m 25 born Ireland.

GARRITY, EDWARD, 25, M, Laborer, -, Ireland, 216, 203, CHAS+.

GARRITY, JAMES, 45, M, Ditcher, -, Ireland, 36, 37, ORNG+. In HH of Samuel Parler m 50 born SC.

GARVIN, ADAM, 7, M, None listed, -, Ireland, 628, 586, CHAS+. In HH of John Garvin m 24 born Ireland.

GARVIN, ELIZABETH, 46, F, None listed, -, Ireland, 628, 586, CHAS+. In HH of John Garvin m 24 born Ireland.

GARVIN, JOHN, 14, M, None listed, -, Ireland, 628, 586, CHAS+. In HH of John Garvin m 24 born Ireland.

GARVIN, JOHN, 16, M, Clerk, -, Ireland, 356, 328, CHAS. In HH of J.F. ONeell 33 m born SC.

GARVIN, JOHN, 24, M, Laborer, -, Ireland, 628, 586, CHAS+.

GARVIN, MARGARET, 10, F, None listed, -, Ireland, 628, 586, CHAS+. In HH of John Garvin m 24 born Ireland.

GARVIN, MARTHA, 16, F, None listed, -, Ireland, 628, 586, CHAS+. In HH of John Garvin m 24 born Ireland.

GARVIN, NANCY, 20, F, None listed, -, Ireland, 628, 586, CHAS+. In HH of John Garvin m 24 born Ireland.

GARVIN, PETER, 18, M, Clerk, -, Ireland, 356, 328, CHAS. In HH of J.F. ONeell 33 m born SC.

GASCOIN, WASHINGTON, 56, M, Laborer, -, Ireland, 624, 582, CHAS+.

GAUT, JAMES, 43, M, Mechanic, -, Ireland, 2084, 2084, GREE.

GEARTY, JAMES, 44, M, Fairer, -, Ireland, 1997, 2003, EDGE.Note; out of order after fam. No. 2000

GEORGE, CAROLINE, 28, F, None listed, -, Ireland, 209, 187, CHAS. In HH of Mary Jeannerell f 28 born SC.

GEORGE, JOHN, 34, M,

Laborer, -, Ireland, 209, 187, CHAS. In HH of Mary Jeannerell f 28 born SC.

GEORGE, MARY, 25, F, None listed, -, Ireland, 1042, 1020, CHAS%. In HH of Reuben George m 35 born SC.

GEORGE, PATRICK, 12, M, None listed, -, Ireland, 209, 187, CHAS. In HH of Mary Jeannerell f 28 born SC.

GEORTY, M.L., 46, M, Tanner, -, Ireland, 1998, 2001, EDGE.

GEORTY, WILLIAM, 40, M, Merchant, -, Ireland, 189, 189, EDGE. In HH of Patrick Moore m 40 born Ireland.

GERENEAU, CATHERINE, 20, F, None listed, -, Ireland, 1003, 981, CHAS-. In HH of L. Watts f 32 born England.

GETTY, JANE, 90, F, None listed, -, Ireland, 539, 522, CHAS-. In HH of Eliza Wilson f 39 born Ireland.

GETTYS, MATILDA, 46, F, None listed, -, Ireland, 105, 105, YORK. In HH of Ebenezer Gettys m 27 born Lancaster, SC.

GIBBES, ANN, 22, F, None listed, -, Ireland, 437, 396, CHAS+. In HH of James Gibbes m 25 born Ireland.

GIBBES, JAMES, 25, M, Wheelwright, -, Ireland, 437, 396, CHAS+.

GIBBON, DOMINIC, 23, M,

Student, -, Ireland, 480, 446, CHAS*. In HH of Rt. Revd. Jgn. A. Reynolds m 51 born KY.

GIBSON, ELIZABETH, 80, F, None listed, -, Ireland, 868, 826, CHAS+.

GILFILLAN, GIZZILA, 55, F, None listed, -, Ireland, 1591, 1591, YORK. In HH of Robert Gilfillan m 48 born Ireland.

GILFILLAN, ROBERT, 48, M, Farmer, -, Ireland, 1591, 1591, YORK.

GILL, JOHN, 19, M, Laborer, -, Ireland, 389, 351, CHAS+. In HH of Edward Collins m 40 born Ireland.

GILL, MARY, 35, F, None listed, -, Ireland, 446, 413, CHAS*. In HH of Sarah McCrady f 20 born Ireland.

GILLAM, JOHN, 40, M, Stone mason, -, Ireland, 1783, 1783, LAU. In HH of Charles Smith m 65 born SC.

GILLESPIE, AGNES, 46, F, None listed, -, Ireland, 1414, 1414, ABB.

GILLINOR, A., 20, M, Iron Padler, -, Ireland, 1618, 1618, SPART.

GILMER, MATILDA, 33, F, None listed, -, Ireland, 2238, 2238, ABB. In HH of James G. Gilmer m 51 born SC.

GILMORE, CATHERINE, 22, F, None listed, -, Ireland, 272, 252, CHAS+. In HH of John McCormick m 40 born

Ireland.

GILMORE, RACHEL, 25, F, None listed, -, Ireland, 545, 528, CHAS-. In HH of Robert A. Clark m 27 born NY.

GILMORE, THOMAS, 21, M, Farmer, -, Ireland, 1611, 1611, SPART. In HH of John Oglesly m 48 born Ireland.

GILROY, EDWARD, 30, M, Store Keeper, -, Ireland, 215, 202, CHAS+. In HH of Peter Kelly m 35 born Ireland.

GILROY, EDWARD, 32, M, Seaman, -, Ireland, 326, 301, CHAS. On Steam Ship Southerner.

GILSON, JOHN, 45, M, Taylor, -, Ireland, 103, 103, Beau+.

GIVEN, ELIZABETH, 22, F, None listed, -, Ireland, 779, 759, CHAS-. In HH of John Ogeman m 26 born Germany.

GIVEN, MARTHA, 22, F, None listed, -, Ireland, 1091, 1068, CHAS-. In HH of William Given m 25 born Ireland.

GIVEN, WILLIAM, 25, M, Shoe dealer, -, Ireland, 1091, 1068, CHAS-.

GLASCOCK, JOHANA, 14, F, None listed, -, Ireland, 207, 195, CHAS+. In HH of John Glasscock m 40 born Ireland.

GLASCOCK, JOHN, 40, M, Laborer, -, Ireland, 207, 195, CHAS+.

GLASCOCK, MARGARET, 32, F, None listed, -, Ireland, 207, 195, CHAS+. In HH of John Glasscock m 40 born Ireland.

GLOVER, ADAM, 22, M, Planter, -, Ireland, 354, 354, FAIR. In HH of Jane Cork f 42 born Ireland

GOETTEE, JOHN G., 43, M, School Teacher, -, Ireland, 18, 18, Beau-.

GOFF, CHARLES, 36, M, Bricklayer, -, Ireland, 1038, 1016, CHAS%.

GOFF, JANE, 25, F, None listed, -, Ireland, 1038, 1016, CHAS%. In HH of Charles Goff m 36 born Ireland.

GOLD, WILLIAM, 27, M, Laborer, -, Ireland, 114, 114, COLL. In HH of Clark Bates m 52 born MA.

GONZALLUS, MARGARET, 29, F, None listed, -, Ireland, 327, 296, CHAS+. In HH of Sarah Logan f 45 born SC.

GOODMAN, MARY A., 40, F, None listed, -, Ireland, 66, 66, SUMT. In HH of Irwin P. Goodman m 40 born SC.

GORCIAN, FANNY, 18, F, None listed, M, Ireland, 12, 12, CHAS+. In HH of Caroline Douglas f 30 born GA.

GORDAN, JAMES, 14, M, None listed, -, Ireland, 1819, 1819, SPART. In HH of

Miredor OShals m 24 born SC.

GORDIN, ROBT., 51, M, Farmer, -, Ireland, 597, 597, CHES.

GORDON, DAVID, 24, M, Bootmaker, -, Ireland, 638, 638, UNION. In HH of Michael Krone? m 46 born SC.

GORDON, DAVID, 51, M, Farmer, -, Ireland, 705, 709, AND.

GORDON, DAVID, 60, M, Laborer, -, Ireland, 978, 979, FAIR.

GORDON, ELIZA, 17, F, None listed, -, Ireland, 549, 549, UNION. In HH of John McIlwain m 49 born Ireland.

GORDON, ELIZABETH, 50, F, None listed, -, Ireland, 473, 473, FAIR. In HH of William Gordon m 25 born Ireland.

GORDON, ELIZABETH, 54, F, None listed, -, Ireland, 978, 979, FAIR. In HH of David Gordon m 60 born Ireland.

GORDON, JANE, 23, F, None listed, -, Ireland, 978, 979, FAIR. In HH of David Gordon m 60 born Ireland.

GORDON, JANE, 28, F, None listed, -, Ireland, 149, 149, CHAS%. In HH of John Gordon m 40 born NY.

GORDON, MARY, 41, F, None listed, -, Ireland, 1576, 1576, ABB. In HH of William Gordon m 46 born Ireland.

GORDON, REBECCA, 73, F, None listed, -, Ireland, 1579, 1579, ABB. In HH of Robert C. Gordon m 78 born SC.

GORDON, ROBERT, 30, M, Shoe maker, -, Ireland, 742, 743, FAIR.

GORDON, SMITH, 28, M, None listed, -, Ireland, 978, 979, FAIR. In HH of David Gordon m 60 born Ireland.

GORDON, THOMAS, 80, M, Farmer, -, Ireland, 2247, 2247, ABB.

GORDON, WILLIAM, 25, M, Shoe maker, -, Ireland, 473, 473, FAIR.

GORDON, WILLIAM, 46, M, Shoemaker, -, Ireland, 1576, 1576, ABB.

GORMAN, BETHIA, 39, F, None listed, -, Ireland, 717, 697, CHAS-. In HH of Felix Gorman m 41 born Ireland.

GORMAN, CATHERINE, 9, F, None listed, -, Ireland, 717, 697, CHAS-. In HH of Felix Gorman m 41 born Ireland.

GORMAN, CHARLES, 6, M, None listed, -, Ireland, 186, 170, CHAS*. In HH of Richard Gorman m 40 born Ireland.

GORMAN, DENNIS, 40, M, Laborer, -, Ireland, 640, 599, CHAS+. In HH of Michael Keenan m 44 born Ireland.

GORMAN, FELIX, 41, M, Laborer, -, Ireland, 717, 697, CHAS-.

GORMAN, JANE, 25, F,

None listed, M, Ireland, 312, 318, RICH. In HH of James Cathcart m 55 born Ireland.

GORMAN, JOHN, 2, M, None listed, -, Ireland, 186,170, CHAS*. In HH of Richard Gorman m 40 born Ireland.

GORMAN, JULIA, 30, F, None listed, -, Ireland, 186, 170, CHAS*. In HH of Richard Gorman m 40 born Ireland.

GORMAN, MARY, 3, F, None listed, -, Ireland, 186, 170, CHAS*. In HH of Richard Gorman m 40 born Ireland

GORMAN, MARY, 12, F, None listed, -, Ireland, 717, 697, CHAS-. In HH of Felix Gorman m 41 born Ireland.

GORMAN, PATRICK, 16, M, Laborer, -, Ireland, 717, 697, CHAS-. In HH of Felix Gorman m 41 born Ireland

GORMAN, PETER O., 45, M, Clerk, -, Ireland, 288, 266, CHAS+.

GORMAN, RICHARD, 5, M, None listed, -, Ireland, 186, 170, CHAS*. In HH of Richard Gorman m 40 born Ireland.

GORMAN, RICHARD, 40, M, Accountant, -, Ireland, 186, 170, CHAS*.

GOUBER, SARAH, 30, F, None listed, -, Ireland, 47, 43, CHAS$. In HH of John Ewing m 50 born MA.

GOULD, PATRICK, 23, M,

Laborer, -, Ireland, 170, 160, CHAS+. In HH of Cornelius Canary m 28 born Ireland.

GOWAN, LIPEY, 18, F, None listed, -, Ireland, 26, 26, CHAS*. In HH of Sarah Gowan f 50 born Ireland.

GOWAN, SARAH, 50, F, None listed, -, Ireland, 26, 26, CHAS*.

GOWDY, ELIZA, 30, F, None listed, -, Ireland, 2244, 2244, ABB. In HH of Jane Gowdy f 68 born Ireland.

GOWDY, JANE, 68, F, None listed, -, Ireland, 2244, 2244, ABB.

GOWEN, BRIGET, 8, F, None listed, -, Ireland, 349, 311, CHAS+. In HH of Patrick Gowen m 40 born Ireland.

GOWEN, BRIGET, 37, F, None listed, -, Ireland, 349, 311, CHAS+. In HH of Patrick Gowen m 40 born Ireland.

GOWEN, CATHERINE, 27, F, None listed, -, Ireland, 349, 311, CHAS+. In HH of Patrick Gowen m 40 born Ireland.

GOWEN, DORA, 3, F, None listed, -, Ireland, 349, 311, CHAS+. In HH of Patrick Gowen m 40 born Ireland.

GOWEN, EDWARD, 29, M, Laborer, -, Ireland, 349, 311, CHAS+. In HH of Patrick Gowen m 40 born Ireland.

GOWEN, KATEY, 10, F, None listed, -, Ireland, 349, 311,

CHAS+. In HH of Patrick
Gowen m 40 born Ireland.

GOWEN, MIKE, 6, M, None
listed, -, Ireland, 349, 311,
CHAS+. In HH of Patrick
Gowen m 40 born Ireland.

GOWEN, PATRICK, 12, M,
None listed, -, Ireland, 349,
311, CHAS+. In HH of Patrick
Gowen m 40 born Ireland.

GOWEN, PATRICK, 40, M,
Pavior, -, Ireland, 349, 311,
CHAS+.

GRACE, JANE, 28, F, None
listed, -, Ireland, 269, 250,
CHAS+. In HH of John Brady
m 50 born Ireland.

GRACE, PATRICK, 32, M,
Clerk, -, Ireland, 269, 250,
CHAS+. In HH of John Brady
m 50 born Ireland.

GRAHAM, JOHN, 35, M,
Clerk, -, Ireland, 188, 192,
RICH. In Hotel.

GRAHAM, JOHN Q., 32, M,
Overseer, -, Ireland, 801, 801,
SUMT.

GRAHAM, JULIA, 28, F,
None listed, -, Ireland, 125,
116, CHAS+. In HH of Alice
OBrian f 30 born Ireland.

GRAHAM, MARGARAET,
87, F, None listed, -, Ireland,
392, 392, YORK. In HH of
Archibald Graham m 44 born
Yok Dist., SC.

GRAHAM, MARIA, 23, F,
None listed, -, Ireland, 984,
963, CHAS-. In HH of Charles

McElleron m 30 born Ireland.

GRAHAM, NELLY, 65, F,
None listed, -, Ireland, 598, 598,
YORK. In HH of Elesinga W.
Smith m 49 born York Dist.,
SC.

GRAHAM, RICHARDSON,
35, M, None listed, -, Ireland,
84, 84, BEAU.

GRANT, CATHERINE, 35,
F, None listed, -, Ireland, 438,
421, CHAS-. In Pavillion
Hotel.

GRANT, MARY C., 23, F,
None listed, -, Ireland, 824, 804,
CHAS-. In HH of N.S. King m
39 born NY.

GRAY, JAMES, 45, M,
Planter, -, Ireland, 1253, 1254,
FAIR.

GREEN, AGNES, 33, F, None
listed, -, Ireland, 529, 565,
RICH.

GREEN, ANN, 33, F, None
listed, -, Ireland, 386, 348,
CHAS+. In HH of Patrick
Green m 33 born Ireland.

GREEN, BRIGET, 8, F,
None listed, -, Ireland, 488, 454,
CHAS*. In HH of Owen Green
m 42 born Ireland.

GREEN, CATHERINE, 39,
F, None listed, -, Ireland, 540,
506, CHAS*.

GREEN, ELLEN, 38, F, None
listed, -, Ireland, 882, 859,
CHAS%. In HH of John Green
m 40 born Ireland.

GREEN, FRANCIS, 13, M,

None listed, -, Ireland, 488, 454, CHAS*. In HH of Owen Green m 42 born Ireland.

GREEN, HUGH, 11, M, None listed, -, Ireland, 488, 454, CHAS*. In HH of Owen Green m 42 born Ireland.

GREEN, JOHN, 40, M, Laborer, -, Ireland, 882, 859, CHAS%.

GREEN, MARGARET, 36, F, None listed, -, Ireland, 488, 454, CHAS*. In HH of Owen Green m 42 born Ireland.

GREEN, MARIA, 25, F, None listed, -, Ireland, 367, 340, CHAS*. In HH of Jose Stevens m 60 born Nassau N.P.

GREEN, MARIA C., 25, F, None listed, -, Ireland, 529, 565, RICH. In HH of Agnes Green f 33 born Ireland.

GREEN, MARY, 4, F, None listed, -, Ireland, 882, 859, CHAS%. In HH of John Green m 40 born Ireland.

GREEN, MICHAEL, 52, M, Finisher, -, Ireland, 665, 657, CHAS%. In HH of James Dewin m 43 born Boston {MA}.

GREEN, OWEN, 42, M, Tailor, -, Ireland, 488, 454, CHAS*.

GREEN, PATRICK, 15, M, None listed, -, Ireland, 488, 454, CHAS*. In HH of Owen Green m 42 born Ireland.

GREEN, PATRICK, 33, M,

Tailor, -, Ireland, 386, 348, CHAS+.

GREEN, PETER, 17, M, None listed, -, Ireland, 488, 454, CHAS*. In HH of Owen Green m 42 born Ireland.

GREER, BENJAMIN, 28, M, None listed, -, Ireland, 82, 82, AND*. In HH of David Greer m 90 born Ireland.

GREER, BENJN., 50, M, Planter, -, Ireland, 459, 457, CHAS%.

GREER, DAVID, 90, M, Farmer, -, Ireland, 82, 82, AND*.

GREER, JOHN M., 42, M, Book seller, -, Ireland, 687, 667, CHAS-.

GREER, MARY, 60, F, None listed, -, Ireland, 82, 82, AND*. In HH of David Greer m 90 born Ireland.

GREER, WM., 25, M, Tavern Keeper, -, Ireland, 186, 169, CHAS.

GRIFFETHS, RACHAEL, 20, F, Servant, -, Ireland, 303, 280, CHAS. In HH of Arthur M. Huger m 30 born SC.

GRIFFITH, ELIZA, 26, F, None listed, -, Ireland, 700, 658, CHAS+. In HH of R.J. Griffith m 36 born Ireland.

GRIFFITH, MARY JANE, 52, F, None listed, -, Ireland, 700, 658, CHAS+. In HH of R.J. Griffith m 36 born Ireland.

GRIFFITH, MATILDA, 25,

F, None listed, -, Ireland, 571, 554, CHAS-. In HH of The Honble. M. King m 66 born Scotland.

GRIFFITH, R.J., 36, M, Merchant, -, Ireland, 700, 658, CHAS+.

GROGARTHY, MICHAEL, 30, M, Laborer, -, Ireland, 312, 296, CHAS-. In HH of Bernard Connely m 26 born Ireland.

GUILFOIL, JOANNA, 11, F, None listed, -, Ireland, 88, 88, ABB. In HH of William Guilfoil m 30 born Ireland.

GUILFOIL, MARGARET, 30, F, None listed, -, Ireland, 88, 88, ABB. In HH of William Guilfoil m 30 born Ireland.

GUILFOIL, WILLIAM, 30, M, Ditcher, -, Ireland, 88, 88, ABB.

GULLATT, JAMES, 18, M, Moulder, -, Ireland, 1136, 1115, CHAS%. In HH of Maria Carpenter f 52 born Ireland.

GUY, MARY, 55, F, None listed, -, Ireland, 518, 518, FAIR. In HH of David Aiken m 65 born Ireland.

H

HACKET, MARY, 27, F, None listed, -, Ireland, 120, 111, CHAS+. In HH of Mary Hays f 50 born Ireland.

HACKET, WILLIAM, 50, M, Hireling, -, Ireland, 1583, 1583, ABB. In HH of Hezekiah Dryman m 32 born NC.

HACKET, WILLIAM, 58, M, Farmer, -, Ireland, 69, 69, YORK+.

HACKETT, WILLIAM K., 20, M, Clerk, -, Ireland, 303, 309, RICH. In Hotel, Davis Caldwell m 51 proprietor.

HADDEN, JANE, 39, F, None listed, -, Ireland, 1303, 1303, ABB. In HH of John T. Haddon m 42 born SC.

HAFSETT, JAMES, 30, M, Carpenter, -, Ireland, 635, 593, CHAS+. In HH of John Moreen m 35 born Ireland.

HAFSETT, MARY, 25, F, None listed, -, Ireland, 635, 593, CHAS+. In HH of John Moreen m 35 born Ireland.

HAGAN, ROSANA, 58, F, None listed, -, Ireland, 194, 182, CHAS-.

HAGERTY, DENNIS O., 40, M, Laborer, -, Ireland, 1187, 1166, CHAS%.

HAGERTY, JANE, 16, F, None listed, -, Ireland, 1187, 1166, CHAS%. In HH of Dennis O Hagerty m 40 born Ireland.

HAGERTY, JOHN, 19, M, Laborer, -, Ireland, 1187, 1166, CHAS%. In HH of Dennis O Hagerty m 40 born Ireland.

HAGERTY, MARY, 36, F, None listed, -, Ireland, 1187,

1166, CHAS%. In HH of Dennis O Hagerty m 40 born Ireland.

HAGERTY, ROBERT, 12, M, None listed, -, Ireland, 1187, 1166, CHAS%. In HH of Dennis O Hagerty m 40 born Ireland.

HAGGERTY, JERRY, 35, M, Farmer, -, Ireland, 1363, 1363, CHES.

HAGGERTY, JOHN, 30, M, Mariner, -, Ireland, 337, 311, CHAS. In HH of William H. Fowler m 38 running Boarding house born England.

HAGIN, MARTHA, 48, F, None listed, -, Ireland, 2236, 2236, ABB. In HH of Thomas Hagin m 50 born Ireland.

HAGIN, MARY, 43, F, None listed, -, Ireland, 2236, 2236, ABB. In HH of Thomas Hagin m 50 born Ireland.

HAGIN, NANCY, 46, F, None listed, -, Ireland, 2236, 2236, ABB. In HH of Thomas Hagin m 50 born Ireland.

HAGIN, THOMAS, 50, M, Farmer, -, Ireland, 2236, 2236, ABB.

HALBINS, JNO., 23, M, Laborer, -, Ireland, 2058, 2061, EDGE. In HH of Richard Sullivan m 27 born Ireland.

HALEY, JOHN, 40, M, Drayman, -, Ireland, 172, 162, CHAS+.

HALEY, MARGARET, 45, F, None listed, -, Ireland, 172, 162, CHAS+. In HH of John Haley m 40 born Ireland.

HALEY, MATTHEW, 37, M, Planter, -, Ireland, 44, 44, RICH+.

HALEY, THOMAS, 45, M, Ditcher, -, Ireland, 910, 910, NEWB. In HH of Joseph Davenport m 43 born SC.

HAMBLETON, WILLIAM N., 30, M, Clerk, -, Ireland, 476, 442, CHAS*.

HAMELLON, ANN, 22, F, None listed, -, Ireland, 821, 801, CHAS-. In HH of August Pelerun m 31 born France.

HAMILTON, JANE, 20, F, None listed, -, Ireland, 178, 178, YORK. In HH of William Hamilton m 24 born York Dist., SC.

HAMILTON, JOHN, 69, M, None listed, -, Ireland, 426, 426, EDGE.

HAMILTON, MARY, 34, F, None listed, -, Ireland, 641, 641, YORK. In HH of William K Hamilton m 42 born York Dist., SC.

HAMLIN, JOSEPHINE, 21, F, None listed, -, Ireland, 709, 701, CHAS%. In HH of Simon Carmes m 38 born Ireland.

HAMLITER, SAMUEL, 50, M, Farmer, -, Ireland, 1433, 1433, LAU.

HAMMELL, MARIA, 28, F, None listed, -, Ireland, 145, 145,

CHAS%. In HH of W.
Hammell m 36 born Germany.
HAMMELL, THOMAS, 56,
M, Wheelwright, -, Ireland,
790, 748, CHAS+. In HH of
George H. King m 24 born SC.
HAMMITTAR, MARTHA,
78, F, None listed, -, Ireland,
634, 634, CHES. In HH of
Wm. Wilson m 44 born Ireland.
HAMSON, ELIZABETH, 20,
F, None listed, -, Ireland, 346,
308, CHAS+. In Boarding
house.
HANAHAN, MARY, 35, F,
None listed, -, Ireland, 542,
557, RICH. Date 1844 by
name. In Lunatic Asylum.
HANCOCK, CATHERINE,
50, F, None listed, -, Ireland,
492, 458, CHAS*. In HH of
Henry Hancock m 56 born
Ireland.
HANCOCK, CHARLES, 20,
M, Clerk, -, Ireland, 492, 458,
CHAS*. In HH of Henry
Hancock m 56 born Ireland.
HANCOCK, HENRY, 56, M,
Baker, -, Ireland, 492, 458,
CHAS*.
HANCOCK, THOMAS, 14,
M, None listed, -, Ireland, 492,
458, CHAS*. In HH of Henry
Hancock m 56 born Ireland.
HANKS, JANE, 66, F, None
listed, -, Ireland, 1532, 1532,
CHES.
HARBESON, JOHN, 48, M,
Merchant, -, Ireland, 788, 768,

CHAS-.
HARBESON, JOHN JR., 22,
M, Clerk, -, Ireland, 788, 768,
CHAS-. In HH of John
Harbeson m 48 born Ireland.
HARBESON, JOSEPH, 17,
M, Clerk, -, Ireland, 788, 768,
CHAS-. In HH of John
Harbeson m 48 born Ireland.
HARDING, MATTHEW, 33,
M, Restorat, -, Ireland, 187,
191, RICH.
HARE, FANNY A., 6, F, None
listed, -, Ireland, 599, 600,
FAIR. In HH of John Hare m
29 born Ireland.
HARE, JOHN, 29, M, Planter,
-, Ireland, 599, 600, FAIR.
HARE, MARGARET, 23, F,
None listed, -, Ireland, 599, 600,
FAIR. In HH of John Hare m
29 born Ireland.
HARE, RICHARD, 38, M,
Stonemason, -, Ireland, 90, 90,
YORK+.
HARE, SARAH, 50, F, None
listed, -, Ireland, 90, 90,
YORK+. In HH of Richard
Hare m 38 born Ireland.
HARE, WILLIAM J., 4, M,
None listed, -, Ireland, 599, 600,
FAIR. In HH of John Hare m
29 born Ireland.
HARKIN, JOHN, 48, M, Attd.
Lunatic A, -, Ireland, 538, 553,
RICH. Attendant at Lunatic
Asylum.
HARKLEY, ANN, 20, F,
None listed, -, Ireland, 883, 860,

CHAS%. In HH of George H. Winges m 21 born SC.

HARKLEY, RICHARD, 30, M, None listed, -, Ireland, 883, 860, CHAS%. In HH of George H. Winges m 21 born SC.

HARKNESS, JOHN, 76, M, Farmer, -, Ireland, 312, 313, AND*.

HARLNETT, WILLIAM, 28, M, Ditcher, -, Ireland, 1375, 1375, EDGE.

HARLOW, ANN, 30, F, None listed, -, Ireland, 1205, 1184, CHAS%. In HH of Michael Harlow m 45 born Ireland.

HARLOW, CATHERINE, 14, F, None listed, -, Ireland, 1205, 1184, CHAS%. In HH of Michael Harlow m 45 born Ireland.

HARLOW, JAMES, 6, M, None listed, -, Ireland, 491, 485, CHAS%. In HH of Mary Harlow f 40 born Ireland.

HARLOW, JOHN, 5, M, None listed, -, Ireland, 491, 485, CHAS%. In HH of Mary Harlow f 40 born Ireland.

HARLOW, MARY, 12, F, None listed, -, Ireland, 491, 485, CHAS%. In HH of Mary Harlow f 40 born Ireland.

HARLOW, MARY, 40, F, None listed, -, Ireland, 491, 485, CHAS%.

HARLOW, MICHAEL, 11, M, None listed, -, Ireland, 1205,

1184, CHAS%. In HH of Michael Harlow m 45 born Ireland.

HARLOW, MICHAEL, 45, M, Laborer, -, Ireland, 1205, 1184, CHAS%.

HARLOW, SARAH, 6, F, None listed, -, Ireland, 1205, 1184, CHAS%. In HH of Michael Harlow m 45 born Ireland.

HARLOW, WINNEY, 9, F, None listed, -, Ireland, 1205, 1184, CHAS%. In HH of Michael Harlow m 45 born Ireland.

HARMON, HANNAH S., 13, F, None listed, -, Ireland, 84, 84, YORK*. In HH of Preston Harmon m 53 born NC.

HARNEY, MARY, 22, F, None listed, -, Ireland, 36, 36, CHAS!. In HH of Nichl. Harney m 30 born Ireland.

HARNEY, NICHL., 30, M, Laborer, -, Ireland, 36, 36, CHAS!.

HARPER, JAMES, 41, M, Planter, -, Ireland, 940, 941, FAIR.

HARPER, JAMES, 75, M, Planter, -, Ireland, 55, 55, FAIR.

HARPER, JANE, 65, F, None listed, -, Ireland, 55, 55, FAIR. In HH of James Harper m 75 born Ireland.

HARPER, JANE, 73, F, None listed, -, Ireland, 267, 267, YORK. In HH of John S.

Harper m 47 born Ireland.

HARPER, JOHN S., 47, M, Laborer, -, Ireland, 267, 267, YORK.

HARPER, MATTHEW, 50, M, Cabinet maker, -, Ireland, 307, 307, YORK.

HARPOLE, JOSEPH, 32, M, Ordinance man, -, Ireland, 1005, 982, CHAS%.Under command of Major P. Hagnes, Comg. Off. U.S. Arnsel.

HARRIS, C., 76, M, None listed, -, Ireland, 1529, 1529, GREE. In HH of John Ford m 34 born SC.

HARRIS, ELIZABETH, 24, F, None listed, -, Ireland, 553, 519, CHAS*. In Catholic Seminary.

HARRISON, CATHARINE, 28, F, None listed, -, Ireland, 98, 98, BEAU. In HH of William Harrison m 25 born Ireland.

HARRISON, WILLIAM, 25, M, Grocer, -, Ireland, 98, 98, BEAU.

HART, BRIDGET, 30, F, None listed, -, Ireland, 1346, 1346, BARN. In HH of Dr. Amory Coffin m 37 born SC.

HARTIN, ROSANNA, 68, F, None listed, -, Ireland, 670, 679, RICH+.

HARVEY, CATHERINE, 25, F, None listed, -, Ireland, 167, 158, CHAS+. In Boarding house.

HARVEY, EDWARD, 50, M, None listed, -, Ireland, 1005, 983, CHAS-. In HH of Jane Harvey f 45 born Ireland.

HARVEY, ISABELLA, 50, F, None listed, -, Ireland, 89, 82, CHAS-.

HARVEY, JAMES, 18, M, None listed, -, Ireland, 988, 965, CHAS%. In HH of James Fitzpatrick m 40 born Ireland.

HARVEY, JANE, 45, F, None listed, -, Ireland, 1005, 983, CHAS-.

HARVEY, MARY, 38, F, None listed, -, Ireland, 988, 965, CHAS%. In HH of James Fitzpatrick m 40 born Ireland.

HARVEY, PATRICK, 32, M, Blacksmith, -, Ireland, 167, 158, CHAS+. In Boarding house.

HARVISON, ROBT., 40, M, Merchant, -, Ireland, 240, 240, CHAS3.

HASACT, CAROLINE, 32, F, None listed, -, Ireland, 369, 339, CHAS. In HH of Larry Hasact m 28 born Ireland.

HASACT, DINAH, 9, F, None listed, -, Ireland, 369, 339, CHAS. In HH of Larry Hasact m 28 born Ireland.

HASACT, LARRY, 38, M, Laborer, -, Ireland, 369, 339, CHAS.

HASACT, MARGARET, 4, F, None listed, -, Ireland, 369, 339, CHAS. In HH of Larry

Hasact m 28 born Ireland.

HASACT, MARY ANN, 6, F, None listed, -, Ireland, 369, 339, CHAS. In HH of Larry Hasact m 28 born Ireland.

HASKET, JANE, 30, F, None listed, -, Ireland, 719, 677, CHAS+. In HH of Phoebe Ann Ellis f 30 born PA.

HASSEY, MICHAEL, 17, M, Driver, -, Ireland, 766, 746, CHAS-. In HH of Patarick Hogan m 37 born Ireland.

HASTEN, HUGH, 60, M, Farmer, -, Ireland, 51, 51, CHES. In HH of Hugh Hener m 65 born Ireland.

HAYNE, EMELINE, 60, F, None listed, -, Ireland, 409, 407, CHAS%.

HAYNIE, ELIZABETH, 23, F, None listed, -, Ireland, 278, 279, AND*. In HH of David Haynie m 20 born GA.

HAYS, HONORU, 16, F, None listed, -, Ireland, 373, 340, CHAS. In HH of Eliza Jervais f 35 born SC.

HAYS, JOHN, 73, M, Farmer, -, Ireland, 1232, 1232, YORK.

HAYS, MARY, 50, F, None listed, -, Ireland, 120, 111, CHAS+.

HAYS, MARY H., 66, F, None listed, -, Ireland, 365, 365, CHAS%. In HH of Thomas H. Hays m 36 born New Orleans {LA}.

HAZARD, JANE, 34, F, None listed, -, Ireland, 816, 799, CHAS%. In HH of John Hazard m 41 born Ireland.

HAZARD, JOHN, 41, M, Laborer, -, Ireland, 816, 799, CHAS%.

HEANEY, JOHN, 25, M, Fireman, -, Ireland, 326, 301, CHAS. In HH of William Rollins m 40 born {-}.

HEDDAS?, ELIZABETH, 58, F, None listed, -, Ireland, 1158, 1158, YORK. In HH of Joseph McLosh m 65 born Ireland.

HEDEN, JAMES, 27, M, Clerk, -, Ireland, 397, 381, CHAS-. In HH of Edward Cassady m 30 born Ireland.

HEDEN, JOHN, 22, M, None listed, -, Ireland, 397, 381, CHAS-. In HH of Edward Cassady m 30 born Ireland.

HEELEY, AMELIA, 25, F, None listed, -, Ireland, 821, 801, CHAS-. In HH of August Pelerun m 31 born France.

HEELEY, JAMES, 25, M, Laborer, -, Ireland, 322, 297, CHAS. In Boarding house.

HEENSON, SARAH, 45, F, None listed, -, Ireland, 718, 676, CHAS+. In HH of Margaret Carlisle f 80 born Ireland.

HEFFERNON, JOHN, 48, M, Mason, -, Ireland, 1820, 1820, ABB.

HEFFERNON, MARY, 50, F, None listed, -, Ireland, 1944, 1944, ABB. In HH of Patrick

D. Heffernon m 45 born SC.

HEILL, MARY, 64, F, None listed, -, Ireland, 2243, 2243, ABB.

HEINZ, CHARLES, 27, M, Instrument maker, -, Ireland, 348, 354, RICH.

HEMPHILL, SAMUEL, 65, M, Farmer, -, Ireland, 821, 821, EDGE.

HENDERSON, SARAH, 16, F, None listed, -, Ireland, 679, 679, ABB. In HH of Ebenezer Hilborn m 32 born SC.

HENDERSON, WILLIAM, 28, F, Farmer, -, Ireland, 696, 696, ABB. In HH of Charles Evens 28 born Ireland.

HENER, HUGH, 65, M, Farmer, -, Ireland, 51, 51, CHES.

HENESSE, CATHERINE, 22, F, None listed, -, Ireland, 412, 395, CHAS-. In HH of H.N. Hart m 36 born Ireland.

HENESSE, ELIZA, 6, F, None listed, -, Ireland, 107, 103, CHAS*. In HH of Thomas Henesse m 32 born Ireland.

HENESSE, ELLEN, 4, F, None listed, -, Ireland, 107, 103, CHAS*. In HH of Thomas Henesse m 32 born Ireland.

HENESSE, JOHN, 2, M, None listed, -, Ireland, 107, 103, CHAS*. In HH of Thomas Henesse m 32 born

Ireland.

HENESSE, MARGARET, 26, F, None listed, -, Ireland, 107, 103, CHAS*. In HH of Thomas Henesse m 32 born Ireland.

HENESSE, THOMAS, 32, M, Shop keeper, -, Ireland, 107, 103, CHAS*.

HENESSEY, ELLEN, 24, F, None listed, -, Ireland, 294, 271, CHAS. In HH of John Gravely m 45 born England.

HENNESEE, MARY, 34, F, None listed, -, Ireland, 153, 155, Rick+.

HENNESSE, CHARLES, 26, M, Shoe maker, -, Ireland, 90, 90, CHAS%.

HENOX, JANE, 54, F, None listed, -, Ireland, 2390, 2390, ABB.

HENRICH, JAMES, 36, M, Baker, -, Ireland, 132, 124, CHAS+. In HH of John McCrale {McCrate} m 30 born Canada.

HENRY, EDWARD, 42, M, Tavern keeper, -, Ireland, 315, 291, CHAS+.

HENRY, JANE, 50, F, None listed, -, Ireland, 315, 291, CHAS+. In HH of Edward Henry m 42 born Ireland.

HENRY, JOHN, 20, M, Mason, -, Ireland, 185, 168, CHAS. In HH of S. Morrison m 30 born Ireland.

HENRY, JOHN, 43, M, Farmer, -, Ireland, 29, 29,

EDGE*.

HENRY, MARY, 50, F, None listed, -, Ireland, 573, 531, CHAS+. In HH of Ann Ross f 45 born SC.

HENRY, MARY, 67, F, None listed, -, Ireland, 1567, 1567, ABB. In HH of Peter Henry m 30 born SC.

HENRY, MARY, 78, F, None listed, -, Ireland, 979, 979, YORK.

HENSSER, JOHN, 35, M, Laborer, -, Ireland, 408, 371, CHAS. In HH of J. McDonald m 50 born SC.

HENSSER, MARY, 60, F, None listed, -, Ireland, 408, 371, CHAS. In HH of J. McDonald m 50 born SC.

HENSSER, WILLIAM, 30, M, Laborer, -, Ireland, 408, 371, CHAS. In HH of J. McDonald m 50 born SC.

HERBERT, JOHN, 21, M, Laborer, -, Ireland, 2007, 2013, EDGE. In HH of William Herbert m 37 born Ireland.

HERBERT, JOHN, 22, M, Laborer, -, Ireland, 2057, 2060, EDGE. In HH of Michael Corner m 27 born Ireland.

HERBERT, MAY L., 31, F, None listed, -, Ireland, 2007, 2013, EDGE. In HH of William Herbert m 37 born Ireland.

HERBERT, THOMAS, 27, M, Laborer, -, Ireland, 409,

368, CHAS+.

HERBERT, WILLIAM, 37, M, Merchant, -, Ireland, 2007, 2013, EDGE.

HERMANS, PATRICK, 30, M, Laborer, -, Ireland, 268, 249, CHAS+. In HH of Thomas Morrison m 36 born Ireland.

HERMON, JANE, 40, F, None listed, -, Ireland, 467, 467, UNION.

HERMON, MARY, 39, F, None listed, -, Ireland, 468, 468, UNION.

HERMON, THOMAS, 65, M, Gunsmith, -, Ireland, 1610, 1610, GREE.

HERRATTY, ANN, 38, F, None listed, -, Ireland, 371, 340, CHAS. In HH of Patrick Herratty m 40 born Ireland.

HERRATTY, PATRICK, 40, M, Laborer, -, Ireland, 371, 340, CHAS.

HERRON, JAMES, 78, M, Farmer, -, Ireland, 657, 661, AND.

HEYER, SOLOMIN, 21, M, Laborer, -, Ireland, 1197, 1176, CHAS%. In Boarding house.

HIGGINS, ANTHONY, 20, M, R.R. Conductor, -, Ireland, 988, 965, CHAS%. In HH of James Fitzpatrick m 40 born Ireland.

HIGGINS, CATHERINE, 35, F, None listed, -, Ireland, 41, 41, CHAS!. In HH of Patrick Higgins m 40 born Ireland.

HIGGINS, HONORE, 40, F, None listed, -, Ireland, 550, 509, CHAS+. In HH of Michael Higgins m 35 born Ireland.

HIGGINS, MICHAEL, 35, M, Laborer, -, Ireland, 550, 509, CHAS+.

HIGGINS, PATRICK, 40, M, Laborer, -, Ireland, 41, 41, CHAS!.

HILBERT, BRIGET, 22, F, None listed, -, Ireland, 250, 235, CHAS-. In HH of Revd. J. Rosenfeld m 36 born Prussia.

HILBERT, JOHN, 35, M, Laborer, -, Ireland, 108, 103, CHAS*. In HH of Patrick Keefe m 40 born Ireland.

HILHORN, ELIZABETH, 19, F, None listed, -, Ireland, 679, 679, ABB. In HH of Ebenezer Hilborn m 32 born SC.

HILL, EDWARD, 36, M, Carpenter, -, Ireland, 100, 100, CHAS^.

HILL, SARAH, 27, F, None listed, -, Ireland, 2255, 2255, ABB. In HH of William C. HIll m 27 born SC.

HILL, WILLIAM, 45, M, Farmer, -, Ireland, 1582, 1582, ABB.

HINDMAN, JANE, 65, F, None listed, -, Ireland, 414, 414, CHES. In HH of J.A. Hindman m 33 born SC.

HINES, JOHN, 28, M, Laborer, -, Ireland, 222, 209, CHAS+. In HH of John Donnahugh m 22 born Ireland.

HINES, MARY C., 25, F, None listed, -, Ireland, 828, 786, CHAS+. In HH of William Hines m 33 born Ireland.

HINES, WILLIAM, 33, M, Drayman, -, Ireland, 828, 786, CHAS+.

HODGE, MARTHA, 65, F, None listed, -, Ireland, 917, 917, ABB. In HH of Thomas Hodge 73 born SC.

HOGAN, BRIDGET, 10, F, None listed, -, Ireland, 347, 321, CHAS. In HH of Michael Hogan m 30 born Ireland.

HOGAN, BRIDGET, 25, F, None listed, -, Ireland, 347, 321, CHAS. In HH of Michael Hogan m 30 born Ireland.

HOGAN, CATHERINE, 6, F, None listed, -, Ireland, 347, 321, CHAS. In HH of Michael Hogan m 30 born Ireland.

HOGAN, DENIS, 29, M, Laborer, -, Ireland, 261, 244, CHAS+. In HH of Hugh McNamara m 28 born Ireland.

HOGAN, EDWARD, 68, M, Farmer, -, Ireland, 2286, 2286, ABB.

HOGAN, ELIZABETH, 14, F, None listed, -, Ireland, 174, 164, CHAS+. In HH of Richard Hogan m 36 born Ireland.

HOGAN, JAMES, 35, M, Laborer, -, Ireland, 240, 226, CHAS+. In HH of William Farley m 38 born Ireland.

HOGAN, JOHN, 21, M, Laborer, -, Ireland, 261, 244, CHAS+. In HH of Hugh McNamara m 28 born Ireland.

HOGAN, JOHN, 28, M, Coal passer, -, Ireland, 326, 301, CHAS. In HH of William Rollins m 40 born {-}. In crew of the Steam Ship Isabel.

HOGAN, JOHN, 35, M, Laborer, -, Ireland, 241, 227, CHAS+. In HH of James Kennedy m 30 born Ireland.

HOGAN, JOHN, 40, M, Laborer, -, Ireland, 46, 46, COLL.

HOGAN, JOHN JR., 18, M, Laborer, -, Ireland, 241, 227, CHAS+. In HH of James Kennedy m 30 born Ireland.

HOGAN, MARGARET, 20, F, None listed, -, Ireland, 166, 148, CHAS. In HH of John Jenkins m 25 born England.

HOGAN, MARGARET, 32, F, None listed, -, Ireland, 174, 164, CHAS+. In HH of Richard Hogan m 36 born Ireland.

HOGAN, MARTIN, 23, M, Laborer, -, Ireland, 261, 244, CHAS+. In HH of Hugh McNamara m 28 born Ireland.

HOGAN, MICHAEL, 30, M, Laborer, -, Ireland, 347, 321, CHAS.

HOGAN, PATRICK, 37, M, Stable keeper, -, Ireland, 766, 746, CHAS-.

HOGAN, PETER, 19, M, Laborer, -, Ireland, 326, 295, CHAS+. In HH of Edwd McLaughlin m 23 born Ireland.

HOGAN, RICHARD, 36, M, Merchant, -, Ireland, 174, 164, CHAS+.

HOGAN, SUSAN, 3, F, None listed, -, Ireland, 347, 321, CHAS. In HH of Michael Hogan m 30 born Ireland.

HOGG, ISABELLA, 75, F, None listed, -, Ireland, 1211, 1211, YORK. In HH of Alexander Hogg m 36 born SC.

HOLDEN, MARY, 42, F, None listed, -, Ireland, 355, 355, ABB. In HH of Daniel Holden 37 m born SC

HOLDING, JANE, 38, F, None listed, -, Ireland, 1301, 1301, EDGE. In HH of James L. Hill m 26 born SC.

HOLLINS, EDWARD, 30, M, Laborer, -, Ireland, 479, 437, CHAS+. In HH of Mary Welch f 32 born NY.

HOLLINS, MARY, 29, F, None listed, -, Ireland, 479, 437, CHAS+. In HH of Mary Welch f 32 born NY.

HOLLINS, WILLIAM, 40, M, Laborer, -, Ireland, 479, 437, CHAS+. In HH of Mary Welch f 32 born NY.

HOLMES, ELIZA A., 16, F, None listed, -, Ireland, 267, 267, YORK*. In HH of Joshua Holmes m 50 born Ireland.

HOLMES, JOSHUA, 50, M, Farmer, -, Ireland, 267, 267, YORK*.

HOLMES, REBECCA, 45, F, None listed, -, Ireland, 267, 267, YORK*. In HH of Joshua Holmes m 50 born Ireland.

HOLMES, REBECCA B., 18, F, None listed, -, Ireland, 267, 267, YORK*. In HH of Joshua Holmes m 50 born Ireland.

HOLMES, SARAH J., 20, F, None listed, -, Ireland, 267, 267, YORK*. In HH of Joshua Holmes m 50 born Ireland.

HOOD, THOMAS, 71, M, None listed, -, Ireland, 427, 396, CHAS*. In HH of Elizabeth Hood f 45 born NY.

HORAN, WILLIAM, 25, M, Laborer, -, Ireland, 389, 351, CHAS+. In HH of Edward Collins m 40 born Ireland.

HORN, BETTY, 22, F, None listed, -, Ireland, 389, 351, CHAS+. In HH of Edward Collins m 40 born Ireland.

HORTY, ELLEN, 5, F, None listed, -, Ireland, 238, 224, CHAS+. In HH of Thomas Quin m 30 born Ireland.

HORTY, JANNA, 4, F, None listed, -, Ireland, 238, 224, CHAS+. In HH of Thomas

Quin m 30 born Ireland.

HORTY, MARY, 8, F, None listed, -, Ireland, 238, 224, CHAS+. In HH of Thomas Quin m 30 born Ireland.

HORTY, MARY, 35, F, None listed, -, Ireland, 238, 224, CHAS+. In HH of Thomas Quin m 30 born Ireland.

HORTY, THOMAS, 2, M, None listed, -, Ireland, 238, 224, CHAS+. In HH of Thomas Quin m 30 born Ireland.

HORTY, THOMAS, 45, M, Laborer, -, Ireland, 238, 224, CHAS+. In HH of Thomas Quin m 30 born Ireland.

HOUSTON, HUGH, 73, M, None, -, Ireland, 1584, 1584, ABB. In HH of William McIlwain m 56 born Ireland.

HOWARD, ANN MARIA, 37, F, None listed, -, Ireland, 996, 973, CHAS%. In HH of Thomas Howard m 43 born Ireland.

HOWARD, JOANA, 21, F, Laborer, -, Ireland, 456, 415, CHAS+. In HH of Michael Howard m 25 born Ireland.

HOWARD, MICHAEL, 25, M, Laborer, -, Ireland, 456, 415, CHAS+.

HOWARD, THOMAS, 43, M, Farmer, -, Ireland, 996, 973, CHAS%.

HOY, PATRICK, 64, M, Gunsmith, -, Ireland, 112, 112, SPART.

HUEY, JAMES, 30, M, Planter, -, Ireland, 741, 742, FAIR. In HH of John Adger m 40 born SC.

HUGHES, MARTHA, 40, F, None listed, -, Ireland, 158, 158, EDGE. In HH of John H. Hughes m 48 born SC.

HUMPHREY, ROBERT B., 40, M, Bricklayer, -, Ireland, 540, 541, ORNG+.

HUMPHREY, ROBERT B., 40, M, Bricklayer, -, Ireland, 540, 541, ORNG+.

HUMPHRY, JOHN, 53, M, Planter, -, Ireland, 393, 393, SUMT.

HUMPHRY, NANCY, 44, F, None listed, -, Ireland, 393, 393, SUMT. In HH of John Humphry m 53 born Ireland.

HUMPSEY, BRIDGET, 20, F, Servant, -, Ireland, 54, 64, CHAS. In HH of William Ravenel m 43 born SC.

HUNTER, ELIZA, 32, F, None listed, -, Ireland, 276, 282, RICH. In HH of Thomas Beggs m 30 born MS.

HUNTER, JOHN B., 47, M, Physician, -, Ireland, 1618, 1618, YORK.

HUNTER, JOHNSON, 24, M, Blacksmith, -, Ireland, 476, 491, RICH.

HUNTER, WILLIAM, 81, M, Farmer, -, Ireland, 1091, 1091, NEWB.

HUNTER, WILLIAM H., 6, M, None listed, -, Ireland, 276, 282, RICH. In HH of Thomas Beggs m 30 born MS.

HURLEY, JOHN, 27, M, Laborer, -, Ireland, 206, 184, CHAS.

HURLEY, MARY, 30, F, None listed, -, Ireland, 206, 184, CHAS. In HH of John Hurley m 27 born Ireland.

HURLEY, TIMOTHY, 21, M, None listed, -, Ireland, 206, 184, CHAS. In HH of John Hurley m 27 born Ireland.

HURST, E., 29, F, None listed, -, Ireland, 482, 439, CHAS. In Planters Hotel.

HUTCHIN, ARCHIBALD, 40, M, Planter, -, Ireland, 711, 712, FAIR. In HH of Richard Cathcart m 55 born Ireland.

HUTCHINSON, JAMES, 27, M, Planter, -, Ireland, 801, 802, FAIR.

HUTCHINSON, JAMES, 51, M, Stone mason, -, Ireland, 771, 772, FAIR.

HUTCHINSON, JOHN, 16, M, None listed, -, Ireland, 771, 772, FAIR. In HH of James Hutchinson m 51 born Ireland.

HUTCHINSON, MARGARET, 13, F, None listed, -, Ireland, 771, 772, FAIR. In HH of James Hutchinson m 51 born Ireland.

HUTCHINSON, ROBERT, 18, M, None listed, -, Ireland, 771, 772, FAIR. In HH of

James Hutchinson m 51 born Ireland.

HUTCHINSON, SARAH, 51, F, None listed, -, Ireland, 771, 772, FAIR. In HH of James Hutchinson m 51 born Ireland.

HUTTINGTON, JOHN, 70, M, Farmer, -, Ireland, 1324, 1324, SPART.

HYDE, MICHAEL, 34, M, Laborer, -, Ireland, 337, 311, CHAS. In HH of William H. Fowler m 38 running Boarding house born England.

HYNDMAN, JANE, 29, F, None listed, -, Ireland, 268, 268, FAIR. In HH of David Milling m 52 born Ireland.

HYNDMAN, JOHN, 28, M, Shoe maker, -, Ireland, 513, 513, FAIR. In HH of J.M. Cranford m 27 born Ireland. At the Fairfield Hotel.

HYNES, P., 27, M, Priv. U.S.A., -, Ireland, 47, 43, CHAS$. In HH of John Ewing m 50 born MA.

I

IMMERSON, MARY, 60, F, None listed, -, Ireland, 946, 950, FAIR.

IMMIS, BRIDGET, 20, F, None listed, -, Ireland, 490, 485, CHAS%. In HH of John Butler m 37 born Ireland.

INGALLS, JOHN, 19, M, Clerk, -, Ireland, 150, 141, CHAS+. In Boarding house.

INGRAHAM, JANE, 63, F, None listed, -, Ireland, 1593, 1593, YORK. In HH of John Ingraham m 64 born England.

INRIGHT, CATHERINE, 23, F, None listed, -, Ireland, 487, 444, CHAS. In HH of Dennis Inright m 32 born Ireland.

INRIGHT, DENNIS, 32, M, City police, -, Ireland, 487, 444, CHAS.

IRVIN, ALEXANDER, 25, M, Laborer, -, Ireland, 978, 979, FAIR. In HH of David Gordon m 60 born Ireland.

IRVIN, ISABELLA, 20, F, None listed, -, Ireland, 978, 979, FAIR. In HH of David Gordon m 60 born Ireland.

IRWIN, AGNES, 8, F, None listed, -, Ireland, 680, 680, ABB. In HH of Arthur Irwin m 56 born Ireland.

IRWIN, ANN J., 13, F, None listed, -, Ireland, 680, 680, ABB. In HH of Arthur Irwin m 56 born Ireland.

IRWIN, ARTHUR, 56, M, Stonemason, -, Ireland, 680, 680, ABB.

IRWIN, CHARLOTTE, 24, F, None listed, -, Ireland, 2222, 2222, ABB. In HH of James Irwin m 30 born SC.

IRWIN, DAVID, 6, M, None listed, -, Ireland, 680, 680, ABB. In HH of Arthur Irwin m 56 born Ireland.

IRWIN, ELIZABETH, 68, F, None listed, -, Ireland, 2222, 2222, ABB. In HH of Samuel Irwin m 70 born Ireland

IRWIN, JANE, 49, F, None listed, -, Ireland, 680, 680, ABB. In HH of Arthur Irwin m 56 born Ireland.

IRWIN, MALCOLM, 25, M, Millwright, -, Ireland, 680, 680, ABB. In HH of Arthur Irwin m 56 born Ireland.

IRWIN, MARGARET, 19, F, None listed, -, Ireland, 2255, 2255, ABB. In HH of William C. HIll m 27 born SC.

IRWIN, SAMUEL, 18, M, Farmer, -, Ireland, 680, 680, ABB. In HH of Arthur Irwin m 56 born Ireland.

IRWIN, SAMUEL, 70, M, Farmer, -, Ireland, 2222, 2222, ABB.

IRWIN, WILLIAM J., 15, M, None listed, -, Ireland, 680, 680, ABB. In HH of Arthur Irwin m 56 born Ireland.

IVERS, SARAH, 21, F, None listed, -, Ireland, 542, 557, RICH. In Lunatic Asylum.

J

JAMERSON, JANE, 58, F, None listed, -, Ireland, 805, 805, CHES. In HH of John Jamerson m 54 born SC.

JAMESON, SARAH, 70, F, None listed, -, Ireland, 259, 259, CHES.

JEANEY, ROBERT, 35, M, Sadler, -, Ireland, 792, 772, CHAS-.

JENKINS, ANNASTACIA, 23, F, None listed, -, Ireland, 166, 148, CHAS. In HH of John Jenkins m 25 born England.

JENKINSON, MARIA, 24, F, None listed, -, Ireland, 249, 234, CHAS+. In HH of John Brown m 36 born Ireland.

JENNING, PATRICK, 40, M, Merchant, -, Ireland, 882, 840, CHAS+. In Charleston Hotel.

JENNINGS, ROWAN, 30, M, Clerk, -, Ireland, 650, 650, UNION.

JERREL, DAVID TITE, 38, M, None, -, Ireland, 1192, 1192, Lex.

JLEFFE, MARY, 24, F, None listed, -, Ireland, 422, 394, CHAS*. In HH of Charles Jleffe m 30 born SC.

JOHNSON, AGNES, 14, F, None listed, -, Ireland, 27, 27, CHES. In HH of John Johnston m 46 born Ireland.

JOHNSON, CATHERINE, 20, F, None listed, -, Ireland, 682, 662, CHAS-. In HH of James Gamble f 50 born Ireland.

JOHNSON, ELIZA, 40, F, None listed, -, Ireland, 682, 662, CHAS-. In HH of James Gamble f 50 born Ireland.

JOHNSON, ELIZABETH, 18, F, None listed, -, Ireland, 682, 662, CHAS-. In HH of James Gamble f 50 born Ireland.

JOHNSON, EUPHEMA, 30, F, None listed, -, Ireland, 1091, 1092, AND*. In HH of David Robbinson m 52 born SC.

JOHNSON, HANNAH, 21, F, None listed, -, Ireland, 181, 181, CHAS%. In HH of William Johnson m 27 born Ireland.

JOHNSON, JANE, 45, F, None listed, -, Ireland, 21, 21, KERS. In HH of Wm. Johnson m 45 born Ireland.

JOHNSON, JOHN, 28, M, Mariner, -, Ireland, 362, 333, CHAS. In Boarding house.

JOHNSON, L.D., 40, M, Brick mason, -, Ireland, 1550, 1550, EDGE. In HH of Harriet Rhodes f 32 born SC.

JOHNSON, M., 17, M, None listed, -, Ireland, 27, 27, CHES. In HH of John Johnston m 46 born Ireland.

JOHNSON, M., 71, M, None listed, -, Ireland, 27, 27, CHES. In HH of John Johnston m 46 born Ireland.

JOHNSON, MARGARET, 15, F, None listed, -, Ireland, 974, 975, FAIR. In HH of William Johnson m 40 born Ireland.

JOHNSON, MARY, 22, F, Servant, -, Ireland, 462, 419, CHAS. In HH of The Hon. T.L. Hutchenson m 38, Mayor of Charleston, born SC.

JOHNSON, MARY, 38, F, Servant, -, Ireland, 355, 327, CHAS. In HH of Col. W.S. King 48 m born CT.

JOHNSON, MARY, 50, F, None listed, -, Ireland, 1061, 1038, CHAS-.

JOHNSON, SARAH, 14, F, None listed, -, Ireland, 27, 27, CHES. In HH of John Johnston m 46 born Ireland.

JOHNSON, SARAH, 25, F, None listed, -, Ireland, 54, 49, CHAS-. In HH of Robert Leckia m 28 born Ireland.

JOHNSON, WILLIAM, 27, M, Musician, -, Ireland, 181, 181, CHAS%.

JOHNSON, WILLIAM, 40, M, Planter, -, Ireland, 974, 975, FAIR.

JOHNSON, WM., 45, M, None listed, -, Ireland, 21, 21, KERS.

JOHNSTON, ANN, 40, F, None listed, -, Ireland, 51, 47, CHAS-. In HH of A.M. Talvand f 40 born Ireland.

JOHNSTON, ELIZABETH, 56, F, None listed, -, Ireland, 477, 477, FAIR. In HH of Samuel Johnston m 80 born Ireland.

JOHNSTON, ELLEN, 50, F, None listed, -, Ireland, 1068, 1068, CHES.

JOHNSTON, J.A., 56, M,

Scribery, -, Ireland, 30, 30, NEWB. In HH of H.K. Boyd 44 m Ordinary born NC.

JOHNSTON, JOHN, 5, M, None listed, -, Ireland, 615, 615, CHES. In HH of John Johnston m 26 born Ireland.

JOHNSTON, JOHN, 26, M, Farmer, -, Ireland, 615, 615, CHES.

JOHNSTON, JOHN, 46, M, Blacksmith, -, Ireland, 27, 27, CHES.

JOHNSTON, JOSEPH, 42, M, None listed, -, Ireland, 208, 208, CHES.

JOHNSTON, M., 48, F, None listed, -, Ireland, 27, 27, CHES. In HH of John Johnston m 46 born Ireland.

JOHNSTON, M.A., 26, F, None listed, -, Ireland, 615, 615, CHES. In HH of John Johnston m 26 born Ireland.

JOHNSTON, MARY, 89, F, None listed, -, Ireland, 32, 32, CHES.

JOHNSTON, ROBERT, 41, M, Farmer, -, Ireland, 61, 61, PICK+.

JOHNSTON, SAMUEL, 80, M, Planter, -, Ireland, 477, 477, FAIR.

JOHNSTON, TOM, 29, M, Clerk, -, Ireland, 261, 244, CHAS+. In HH of Hugh McNamara m 28 born Ireland.

JOHNSTON, WILLIAM B., 32, M, Editor, -, Ireland, 240, 245, RICH.

JOICE, EDWARD, 24, M, Clerk, -, Ireland, 61, 61, GEOR. In HH of Nathan Emanuel m 36 born VA.

JOICE, JOHN, 28, M, Taylor, -, Ireland, 178, 178, GEOR.

JONES, GEORGE, 25, M, None listed, -, Ireland, 1192, 1171, CHAS%. In HH of Mary Constance f 32 mulatto born SC

JONES, MARY, 25, F, None listed, -, Ireland, 469, 427, CHAS. In HH of Thomas Kinney m 74 born Ireland.

JONES, SARAH, 22, F, Servant, -, Ireland, 462, 419, CHAS. In HH of The Hon. T.L. Hutchenson m 38, Mayor of Charleston, born SC.

JORDAN, AUGUSTUS, 19, M, Clerk, -, Ireland, 89, 99, CHAS. In HH of Edward Jordan m 34 born Ireland.

JORDAN, EDWARD, 34, M, Sail maker, -, Ireland, 89, 99, CHAS.

JORDAN, FRANCIS E., 29, F, None listed, -, Ireland, 501, 501, FAIR. In HH of Thomas Jordan m 35 born SC.

JORDAN, SARAH, 39, F, None listed, -, Ireland, 89, 99, CHAS. In HH of Edward Jordan m 34 born Ireland.

JUICE, MICHAEL, 27, M, Tailor, -, Ireland, 68, 68, MARL. In HH of W.J. Daniels m 29 Tailor born SC.

JUNKIN, DAVID, 28, M, Hireling, -, Ireland, 1435, 1435, ABB.

JUNKIN, ROBERT, 24, M, Carriage maker, -, Ireland, 857, 861, AND. In HH of A.S. McClinton m 51, Waggon maker born SC.

JUNKIN, SARAH, 28, F, None listed, -, Ireland, 1435, 1435, ABB. In HH of David Junkin m 28 born Ireland.

K

KAHAL, JOHN, 29, M, Laborer, -, Ireland, 31, 27, CHAS$. In HH of E. Reynolds m 33 mulatto born Ireland.

KAICY?, JAS., 34, F, Planter, -, Ireland, 1426, 1426, BARN.

KANE, ELIZABETH M., 32, F, None listed, -, Ireland, 604, 621, RICH.

KANE, WILLIAM, 34, M, Laborer, -, Ireland, 337, 311, CHAS. In HH of William H. Fowler m 38 running Boarding house born England.

KARVIN, JAMES, 30, M, Laborer, -, Ireland, 457, 415, CHAS+.

KAVANAGH, B., 50, M, Ditcher, -, Ireland, 1843, 1843, SUMT.

KEANAN, THOMAS, 40, M, Carpenter, -, Ireland, 2002, 2005, EDGE.

KEANNY, RICHARD, 22, M, Farmer, -, Ireland, 912, 912, CHES. In HH of James Finney m 36 born SC.

KEARNEY, MICHAEL, 24, M, Laborer, -, Ireland, 312, 296, CHAS-. In HH of Bernard Connely m 26 born Ireland.

KEEARN, J.J., 30, M, Plasterer, -, Ireland, 59, 59, EDGE. In HH of Thomas W. Blease m 26 born SC.

KEEFE, ALICE, 35, F, None listed, -, Ireland, 108, 103, CHAS*. In HH of Patrick Keefe m 40 born Ireland.

KEEFE, PATRICK, 40, M, None listed, -, Ireland, 108, 103, CHAS*.

KEEGAN, ANN, 11, F, None listed, -, Ireland, 778, 761, CHAS%. In HH of Thomas Keegan m 39 born Ireland.

KEEGAN, ELIZABETH, 34, F, None listed, -, Ireland, 778, 761, CHAS%. In HH of Thomas Keegan m 39 born Ireland.

KEEGAN, HOLME, 53, M, Laborer, -, Ireland, 172, 162, CHAS+. In HH of John Haley m 40 born Ireland.

KEEGAN, JAMES, 16, M, None listed, -, Ireland, 37, 37, CHAS!. In HH of Mary Keegan f 30 born Ireland.

KEEGAN, MARY, 30, F, None listed, -, Ireland, 37, 37, CHAS!.

KEEGAN, PATRICK, 24, M, Laborer, -, Ireland, 337, 311, CHAS. In HH of William H. Fowler m 38 running Boarding house born England.

KEEGAN, THOMAS, 14, M, None listed, -, Ireland, 778, 761, CHAS%. In HH of Thomas Keegan m 39 born Ireland.

KEEGAN, THOMAS, 39, M, Laborer, -, Ireland, 778, 761, CHAS%.

KEENAN, ALEXANDER, 42, M, Mechanic, -, Ireland, 525, 540, RICH.

KEENAN, ANN, 40, F, None listed, -, Ireland, 4, 4, BARN. In HH of Re Keenan m 58 born Ireland.

KEENAN, EDWARD, 30, M, Laborer, -, Ireland, 31, 27, CHAS$. In HH of E. Reynolds m 33 mulatto born Ireland.

KEENAN, ELEANOR, 35, F, None listed, -, Ireland, 525, 540, RICH. In HH of Alexander Keenan m 42 born Ireland.

KEENAN, GEORGE, 22, M, Farmer, -, Ireland, 900, 900, CHES. In HH of Saml. Keenan m 51 born Ireland.

KEENAN, JAMES, 20, M, Clerk, -, Ireland, 322, 294, CHAS+. In HH of John Dowling m 34 born Ireland.

KEENAN, JANE, 24, F, None listed, -, Ireland, 1055, 1033, CHAS%.

KEENAN, MARY, 24, F, None listed, -, Ireland, 31, 27, CHAS$. In HH of E. Reynolds m 33 mulatto born Ireland.

KEENAN, MARY, 39, F, None listed, -, Ireland, 31, 27, CHAS$. In HH of E. Reynolds m 33 mulatto born Ireland.

KEENAN, MICHAEL, 44, M, Laborer, -, Ireland, 640, 599, CHAS+.

KEENAN, RE, 58, M, Plant., -, Ireland, 4, 4, BARN.

KEENAN, SAML., 57, M, Farmer, -, Ireland, 900, 900, CHES.

KEENAN, WILLIAM, 21, M, Laborer, -, Ireland, 1055, 1033, CHAS%. In HH of Jane Keenan f 24 born Ireland.

KEENMAN?, SUSAN, 52, F, None listed, -, Ireland, 996, 996, CHES.

KEILY, U., 26, M, Priv. U.S.A., -, Ireland, 47, 43, CHAS$. In HH of John Ewing m 50 born MA.

KELLER, LEWIS, 45, M, Laborer, -, Ireland, 200, 181, CHAS.

KELLER, MARGARET, 37, F, None listed, -, Ireland, 200, 181, CHAS. In HH of Lewis Keller m 45 born Ireland.

KELLY, ANN, 18, F, None listed, -, Ireland, 250, 235, CHAS-. In HH of Revd. J. Rosenfeld m 36 born Prussia.

KELLY, ANN, 26, F, None listed, -, Ireland, 731, 722, CHAS%. In HH of Michael Kelly m 28 born Ireland.

KELLY, ANN, 30, F, None listed, -, Ireland, 215, 202, CHAS+. In HH of Peter Kelly m 35 born Ireland.

KELLY, BRIDGET, 19, F, None listed, -, Ireland, 1007, 1008, AND*. In HH of Samuel Mavrick m 77 born SC.

KELLY, BRIDGET, 27, F, None listed, -, Ireland, 714, 704, CHAS%. In HH of John Burns m 28 born Ireland.

KELLY, CATHERINE, 7, F, None listed, -, Ireland, 714, 704, CHAS%. In HH of John Burns m 28 born Ireland.

KELLY, CATHERINE, 24, F, None listed, -, Ireland, 515, 474, CHAS+. In HH of Joseph Walker m 30 born NY.

KELLY, CATHERINE, 25, F, None listed, -, Ireland, 207, 189, CHAS*. In HH of Patrick Brady m 49 born Ireland.

KELLY, CATHERINE, 25, F, None listed, -, Ireland, 5, 5, CHAS$. In HH of Patric (sic) Kelly m 38 born Ireland.

KELLY, CHS., 30, M, Laborer, -, Ireland, 260, 238, CHAS. In HH of Dunham Watson m 60 born MA.

KELLY, JAMES, 4, M, None listed, -, Ireland, 714, 704, CHAS%. In HH of John Burns m 28 born Ireland.

KELLY, JOANA, 30, F, None listed, -, Ireland, 745, 732, CHAS%. In HH of Owen Kelly m 34 born Ireland.

KELLY, JOHN, 9, M, None listed, -, Ireland, 714, 704, CHAS%. In HH of John Burns m 28 born Ireland.

KELLY, JOHN, 45, M, Well Digger, -, Ireland, 1777, 1777, LAU. In HH of Archey M. Smith m 26 born SC.

KELLY, MARY, 36, F, None listed, -, Ireland, 2051, 2054, EDGE. In HH of Thomas Kelly m 38 born Ireland.

KELLY, MARY ANN, 13, F, None listed, -, Ireland, 2051, 2054, EDGE. In HH of Thomas Kelly m 38 born Ireland.

KELLY, MARY K., 38, F, None listed, -, Ireland, 297, 281, CHAS-. In HH of William Kelly m 51 born Ireland.

KELLY, MICHAEL, 28, M, Laborer, -, Ireland, 731, 722, CHAS%.

KELLY, MICHAEL, 34, M, Laborer, -, Ireland, 322, 297, CHAS. In Boarding house.

KELLY, OAN {Owen?}, 30, M, Laborer, -, Ireland, 934, 911, CHAS%. In HH of Joana Tinen f 28 born Ireland.

KELLY, OWEN, 34, M, Laborer, -, Ireland, 745, 732, CHAS%.

KELLY, PAT. J., 28, M, Clerk, -, Ireland, 685, 665, CHAS-. In Victoria Hotel.

KELLY, PATRICK, 27, M, Mariner, -, Ireland, 337, 311, CHAS. In HH of William H. Fowler m 38 running Boarding house born England.

KELLY, PATRICK, 30, M, Laborer, -, Ireland, 714, 704, CHAS%. In HH of John Burns m 28 born Ireland.

KELLY, PATRICK, 38, M, Laborer, -, Ireland, 5, 5, CHAS$.

KELLY, PETER, 35, M, Laborer, -, Ireland, 215, 202, CHAS+.

KELLY, THOMAS, 11, M, None listed, -, Ireland, 714, 704, CHAS%. In HH of John Burns m 28 born Ireland.

KELLY, THOMAS, 38, M, Merchant/clerk, -, Ireland, 2051, 2054, EDGE.

KELLY, WILLIAM, 51, M, Plasterer, -, Ireland, 297, 281, CHAS-.

KENAN, ROSA, 35, F, None listed, -, Ireland, 1426, 1426, BARN. In HH of Jas. Kaicy? m 34 born Ireland.

KENEFEE, D.C., 54, M, Hospital Nurse, -, Ireland, 237, 222, CHAS-. Works in Poor House.

KENNAN, ENORA, 20, F, None listed, -, Ireland, 1003, 981, CHAS-. In HH of L.

Watts f 32 born England.

KENNAN, JAMES, 24, M, Laborer, -, Ireland, 292, 269, CHAS+. In HH of Michael McMurray m 50 born Ireland.

KENNEDY, ALICE, 13, F, None listed, -, Ireland, 992, 971, CHAS-. In HH of S.B. Bernard m 38 born France.

KENNEDY, BRIDGET, 25, F, None listed, -, Ireland, 1145, 1124, CHAS%. In HH of John Kennedy m 31 born Ireland.

KENNEDY, BRIGET, 34, F, None listed, -, Ireland, 325, 295, CHAS+. In HH of Michl Kennedy m 28 born Ireland.

KENNEDY, C.M., 42, M, Farmer, -, Ireland, 435, 435, LAU.

KENNEDY, CATHERINE, 21, F, None listed, -, Ireland, 317, 291, CHAS+. In HH of Tim Kennedy m 71 born Ireland.

KENNEDY, DENNIS, 34, M, Butcher, -, Ireland, 1144, 1123, CHAS%.

KENNEDY, ELLEN, 27, F, None listed, -, Ireland, 39, 39, CHAS!.

KENNEDY, ELLEN, 28, F, None listed, -, Ireland, 1144, 1123, CHAS%. In HH of Dennis Kennedy m 34 born Ireland.

KENNEDY, ELLEN, 30, F, None listed, -, Ireland, 221, 208, CHAS+. In HH of Michael

Kennedy m 50 born Ireland.

KENNEDY, ELLEN, 30, F, None listed, -, Ireland, 1075, 1052, CHAS-. In HH of C.M. Arnold m 34 born GA.

KENNEDY, ELLEN, 36, F, None listed, -, Ireland, 537, 496, CHAS+.

KENNEDY, JAMES, 30, M, Laborer, -, Ireland, 241, 227, CHAS+.

KENNEDY, JAMES, 40, M, Laborer, -, Ireland, 537, 496, CHAS+. In HH of Ellen Kennedy f 36 born Ireland.

KENNEDY, JOHN, 12, M, None listed, -, Ireland, 752, 732, CHAS-. In HH of John McAllister m 37 born Ireland.

KENNEDY, JOHN, 15, M, Farmer, -, Ireland, 572, 572, CHES.

KENNEDY, JOHN, 31, M, Butcher, -, Ireland, 1145, 1124, CHAS%.

KENNEDY, JOHN D., 35, M, State Constable, -, Ireland, 324, 295, CHAS+.

KENNEDY, JULIA, 22, F, None listed, -, Ireland, 150, 141, CHAS+. In Boarding house.

KENNEDY, MARGARET, 25, F, None listed, -, Ireland, 241, 227, CHAS+. In HH of James Kennedy m 30 born Ireland.

KENNEDY, MARY, 19, F, None listed, -, Ireland, 222,

209, CHAS+. In HH of John Donnahugh m 22 born Ireland.

KENNEDY, MARY, 37, F, None listed, -, Ireland, 292, 269, CHAS+. In HH of Michael McMurray m 50 born Ireland.

KENNEDY, MICHAEL, 50, M, City Police, -, Ireland, 221, 208, CHAS+.

KENNEDY, MICHL., 28, M, Mason, -, Ireland, 325, 295, CHAS+.

KENNEDY, THOS., 25, M, Farmer, -, Ireland, 420, 420, CHES. In HH of J.B. McGill m 49 born Ireland.

KENNEDY, TIM, 71, M, None, -, Ireland, 317, 291, CHAS+.

KENNEDY, TIMOTHY, 3, M, None listed, -, Ireland, 325, 295, CHAS+. In HH of Michl Kennedy m 28 born Ireland.

KENNEDY, WILLIAM, 30, M, Ordinance man, -, Ireland, 1005, 982, CHAS%.Under command of Major P. Hagnes, Commanding Officer U.S. Arsenal.

KENNERLY, JOHN, 38, M, Shop keeper, -, Ireland, 987, 964, CHAS%.

KENNERLY, SARAH, 30, F, None listed, -, Ireland, 987, 964, CHAS%. In HH of John Kennerly m 38 born Ireland.

KENNEY, ANN, 60, F, None listed, -, Ireland, 39, 35, CHAS$. In HH of John Kenney

m 27 born Ireland.

KENNEY, BRIGET, 4, F, None listed, -, Ireland, 11, 10, CHAS-. In HH of John Nolan m 35 born Ireland.

KENNEY, EDMUND, 62, M, Merchant, -, Ireland, 743, 743, SUMT.

KENNEY, ELLEN, 17, F, None listed, -, Ireland, 743, 743, SUMT. In HH of Edmund Kenney m 62 born Ireland.

KENNEY, JANE, 27, F, None listed, -, Ireland, 39, 35, CHAS$. In HH of John Kenney m 27 born Ireland.

KENNEY, JOHN, 11, M, None listed, -, Ireland, 743, 743, SUMT. In HH of Edmund Kenney m 62 born Ireland.

KENNEY, JOHN, 27, M, Bricklayer, -, Ireland, 39, 35, CHAS$.

KENNEY, JOHN, 80, M, Shop keeper, -, Ireland, 12, 10, CHAS-.

KENNEY, MARY, 53, F, None listed, -, Ireland, 743, 743, SUMT. In HH of Edmund Kenney m 62 born Ireland.

KENNEY, SARAH, 25, F, None listed, -, Ireland, 11, 10, CHAS-. In HH of John Nolan m 35 born Ireland.

KENNEY, TIRESA, 22, F, None listed, -, Ireland, 346, 308, CHAS+. In Boarding house.

KENNY, BRIGET, 21, F, Laborer, -, Ireland, 167, 158, CHAS+. In Boarding house.

KENNY, ELIZABETH, 35, F, None listed, -, Ireland, 279, 259, CHAS+. In HH of James Kenny m 43 born Ireland.

KENNY, JAMES, 25, M, Laborer, -, Ireland, 934, 911, CHAS%. In HH of Joana Tinen f 28 born Ireland.

KENNY, JAMES, 43, M, Carpenter, -, Ireland, 279, 259, CHAS+.

KENNY, JOHN, 17, M, Clerk, -, Ireland, 223, 201, CHAS. In HH of Charlotte Murray f 38 born Ireland.

KENNY, JOHN, 25, M, Laborer, -, Ireland, 167, 158, CHAS+. In Boarding house.

KENNY, JOHN, 56, M, Farmer, -, Ireland, 1004, 1004, CHES.

KENNY, MARY, 20, F, None listed, -, Ireland, 223, 201, CHAS. In HH of Charlotte Murray f 38 born Ireland.

KENNY, ROBT., 68, M, Wheelwright, -, Ireland, 84, 84, EDGE.

KEOUN, NANCY, 48, F, None listed, -, Ireland, 541, 541, ABB.

KERNEY, ELLEN, 16, F, None listed, -, Ireland, 312, 296, CHAS-. In HH of Bernard Connely m 26 born Ireland.

KEYS, MARTHA, 70, F, None listed, -, Ireland, 69, 71, AND. In HH of J.C. Keys 37 m born SC.

KIDD, JOHN, 32, M, Laborer, -, Ireland, 322, 297, CHAS. In Boarding house.

KILLROY, MARY, 35, F, None listed, -, Ireland, 329, 297, CHAS+. In HH of Patrick Killroy m 40 born Ireland.

KILLROY, PATRICK, 40, M, Laborer, -, Ireland, 329, 297, CHAS+.

KILLROY, THOMAS, 9, M, None listed, -, Ireland, 1106, 1083, CHAS-. In Charleston Orphan House.

KILPATRICK, ALEX-ANDER, 30, M, None listed, -, Ireland, 982, 983, FAIR. In HH of Thomas Kilpatrick m 35 born Ireland.

KILPATRICK, ELIZA-BAETH, 23, F, None listed, -, Ireland, 982, 983, FAIR. In HH of Thomas Kilpatrick m 35 born Ireland.

KILPATRICK, THOMAS, 35, M, Planter, -, Ireland, 982, 983, FAIR.

KIMBALL, JANE, 46, F, None listed, -, Ireland, 523, 523, CHES. In HH of E.Elliot m 35 born MD.

KINEY, EDWARD, 21, M, Bricklayer, -, Ireland, 479, 437, CHAS+. In HH of Mary Welch f 32 born NY.

KINEY, JOHN, 14, M, None listed, -, Ireland, 479, 437, CHAS+. In HH of Mary Welch f 32 born NY.

KINEY, JOHN, 50, M, Laborer, -, Ireland, 479, 437, CHAS+. In HH of Mary Welch f 32 born NY.

KINEY, PATRICK, 12, M, None listed, -, Ireland, 479, 437, CHAS+. In HH of Mary Welch f 32 born NY.

KING, ANNA, 38, F, None listed, -, Ireland, 824, 804, CHAS-. In HH of N.S. King m 39 born NY.

KING, CATHERINE, 60, F, None listed, -, Ireland, 349, 322, CHAS.

KING, CHRISTOPHER, 23, M, Laborer, -, Ireland, 412, 372, CHAS.

KING, ELIZA, 38, F, None listed, -, Ireland, 237, 222, CHAS-.Poor House.

KING, FRANCES, 79, F, None listed, -, Ireland, 150, 150, PICK+. In HH of T.Y. King m 39 born SC.

KING, JEREMIAH, 34, M, Blacksmith, -, Ireland, 81, 81, CHAS^.

KING, MARY, 20, F, None listed, -, Ireland, 412, 372, CHAS. In HH of Christopher King m 23 born Ireland.

KINNEY, THOMAS, 74, M, Tavern keeper, -, Ireland, 469, 427, CHAS.

KINSEY, ANN, 50, F, None listed, -, Ireland, 467, 450, CHAS-. In HH of Martha Mitchell f 30 born SC.

KINSEY, ELIZABETH, 70, F, None listed, -, Ireland, 1723, 1724, EDGE. In HH of Hiram Jordan m 36, landlord, born SC.

KINSLEY, ANN, 9, F, None listed, -, Ireland, 265, 248, CHAS+. In HH of P.E. Kinsley m 34 born Ireland.

KINSLEY, CATHERINE, 30, F, None listed, -, Ireland, 265, 248, CHAS+. In HH of P.E. Kinsley m 34 born Ireland.

KINSLEY, P.E., 34, M, Shop keeper, -, Ireland, 265, 248, CHAS+.

KIRK, FELIZ, 70, M, Stone Mason, -, Ireland, 1957, 1957, LAU. In HH of James Parks m 64 born SC.

KIRK, JOHN, 30, M, Laborer, -, Ireland, 199, 182, CHAS*.

KIRK, SUSAN, 21, F, None listed, -, Ireland, 199, 182, CHAS*. In HH of John Kirk m 30 born Ireland.

KIRKPATRICK, MAR-GARET, 74, F, None listed, -, Ireland, 481, 481, CHES.

KLEARNEY, JOHN, 17, M, Engineer, -, Ireland, 269, 250, CHAS+. In HH of John Brady m 50 born Ireland.

KNOW, ROBERT, 11, M, None listed, -, Ireland, 2390, 2390, ABB. In HH of Jane Knox f 54 born Ireland.

KNOW, SAMUEL, 14, M, None listed, -, Ireland, 2390, 2390, ABB. In HH of Jane Knox f 54 born Ireland.

KNOW, WILLIAM, 18, M, Blacksmith, -, Ireland, 2390, 2390, ABB. In HH of Jane Knox f 54 born Ireland.

KNOWLES, WILLIAM, 45, M, Laborer, -, Ireland, 237, 222, CHAS-.Poor House.

KNOX, DAVID, 29, M, Blacksmith, -, Ireland, 667, 667, ABB.

KNOX, JANE, 54, F, None listed, -, Ireland, 2390, 2390, ABB.

KNOX, MATHEW, 15, M, Student, -, Ireland, 2347, 2347, ABB. In HH of Robert Carlile m 65 born VA.

KNOX, THOMAS, 18, M, Printer, -, Ireland, 754, 754, ABB. In HH of Henry Kerr m 26 born NC.

KOGERS, F.H., 37, F, None listed, -, Ireland, 1101, 1078, CHAS-. In HH of Thos. L. Kogers m 42 born SC.

KYLE, JOHN, 27, M, Clerk, -, Ireland, 848, 858, RICH+.

KYLE, MARY A., 26, F, None listed, -, Ireland, 848, 858, RICH+. In HH of John Kyle m 27 born Ireland.

KYLE, WILLIAM B., 28, M, None, -, Ireland, 90, 90, LAU.

In HH of John P. Holland m 28 born SC.

L

LACKA, JOHN, 26, M, Clerk, -, Ireland, 78, 79, ORNG+. In HH of Sylvister Beach m 54 born CT.

LACKEY, KATE, 30, F, Servant, -, Ireland, 882, 840, CHAS+. In Charleston Hotel.

LAFAN, CATHERINE, 35, F, None listed, -, Ireland, 136, 125, CHAS*. In HH of James Lafan m 45 born SC.

LAFTUS, LARRY, 22, M, Laborer, -, Ireland, 170, 160, CHAS+. In HH of Cornelius Canary m 28 born Ireland.

LAFTUS, PATRICK, 25, M, Laborer, -, Ireland, 170, 160, CHAS+. In HH of Cornelius Canary m 28 born Ireland.

LAIRD, J.S., 28, M, Laborer, -, Ireland, 292, 269, CHAS+. In HH of Michael McMurray m 50 born Ireland.

LAIRD, THOMAS, 22, M, Laborer, -, Ireland, 292, 269, CHAS+. In HH of Michael McMurray m 50 born Ireland.

LAMB, OWEN, 28, M, Laborer, -, Ireland, 338, 303, CHAS+. In HH of Bernard Sweeney m 37 born Ireland.

LAMBERT, ROBERT, 43, M, Merchant, -, Ireland, 850,
808, CHAS+.

LAMBERT, WALTER, 22, M, Clerk, -, Ireland, 693, 673, CHAS-.

LANAGAN, ALICE, 29, F, None listed, -, Ireland, 911, 888, CHAS%. In HH of Patrick Lanagan m 33 born Ireland.

LANAGAN, JOHN, 6, M, None listed, -, Ireland, 911, 888, CHAS%. In HH of Patrick Lanagan m 33 born Ireland.

LANAGAN, NORA, 9, F, None listed, -, Ireland, 911, 888, CHAS%. In HH of Patrick Lanagan m 33 born Ireland.

LANAGAN, PATRICK, 33, M, None listed, -, Ireland, 911, 888, CHAS%.

LANCHREY, WILLIAM, 80, M, Hatter, -, Ireland, 455, 453, CHAS%.

LANDAY?, MARGARET, 45, F, None listed, -, Ireland, 1317, 1317, YORK.

LANE, CON., 18, M, Laborer, -, Ireland, 261, 244, CHAS+. In HH of Hugh McNamara m 28 born Ireland.

LANE, DENNIS, 26, M, Ditcher, -, Ireland, 1997, 2003, EDGE. Note; out of order after family No. 2000 . In HH of James Gearty m 44born Ireland.

LANFAIR, HANNY, 24, F, None listed, -, Ireland, 2106, 2106, BARN. In HH of Patrick Quinn m 30 born Ireland.

LANG, MICHAEL, 30, M, Laborer, -, Ireland, 227, 205, CHAS. In HH of John Patterson m 35 born Scotland.

LANGAN, JAS., 45, M, Planter, -, Ireland, 460, 460, SUMT.

LANGLEY, J.T., 57, F, None listed, -, Ireland, 381, 345, CHAS.

LANGLEY, WM., 34, M, None, -, Ireland, 381, 345, CHAS. In HH of J.T. Langley f 57 born Ireland.

LANGTON, WILLIAM, 32, M, Taylor, -, Ireland, 38, 38, CHAS!.

LARKIN, CATHERINE, 25, F, None listed, -, Ireland, 90, 83, CHAS-. In HH of Margaret Larkin m 60 born Ireland.

LARKIN, CATHERINE, 34, F, Boarding house, -, Ireland, 124, 115, CHAS+.

LARKIN, JANE, 19, F, None listed, -, Ireland, 90, 83, CHAS-. In HH of Margaret Larkin m 60 born Ireland.

LARKIN, JULIA, 17, F, None listed, -, Ireland, 90, 83, CHAS-. In HH of Margaret Larkin m 60 born Ireland.

LARKIN, MARGARET, 20, F, None listed, -, Ireland, 90, 83, CHAS-. In HH of Margaret Larkin m 60 born Ireland.

LARKIN, MARGARET, 60, F, None listed, -, Ireland, 90, 83, CHAS-.

LARMINA, MARGARET, 48, F, None listed, -, Ireland, 544, 544, FAIR. In HH of James McCreight m 51 born Ireland.

LARNON, JAMES M., 29, M, Clerk, -, Ireland, 188, 192, RICH. In Hotel.

LARRY, DANIEL, 30, M, Laborer, -, Ireland, 144, 135, CHAS+.

LARRY, ELIZA, 32, F, None listed, -, Ireland, 144, 135, CHAS+. In HH of Daniel Larry m 30 born Ireland.

LATHAIM, SARAH, 56, F, None listed, -, Ireland, 1227, 1227, YORK.

LATHERS, AGNES, 68, F, None listed, -, Ireland, 2242, 2242, ABB. In HH of John Lathers m 77 born Ireland.

LATHERS, JOHN, 77, M, Farmer, -, Ireland, 2242, 2242, ABB.

LATTA, CATHARINE, 65, F, None listed, -, Ireland, 936, 936, YORK. In HH of John Latta m 33 born Ireland.

LATTA, JOHN, 33, M, Farmer, -, Ireland, 936, 936, YORK.

LATTA, ROBERT, 67, M, None, -, Ireland, 878, 888, RICH+.

LATTA, WILLIAM, 63, M, Farmer, -, Ireland, 936, 936, YORK. In HH of John Latta m 33 born Ireland.

LAUGHLIN, CHARLES, 58, M, Blacksmith, -, Ireland, 522, 522, FAIR.

LAUGHLIN, MARY A., 45, F, None listed, -, Ireland, 522, 522, FAIR. In HH of Charles Laughlin m 58 born Ireland.

LAW, AGNES, 57, F, None listed, -, Ireland, 309, 315, RICH. In HH of William Law m 71 born Ireland.

LAW, WILLIAM, 71, M, Merchant, -, Ireland, 309, 315, RICH.

LAWLER, JAMES, 32, M, Farmer, -, Ireland, 176, 176, HORR.

LAWRENCE, ANN, 28, F, Servant, -, Ireland, 8, 8, CHAS*. In HH of Jos. Dougherty m 70 born Ireland.

LAWRENCE, JOHN, 22, M, Clerk, -, Ireland, 472, 455, CHAS-. In HH of Mary Cooper f 50 born SC.

LAWYER, MARY, 22, F, None listed, -, Ireland, 167, 158, CHAS+. In Boarding house.

LEARY, JOSEPH, 36, M, Painter, -, Ireland, 542, 557, RICH. Date 1850 by name. In Lunatic Asylum.

LEARY, MARY, 28, F, None listed, -, Ireland, 537, 552, RICH. In HH of Thomas Leary m 34 born Ireland.

LEARY, THOMAS, 34, M, Atdt. Lunatic A, -, Ireland, 537, 552, RICH. Attendant at Lunatic Assylm.

LEARY, W.B., 51, M, School master, -, Ireland, 2302, 2302, GREE. In Hotel.

LECKIA, CLARK, 21, M, Umbrella maker, -, Ireland, 54, 49, CHAS-. In HH of Robert Leckia m 28 born Ireland.

LECKIA, JOHN, 76, M, Umbrella maker, -, Ireland, 54, 49, CHAS-. In HH of Robert Leckia m 28 born Ireland.

LECKIA, ROBERT, 28, M, Umbrella maker, -, Ireland, 54, 49, CHAS-.

LEE, ANDREW, 36, M, Blacksmith, -, Ireland, 602, 560, CHAS+.

LEE, ANN, 36, F, None listed, -, Ireland, 1940, 1943, EDGE. In HH of Christopher Lee m 45 born Ireland.

LEE, BRIGET, 36, F, None listed, -, Ireland, 602, 560, CHAS+. In HH of Andrew Lee m 36 born Ireland.

LEE, CHRISTOPHER, 45, M, Ditcher, -, Ireland, 1940, 1943, EDGE.

LEE, ELIZABETH, 30, F, None listed, -, Ireland, 718, 719, FAIR. In HH of John Lee m 93 born Ireland.

LEE, JAMES, 25, M, Laborer, -, Ireland, 982, 959, CHAS%. In HH of Alexander Paul m 21 born Scotland.

LEE, JANE M., 73, F, None

listed, -, Ireland, 718, 719, FAIR. In HH of John Lee m 93 born Ireland.

LEE, JOHN, 93, M, Planter, -, Ireland, 718, 719, FAIR.

LEE, PETER, 25, M, None listed, -, Ireland, 584, 542, CHAS+. In HH of Henry C. Street m 30 born SC.

LEE, WILLIAM, 39, M, None listed, -, Ireland, 718, 719, FAIR. In HH of John Lee m 93 born Ireland.

LEGARE, ABIGAIL, 48, F, None listed, -, Ireland, 886, 844, CHAS+.

LEGARE, C.J., 23, F, None listed, -, Ireland, 886, 844, CHAS+. In HH of Abigail Legare f 48 born Ireland.

LEGARE, MARY J., 15, F, None listed, -, Ireland, 886, 844, CHAS+. In HH of Abigail Legare f 48 born Ireland.

LEGARE, S.J., 28, M, Merchant, -, Ireland, 886, 844, CHAS+. In HH of Abigail Legare f 48 born Ireland.

LEITCH, JAMES, 39, M, Merchant, -, Ireland, 568, 534, CHAS*. In HH of David McDugal m 30 born Scotland.

LEMMON, JANE, 27, F, None listed, -, Ireland, 521, 521, FAIR.

LEMMONS, JAMES, 53, M, Planter, -, Ireland, 381, 381, FAIR.

LEMMONS, MARY A., 47, F, None listed, -, Ireland, 381, 381, FAIR. In HH of James Lemmons m 53 born Ireland.

LENIN, MARY, 28, F, None listed, -, Ireland, 291, 291, CHAS%. In HH of Philip Lenin m 35 born Ireland.

LENIN, PHILIP, 35, M, Laborer, -, Ireland, 291, 291, CHAS%.

LENN, ELLEN, 30, F, None listed, -, Ireland, 758, 738, CHAS-. In HH of John Lenn m 35 born Ireland.

LENN, JOHN, 35, M, Drayman, -, Ireland, 758, 738, CHAS-.

LENOX, MARY, 35, F, None listed, -, Ireland, 438, 421, CHAS-. In Pavillion Hotel.

LENOX, WM., 38, M, Clerk, -, Ireland, 270, 254, CHAS-. In HH of Thomas E. Baker m 50 born VA.

LEONARD, CATHERINE, 22, F, None listed, -, Ireland, 87, 81, CHAS-. In HH of Edward Leonard m 30 born Ireland.

LEONARD, CATHERINE, 46, F, None listed, -, Ireland, 700, 720, RICH. In HH of Thomas Leonard m 50 born Ireland.

LEONARD, EDWARD, 30, M, Laborer, -, Ireland, 87, 81, CHAS-.

LEONARD, ELLEN, 30, F, None listed, -, Ireland, 292, 269,

CHAS+. In HH of Michael McMurray m 50 born Ireland.

LEONARD, J. J., 14, M, None listed, -, Ireland, 261, 235, CHAS*. In HH of Mary McNeill f 47 born SC.

LEONARD, MARY A., 30, F, None listed, -, Ireland, 121, 124, RICH.

LEONARD, PATRICK, 40, M, Light keeper, -, Ireland, 27, 24, CHAS$. In HH of Philip Doyle m 30 born Ireland.

LEONARD, SAML., 48, M, Ditcher, -, Ireland, 669, 669, COLL.

LEONARD, THOMAS, 50, M, Gardner, -, Ireland, 700, 720, RICH.

LESLEY, WILLIAM, 87, M, None listed, -, Ireland, 986, 986, ABB.

LESLY, JOSEPH, 86, M, Farmer, -, Ireland, 1021, 1021, ABB.

LESLY, MARY, 80, F, None listed, -, Ireland, 1021, 1021, ABB. In HH of Joseph Lesly m 86 born Ireland.

LEWIS, NANCY R., 42, F, None listed, -, Ireland, 217, 217, FAIR. In HH of John Lewis m 40 born SC.

LEYMON, WILLIAM D., 51, M, Planter, -, Ireland, 614, 615, FAIR.

LICKIE, CHARLES L., 23, M, Clerk, -, Ireland, 300, 306, RICH. In Boarding house.

LIGHTBURN, WILLIAM, 44, M, Laborer, -, Ireland, 1189, 1168, CHAS%.

LINCH, JAS., 28, M, Laborer, -, Ireland, 2052, 2058, EDGE.

LINES, BRIGET, 6, F, None listed, -, Ireland, 252, 237, CHAS+. In HH of Michael Lines m 30 born Ireland.

LINES, MARGARET, 25, F, None listed, -, Ireland, 252, 237, CHAS+. In HH of Michael Lines m 30 born Ireland.

LINES, MARY, 1, F, None listed, -, Ireland, 252, 237, CHAS+. In HH of Michael Lines m 30 born Ireland.

LINES, MICHAEL, 30, M, Laborer, -, Ireland, 252, 237, CHAS+.

LINES, PATRICK, 4, M, None listed, -, Ireland, 252, 237, CHAS+. In HH of Michael Lines m 30 born Ireland.

LINES, THOMAS, 3, M, None listed, -, Ireland, 252, 237, CHAS+. In HH of Michael Lines m 30 born Ireland.

LINNEHAN, CORCHO-RAN, 32, M, Laborer, -, Ireland, 67, 68, RICH. In HH of William Sally m 35 born Ireland.

LOGAN, CHARLES, 31, M, Shoemaker, -, Ireland, 357, 366, RICH. In HH of Thomas Boyone m 30 born Scotland.

LOGAN, J., 35, M, Overseer,

-, Ireland, 1152, 1152, BARN. In HH of Jas. Roberts m 34 born SC.

LOGUE, JOHN, 50, M, Tailor, -, Ireland, 1815, 1815, ABB. In HH of Ephrain P. Calhoun m 48 born SC.

LOGUE, WILLIAM H., 24, M, Clerk, -, Ireland, 188, 192, RICH. In Hotel.

LOMBODY, JAMES, 40, M, Servant, -, Ireland, 78, 88, CHAS. In HH of Otis Mills m 53 born MA.

LONEYAN, WILLIAM A., 22, M, None listed, -, Ireland, 603, 604, FAIR. In HH of J.C.C. Feaster m 31 born SC.

LONGBRIDGE, MARY, 77, F, None listed, -, Ireland, 1489, 1489, YORK. In HH of James Longbridge m 55 born York Dist., SC.

LONGHTY, JANE, 27, F, None listed, -, Ireland, 987, 964, CHAS%. In Boarding house.

LONGRAIN, WILLIAM, 60, M, Stonemason, -, Ireland, 355, 355, YORK.

LOVE, SARAH, 60, F, None listed, -, Ireland, 185, 185, YORK*.

LOVE, WILLIAM, 50, M, Laborer, -, Ireland, 58, 58, YORK.

LOW, ELIZABETH, 60, F, None listed, -, Ireland, 68, 68, FAIR. In HH of Isaac Low m

58 born SC.

LOWDEON, J., 52, M, Shoe maker, -, Ireland, 2, 2, LANC*. In HH of Thomas K. Cureton m 48 born NC.

LOWERY, JAS., 35, M, Planter, -, Ireland, 998, 998, SUMT.

LOWERY, ROBT., 31, M, Planter, -, Ireland, 90, 90, SUMT.

LOWRY, JOHN, 70, M, Farmer, -, Ireland, 226, 226, YORK*.

LOWRY, MARY, 28, F, None listed, -, Ireland, 194, 182, CHAS+. In HH of Patrick Lowry m 33 born Ireland.

LOWRY, MARY, 70, F, None listed, -, Ireland, 226, 226, YORK*. In HH of John Lowry m 70 born Ireland.

LOWRY, PATRICK, 33, M, Laborer, -, Ireland, 194, 182, CHAS+.

LOWTHER, JAMES, 14, M, None listed, -, Ireland, 228, 214, CHAS-. In HH of Mary Roddy f 60 born Ireland.

LUCAS, AUGUSTA, 30, M, None listed, -, Ireland, 438, 407, CHAS*. In HH of John Lucas m 35 born England.

LUCAS, JONATHAN, 26, M, Planter, -, Ireland, 1146, 1125, CHAS%. In HH of Harris Simons m 43 born Ireland.

LUCAS, MARY JON, 20, F, None listed, -, Ireland, 1146,

1125, CHAS%. In HH of Harris Simons m 43 born Ireland.

LYLES, DAVID, 56, M, Farmer, -, Ireland, 995, 995, CHES.

LYLES, ISABELLA, 48, F, None listed, -, Ireland, 326, 332, RICH. In HH of William Lyles m 43 born Ireland.

LYLES, JANE, 56, F, None listed, -, Ireland, 995, 995, CHES. In HH of David Lyles m 56 born Ireland.

LYLES, THOMAS, 32, M, Teacher, -, Ireland, 994, 994, CHES.

LYLES, WILLIAM, 43, M, Merchant, -, Ireland, 326, 332, RICH.1849 by name.

LYNAP, B., 33, M, Merchant, -, Ireland, 845, 825, CHAS-.

LYNAP, MARY, 26, F, None listed, -, Ireland, 845, 825, CHAS-. In HH of B. Lynap m 33 born Ireland.

LYNCH, BELNER, 35, M, Gass fitter, -, Ireland, 264, 247, CHAS+. In HH of John Russel m 31 born MA.

LYNCH, JOHN, 45, M, Laborer, -, Ireland, 1226, 1226, SUMT.

LYNCH, MARIA, 20, F, None listed, -, Ireland, 264, 247, CHAS+. In HH of John Russel m 31 born MA.

LYNCH, MARY, 20, F, None listed, -, Ireland, 584, 542, CHAS+. In HH of Henry C. Street m 30 born SC.

LYNCH, P., 25, M, Priv. U.S.A., -, Ireland, 47, 43, CHAS$. In HH of John Ewing m 50 born MA.

LYNCH, THOMAS, 25, M, Laborer, -, Ireland, 110, 102, CHAS+. In HH of John May m 30 born Ireland.

LYNCH, THOMAS F., 43, M, Farmer, -, Ireland, 989, 966, CHAS%.

LYNN JAMES, 86, M, None, -, Ireland, 503, 503, CHES. In HH of Mary Ralph f 41 born SC.

LYNN, GUZILDA, 75, F, None listed, -, Ireland, 619, 619, CHES. In HH of Richard McAliley m 25 born SC.

LYNOT, MARTIN, 45, M, Ditcher, -, Ireland, 742, 742, SUMT. In HH of Jas. Lawrence m 45 born NC.

LYON, CATHERINE, 12, F, None listed, -, Ireland, 220, 207, CHAS+. In HH of Daraby Lyon m 40 born Ireland.

LYON, CATHERINE, 20, F, None listed, -, Ireland, 752, 710, CHAS+. In HH of Theodore D. Ruddock m 30 born SC.

LYON, DARBY, 40, M, Laborer, -, Ireland, 220, 207, CHAS+.

LYON, DENNIS, 8, M, None listed, -, Ireland, 220, 207, CHAS+. In HH of Daraby

Lyon m 40 born Ireland.

LYON, ENORA, 6, F, None listed, -, Ireland, 220, 207, CHAS+. In HH of Daraby Lyon m 40 born Ireland. *Darby not Daraby change...

LYON, JOANA, 10, F, None listed, -, Ireland, 220, 207, CHAS+. In HH of Daraby Lyon m 40 born Ireland.

LYON, JOANA, 40, F, None listed, -, Ireland, 220, 207, CHAS+. In HH of Daraby Lyon m 40 born Ireland.

LYON, MARY, 16, F, None listed, -, Ireland, 220, 207, CHAS+. In HH of Daraby Lyon m 40 born Ireland.

LYON, THOMAS, 14, M, None listed, -, Ireland, 220, 207, CHAS+. In HH of Daraby Lyon m 40 born Ireland.

LYON, THOMAS, 17, M, Clerk, -, Ireland, 814, 794, CHAS-. In HH of John G. Willis m 45 born NC.

LYONS, ANN, 17, F, None listed, -, Ireland, 215, 202, CHAS+. In HH of Peter Kelly m 35 born Ireland.

LYONS, MARGARET, 28, F, Servant, -, Ireland, 55, 65, CHAS. In HH of John Ravenel m 53 born SC.

LYONS, THOMAS, 50, M, Laborer, -, Ireland, 215, 202, CHAS+.

M

MACAT, JANE, 49, F, None listed, -, Ireland, 84, 84, YORK+. In HH of James J. Snider m 30 born Yorkville, SC.

MACHER, JAMES, 30, M, Laborer, -, Ireland, 271, 252, CHAS+. In HH of Mary Campbell f 49 born Ireland.

MACK, ALEXANDER, 25, M, Planter, -, Ireland, 343, 343, SUMT. In HH of Jas. Mack m 35 born Ireland.

MACK, BRIDGET, 35, F, Shop keeper, -, Ireland, 19, 22, CHAS.

MACK, JAS., 35, M, Planter, -, Ireland, 343, 343, SUMT.

MACK, MARY ANN, 41, F, None listed, -, Ireland, 292, 269, CHAS+. In HH of Michael McMurray m 50 born Ireland.

MACKAY, DENNIS, 35, M, Laborer, -, Ireland, 144, 135, CHAS+. In HH of Daniel Larry m 30 born Ireland.

MACKAY, LAURENCE, 8, M, None listed, -, Ireland, 267, 249, CHAS+. In HH of Patrick Mackay m 35 born Ireland.

MACKAY, MARY, 28, F, None listed, -, Ireland, 267, 249, CHAS+. In HH of Patrick Mackay m 35 born Ireland.

MACKAY, PATRICK, 35, M, Laborer, -, Ireland, 267, 249, CHAS+.

MACKLIN, MARY, 60, F, None listed, -, Ireland, 68, 62, CHAS-. In HH of Mary Torlay f 34 born NY.

MACNAMARA, DANIEL, 28, M, Laborer, -, Ireland, 292, 269, CHAS+. In HH of Michael McMurray m 50 born Ireland.

MACNAMARA, MARGARET, 28, F, None listed, -, Ireland, 687, 645, CHAS+. In HH of P.A. Avelhie m 47 born SC..

MACNAMARA, MICHAEL, 50, M, Planter, -, Ireland, 2064, 2064, BARN.

MACOLEY, MICHEL, 30, M, Laborer, -, Ireland, 24, 24, CHAS3. In HH of Hamilton S. Hart m 33 born SC.

MADDEN, ANN, 13, F, None listed, -, Ireland, 844, 824, CHAS-. In HH of Rachel Norton f 26 born NY.

MADDEN, JANE, 48, F, None listed, -, Ireland, 928, 829, FAIR. In HH of Charles Cathcart m 40 born Ireland.

MADDEN, MARGARET, 25, F, None listed, -, Ireland, 25, 25, CHAS*. In HH of David Stokes m 30 born SC.

MADDEN, MARY A., 25, F, None listed, -, Ireland, 928, 829, FAIR. In HH of Charles Cathcart m 40 born Ireland.

MADDEN, THOMAS B., 22, M, Medical Student, -, Ireland, 312, 318, RICH. In HH of James Cathcart m 55 born Ireland.

MAGEE, ELLEN, 31, F, None listed, -, Ireland, 427, 410, CHAS-.

MAGEE, TILMAN, 80, M, Farmer, -, Ireland, 1137, 1188, PICK.

MAGEE, TILMAN, 88, M, Farmer, -, Ireland, 1137, 1188, PICK.

MAGILL, DAVID, 16, M, Student, -, Ireland, 2349, 2349, ABB. In HH of William Magill m 53 born Ireland.

MAGILL, JOHN, 27, M, Overseer, -, Ireland, 2377, 2377, ABB.

MAGILL, MARGARET, 28, F, None listed, -, Ireland, 2349, 2349, ABB. In HH of William Magill m 53 born Ireland.

MAGILL, MARGARET, 51, F, None listed, -, Ireland, 2349, 2349, ABB. In HH of William Magill m 53 born Ireland.

MAGILL, MARY, 12, F, None listed, -, Ireland, 2349, 2349, ABB. In HH of William Magill m 53 born Ireland.

MAGILL, SAMUEL, 14, M, None listed, -, Ireland, 2349, 2349, ABB. In HH of William Magill m 53 born Ireland.

MAGILL, THOMAS, 18, M, Shoemaker, -, Ireland, 2349, 2349, ABB. In HH of William Magill m 53 born Ireland.

MAGILL, WILLIAM, 26, M, Manager, -, Ireland, 668, 668, ABB.

MAGILL, WILLIAM, 53, M, Shoemaker, -, Ireland, 2349, 2349, ABB.

MAGRATH, CATHERINE, 20, F, None listed, -, Ireland, 29, 37, CHAS. In HH of Michael Magrath m 25 born Ireland.

MAGRATH, CATHERINE, 37, F, None listed, -, Ireland, 3, 3, CHAS$. In HH of Joseph Hewot m 47 born NY.

MAGRATH, JOHN, 72, M, Merchant, -, Ireland, 1076, 1054, CHAS%.

MAGRATH, MICHAEL, 25, M, Laborer, -, Ireland, 29, 37, CHAS.

MAGUIRE, ANN, 27, F, None listed, -, Ireland, 1116, 1094, CHAS%. In HH of Thomas Maguire m 30 born Ireland.

MAGUIRE, BRIDGET, 30, F, None listed, -, Ireland, 397, 395, CHAS%. In HH of John Maguire m 34 born Ireland.

MAGUIRE, JAMES, 7, M, None listed, -, Ireland, 1116, 1094, CHAS%. In HH of Thomas Maguire m 30 born Ireland.

MAGUIRE, JOHN, 34, M, Gardner, -, Ireland, 397, 395, CHAS%.

MAGUIRE, MARY ANN, 30, F, None listed, -, Ireland, 369, 342, CHAS*. In HH of Charles Grove m 26 born PA.

MAGUIRE, PATHERINA, 35, F, None listed, -, Ireland, 850, 808, CHAS+. In HH of Robert Lambert m 43 born Ireland.

MAGUIRE, PATRICK, 10, M, None listed, -, Ireland, 397, 395, CHAS%. In HH of John Maguire m 34 born Ireland.

MAGUIRE, THOMAS, 4, M, None listed, -, Ireland, 1116, 1094, CHAS%. In HH of Thomas Maguire m 30 born Ireland.

MAGUIRE, THOMAS, 30, M, Gardner, -, Ireland, 1116, 1094, CHAS%.

MAGUKIN, HUGH, 45, M, Mechanic, -, Ireland, 1447, 1447, ABB.

MAHAN, JOHN, 29, M, Laborer, -, Ireland, 351, 324, CHAS. In Boarding house.

MAHAR, JULIA, 45, F, None listed, -, Ireland, 748, 706, CHAS+. In HH of H.A. Mayer m 45 born Ireland.

MAHER, ELLEN, 44, F, None listed, -, Ireland, 759, 759, BARN. In HH of M.W. Maher m 52 born Ireland.

MAHER, M.W., 52, M, Merchant, -, Ireland, 759, 759, BARN.

MAHER, MARY M., 52, F, None listed, -, Ireland, 204, 192,

CHAS+.

MAHONEY, BETSEY, 13, F, None listed, -, Ireland, 628, 586, CHAS+. In HH of John Garvin m 24 born Ireland.

MAHONEY, BRIGET, 21, F, None listed, -, Ireland, 882, 840, CHAS+. In Charleston Hotel.

MAHONEY, BRIGET, 25, M, None listed, -, Ireland, 763, 721, CHAS+. In HH of William D. Gilleland m 40 born SC

MAHONEY, BRIGET, 32, F, None listed, -, Ireland, 391, 353, CHAS+. In HH of Dennis Mahoney m 34 born Ireland.

MAHONEY, CATHERINE, 8, F, None listed, -, Ireland, 737, 695, CHAS+. In HH of John Mahoney m 30 born Ireland.

MAHONEY, CATHERINE, 29, F, None listed, -, Ireland, 737, 695, CHAS+. In HH of John Mahoney m 30 born Ireland.

MAHONEY, CORNELIUS, 16, M, None listed, -, Ireland, 79, 77, CHAS*. In HH of John Mahoney m 40 born Ireland.

MAHONEY, DAN, 17, M, Laborer, -, Ireland, 628, 586, CHAS+. In HH of John Garvin m 24 born Ireland.

MAHONEY, DENNIS, 14, M, None listed, -, Ireland, 634, 615, CHAS-. In HH of Dennis Mahoney m 42 born Ireland.

MAHONEY, DENNIS, 30, M, Laborer, -, Ireland, 756, 741, CHAS%.

MAHONEY, DENNIS, 34, M, Carpenter, -, Ireland, 391, 353, CHAS+.

MAHONEY, DENNIS, 42, M, Slater, -, Ireland, 634, 615, CHAS-.

MAHONEY, EDWARD, 11, M, None listed, -, Ireland, 628, 586, CHAS+. In HH of John Garvin m 24 born Ireland.

MAHONEY, ELIZABETH, 26, F, None listed, -, Ireland, 628, 586, CHAS+. In HH of John Garvin m 24 born Ireland.

MAHONEY, JAMES, 25, M, Laborer, -, Ireland, 108, 103, CHAS*. In HH of Patrick Keefe m 40 born Ireland.

MAHONEY, JOHN, 9, M, None listed, -, Ireland, 628, 586, CHAS+. In HH of John Garvin m 24 born Ireland.

MAHONEY, JOHN, 23, M, Laborer, -, Ireland, 108, 103, CHAS*. In HH of Patrick Keefe m 40 born Ireland.

MAHONEY, JOHN, 23, M, Laborer, -, Ireland, 108, 103, CHAS*. In HH of Patrick Keefe m 40 born Ireland.

MAHONEY, JOHN, 26, M, Sargt. U.S.A., -, Ireland, 47, 43, CHAS$. In HH of John Ewing m 50 born MA.

MAHONEY, JOHN, 30, M, Blacksmith, -, Ireland, 737, 695,

CHAS+.

MAHONEY, JOHN, 40, M, Clerk, -, Ireland, 79, 77, CHAS*.

MAHONEY, KATE, 16, F, None listed, -, Ireland, 628, 586, CHAS+. In HH of John Garvin m 24 born Ireland.

MAHONEY, KATHLEEN, 15, F, None listed, -, Ireland, 391, 353, CHAS+. In HH of Dennis Mahoney m 34 born Ireland.

MAHONEY, MARGARET, 27, F, None listed, -, Ireland, 336, 310, CHAS*. In HH of Charles Kerrison m 35 born England.

MAHONEY, MARGARET, 28, F, None listed, -, Ireland, 79, 77, CHAS*. In HH of John Mahoney m 40 born Ireland.

MAHONEY, MARGARET, 43, F, None listed, -, Ireland, 634, 615, CHAS-. In HH of Dennis Mahoney m 42 born Ireland.

MAHONEY, MARY, 8, F, None listed, -, Ireland, 79, 77, CHAS*. In HH of John Mahoney m 40 born Ireland.

MAHONEY, MARY, 16, F, None listed, -, Ireland, 634, 615, CHAS-. In HH of Dennis Mahoney m 42 born Ireland.

MAHONEY, MARY, 40, F, None listed, -, Ireland, 82, 82, CHAS%. In HH of S.H. Mortemore m 43 born SC.

MAHONEY, MARY ANN, 6, F, None listed, -, Ireland, 737, 695, CHAS+. In HH of John Mahoney m 30 born Ireland.

MAHONEY, PATRICK, 18, M, Laborer, -, Ireland, 391, 353, CHAS+. In HH of Dennis Mahoney m 34 born Ireland.

MAHONEY, PATRICK, 26, M, Pavior, -, Ireland, 634, 615, CHAS-. In HH of Dennis Mahoney m 42 born Ireland.

MAHONEY, PETER, 36, M, Laborer, -, Ireland, 628, 586, CHAS+. In HH of John Garvin m 24 born Ireland.

MAHONEY, ROSELLA, 23, F, None listed, -, Ireland, 634, 615, CHAS-. In HH of Dennis Mahoney m 42 born Ireland.

MAHONEY, SUSAN, 30, F, None listed, -, Ireland, 838, 818, CHAS-. In HH of T.M. Bristol m 30 born CT.

MAHONY, DANIEL, 16, M, None listed, -, Ireland, 1039, 1017, CHAS%. In HH of Manhew Mahony m 18 born Ireland.

MAHONY, JOANA, 22, F, None listed, -, Ireland, 548, 540, CHAS%.

MAHONY, JUDY, 50, F, None listed, -, Ireland, 1039, 1017, CHAS%. In HH of Manhew Mahony m 18 born Ireland.

MAHONY, MANHEW, 18, M, Blacksmith, -, Ireland, 1039,

1017, CHAS%.

MAHONY, MARGARET, 20, F, None listed, -, Ireland, 1039, 1017, CHAS%. In HH of Manhew Mahony m 18 born Ireland.

MAHONY, MICHAEL, 3, M, None listed, -, Ireland, 1039, 1017, CHAS%. In HH of Manhew Mahony m 18 born Ireland.

MAHONY, WILLIAM, 14, M, None listed, -, Ireland, 1039, 1017, CHAS%. In HH of Manhew Mahony m 18 born Ireland.

MAHOONEY, BRIGET, 38, F, None listed, -, Ireland, 558, 516, CHAS+. In HH of Patrick Mahooney m 44 born Ireland.

MAHOONEY, DAN, 14, M, None listed, -, Ireland, 558, 516, CHAS+. In HH of Patrick Mahooney m 44 born Ireland.

MAHOONEY, DENNIS, 10, M, None listed, -, Ireland, 558, 516, CHAS+. In HH of Patrick Mahooney m 44 born Ireland.

MAHOONEY, ELIZA-BETH, 12, F, None listed, -, Ireland, 558, 516, CHAS+. In HH of Patrick Mahooney m 44 born Ireland.

MAHOONEY, ELLEN, 16, F, None listed, -, Ireland, 558, 516, CHAS+. In HH of Patrick Mahooney m 44 born Ireland.

MAHOONEY, MARY, 18, F, None listed, -, Ireland, 558,

516, CHAS+. In HH of Patrick Mahooney m 44 born Ireland.

MAHOONEY, MARY, 32, F, None listed, -, Ireland, 393, 366, CHAS*. In HH of James J.B. Heyward m 35 born SC.

MAHOONEY, PATRICK, 44, M, Stone cutter, -, Ireland, 558, 516, CHAS+.

MAIN, CATHERINE, 11, F, None listed, -, Ireland, 553, 519, CHAS*. In Catholic Seminary.

MAIN, MARY ANN, 14, F, None listed, -, Ireland, 553, 519, CHAS*. In Catholic Seminary.

MAIS, JEAN, 25, F, None listed, -, Ireland, 24, 24, CHAS*. In HH of D.E. Huger, Jr. m 44 born SC.

MAISENMAN, WILLIAM, 34, M, Painter, -, Ireland, 417, 376, CHAS+.

MAJOR, MARY, 67, F, None listed, -, Ireland, 954, 955, AND*. In HH of John P. Major m 75 born VA.

MAKER, MICHAEL, 40, M, Ordinance man, -, Ireland, 1005, 982, CHAS%.Under command of Major P. Hagnes, Comg. Off. U.S. Arnsel.

MAKWELL, JAMES, 22, M, Sergt. U.S.A., -, Ireland, 47, 43, CHAS$. In HH of John Ewing m 50 born MA.

MALLONEY, FANNY, 30, F, None listed, -, Ireland, 260, 244, CHAS+. In HH of John

Malloney m 35 born Ireland.

MALLONEY, JOHN, 35, M, Shop keeper, -, Ireland, 260, 244, CHAS+.

MALLONEY, MARY, 25, F, None listed, -, Ireland, 260, 244, CHAS+. In HH of John Malloney m 35 born Ireland.

MALLONEY, MARY, 30, F, None listed, -, Ireland, 260, 244, CHAS+. In HH of John Malloney m 35 born Ireland.

MALLOY, BRIGET, 20, F, None listed, -, Ireland, 768, 748, CHAS-. In HH of Owen Campbell m 25 born Ireland.

MALLOY, CATHERINE, 30, F, None listed, -, Ireland, 1086, 1064, CHAS%. In HH of A.G. Rose m 57 born SC.

MALONE, JAMES, 31, M, Well/ditch digger, -, Ireland, 1682, 1682, ABB. In HH of July Welch f 40 born Ireland.

MALONE, PATRICK, 28, M, Well/ditch digger, -, Ireland, 1682, 1682, ABB. In HH of July Welch f 40 born Ireland.

MALONEY, CATHERINE, 48, F, None listed, -, Ireland, 396, 394, CHAS%. In HH of Charles Maloney m 52 born Ireland.

MALONEY, CHARLES, 52, M, Shop keeper, -, Ireland, 396, 394, CHAS%.

MALONEY, ELLEN, 17, F, None listed, -, Ireland, 261,

244, CHAS+. In HH of Hugh McNamara m 28 born Ireland.

MALONEY, FANNY, 19, F, None listed, -, Ireland, 261, 244, CHAS+. In HH of Hugh McNamara m 28 born Ireland.

MALONEY, JANE, 25, F, None listed, -, Ireland, 396, 394, CHAS%. In HH of Charles Maloney m 52 born Ireland.

MALONEY, KATHERINE, 25, F, None listed, -, Ireland, 698, 678, CHAS-. In HH of James E. Spear m 31 born NJ.

MALONEY, LAWRENCE, 34, M, Mariner, -, Ireland, 334, 308, CHAS. In HH of William Bennett m 40 born NY.

MALONEY, MARIA, 40, F, None listed, -, Ireland, 882, 862, CHAS-. In HH of James Maloney m 47 born NC.

MALONEY, MARY, 11, F, None listed, -, Ireland, 396, 394, CHAS%. In HH of Charles Maloney m 52 born Ireland.

MALONEY, MARY, 21, F, None listed, -, Ireland, 863, 843, CHAS-. In HH of G. Lazarus m 46 born NC.

MALONEY, MARY, 40, F, None listed, -, Ireland, 90, 83, CHAS-. In HH of Margaret Larkin m 60 born Ireland.

MALONEY, MARY ANN, 21, F, None listed, -, Ireland, 882, 862, CHAS-. In HH of James Maloney m 47 born NC.

MALONEY, PHILIP, 19, M, Mason, -, Ireland, 396, 394, CHAS%. In HH of Charles Maloney m 52 born Ireland.

MALONEY, THOMAS, 14, M, Clerk, -, Ireland, 396, 394, CHAS%. In HH of Charles Maloney m 52 born Ireland.

MALONY, CATHERINE, 50, F, None listed, -, Ireland, 23, 23, BARN. In HH of James Malony m 65 born Ireland.

MALONY, JAMES, 65, M, Plant., -, Ireland, 23, 23, BARN.

MALOONEY, BRIGET, 28, F, None listed, -, Ireland, 301, 278, CHAS+. In HH of Jim Malooney m 32 born Ireland.

MALOONEY, CON, 18, M, Laborer, -, Ireland, 301, 278, CHAS+. In HH of Jim Malooney m 32 born Ireland.

MALOONEY, DAN, 26, M, Laborer, -, Ireland, 301, 278, CHAS+. In HH of Jim Malooney m 32 born Ireland.

MALOONEY, JIM, 32, M, Gassfitter, -, Ireland, 301, 278, CHAS+.

MALOONEY, MARGERY, 14, F, None listed, -, Ireland, 301, 278, CHAS+. In HH of Jim Malooney m 32 born Ireland.

MALVY, JAMES, 55, M, School master, -, Ireland, 1738, 1738, GREE.

MANGIN, PETER, 39, M, Blacksmith, -, Ireland, 1030, 1008, CHAS%.

MANN, JAMES, 29, M, R.R. Laborer, -, Ireland, 987, 964, CHAS%. In Boarding house.

MANSEY, JOHN, 35, M, Laborer, -, Ireland, 348, 322, CHAS. In HH of Stephen Croughton m 35 born Ireland.

MANSEY, SARAH, 20, F, None listed, -, Ireland, 348, 322, CHAS. In HH of Stephen Croughton m 35 born Ireland.

MANSFIELD, ANN, 35, F, None listed, -, Ireland, 1219, 1219, EDGE. Note: out of order after fam. 1221. In HH of Tarry Mansfield m 40born Ireland.

MANSFIELD, TARRY, 40, M, Brick mason, -, Ireland, 1219, 1219, EDGE. Note: out of order after fam. 1221

MAQUIRE, ANN, 30, F, None listed, -, Ireland, 411, 394, CHAS-. In HH of S.N. Hart m 42 born SC.

MAQUIRE, MARY, 11, F, None listed, -, Ireland, 553, 519, CHAS*. In Catholic Seminary.

MARCHALL, HECTOR, 20, M, Shoemaker, -, Ireland, 560, 560, CHES. In HH of E. McCusker m 25 born Ireland.

MARGART, CATHERINE, 24, F, Servant, -, Ireland, 299, 273, CHAS*. In HH of Samuel

Gilman m 60 born MA.

MARIE, PATRICK, 22, M, Laborer, -, Ireland, 67, 68, RICH. In HH of William Sally m 35 born Ireland.

MARION, J.A., 30, F, None listed, -, Ireland, 437, 437, CHES. In HH of Patrick Marrion m 77 born Ireland.

MARKIE, MARY, 25, F, None listed, -, Ireland, 304, 288, CHAS-. In HH of C.T. Dunham m 29 born MA.

MARLIN, DAVID, 20, M, Farmer, -, Ireland, 475, 475, CHES. In HH of John Marlin m 56 born Ireland

MARLIN, H., 21, M, Farmer, -, Ireland, 475, 475, CHES. In HH of John Marlin m 56 born Ireland

MARLIN, HENRY, 18, M, Farmer, -, Ireland, 475, 475, CHES. In HH of John Marlin m 56 born Ireland

MARLIN, JOHN, 26, M, Farmer, -, Ireland, 441, 441, CHES.

MARLIN, JOHN, 56, M, Farmer, -, Ireland, 475, 475, CHES.

MARLIN, M.J., 25, F, None listed, -, Ireland, 475, 475, CHES. In HH of John Marlin m 56 born Ireland

MARLIN, RACHEAL, 23, F, None listed, -, Ireland, 475, 475, CHES. In HH of John Marlin m 56 born Ireland

MARLIN, RACHEAL, 56, F, None listed, -, Ireland, 475, 475, CHES. In HH of John Marlin m 56 born Ireland

MARRION, PATRICK, 77, M, None, -, Ireland, 437, 437, CHES.

MARRY, CATHERINE, 30, F, Servant, -, Ireland, 56, 66, CHAS. In HH of David Ravenel m 60, Bank President, born SC.

MARS, JAMES, 80, M, None listed, -, Ireland, 2359, 2359, ABB.

MARSHAL, ARCHIBALD, 21, M, None listed, -, Ireland, 981, 982, FAIR. In HH of Archibald Marshal m 50 born Ireland.

MARSHAL, ARCHIBALD, 50, M, Planter, -, Ireland, 981, 982, FAIR.

MARSHAL, CATHARINE, 50, F, None listed, -, Ireland, 981, 982, FAIR. In HH of Archibald Marshal m 50 born Ireland.

MARSHAL, MARY, 28, F, None listed, -, Ireland, 222, 209, CHAS+. In HH of John Donnahugh m 22 born Ireland.

MARSHAL, NANCY, 23, F, None listed, -, Ireland, 981, 982, FAIR. In HH of Archibald Marshal m 50 born Ireland.

MARSHAL, ROBERT, 13, M, None listed, -, Ireland, 981, 982, FAIR. In HH of Archibald

Marshal m 50 born Ireland.

MARSHAL, WILLIAM, 35, M, Laborer, -, Ireland, 222, 209, CHAS+. In HH of John Donnahugh m 22 born Ireland.

MARSHALL, GEORGE, 71, M, Farmer, -, Ireland, 1749, 1749, ABB.

MARSHALL, JOHN, 28, M, Coal passer, -, Ireland, 326, 301, CHAS. In HH of William Rollins m 40 born {-}. In crew of the Steam Ship Isabel.

MARSHALL, JOSEPH, 64, M, Farmer, -, Ireland, 1735, 1735, ABB.

MARSHALL, ROBERT, 52, M, Boot/Shoemaker, -, Ireland, 1238, 1238, ABB. In HH of Thomas Taylor m 52, born SC.

MARSHALL, SAMUEL, 61, M, MD, -, Ireland, 1733, 1733, ABB.

MARSHELL, ANN, 44, F, None listed, -, Ireland, 1697, 1697, GREE. In HH of Jane Marshell f 54 born Ireland.

MARSHELL, JANE, 54, F, None listed, -, Ireland, 1697, 1697, GREE.

MARSHELL, MARY, 52, F, None listed, -, Ireland, 1697, 1697, GREE. In HH of Jane Marshell f 54 born Ireland.

MARSSON, MARY, 63, F, None listed, -, Ireland, 1680, 1680, GREE.

MARTIN, ALICE, 40, F, None listed, -, Ireland, 47, 43,

CHAS$. In HH of John Ewing m 50 born MA.

MARTIN, CHS. G., 20, M, Carpenter, -, Ireland, 390, 354, CHAS. In HH of Hugh ONeile m 30 born Ireland.

MARTIN, ELIZA, 25, F, Confectioner, -, Ireland, 796, 754, CHAS+.

MARTIN, HENRY W., 17, M, None listed, -, Ireland, 498, 498, ABB. In HH of Nancy Martin f 23 born Ireland.

MARTIN, ISAAC, 27, M, Shoe dealer, -, Ireland, 261, 246, CHAS-.

MARTIN, J., 20, M, Priv. U.S.A., -, Ireland, 47, 43, CHAS$. In HH of John Ewing m 50 born MA.

MARTIN, JAMES, 28, M, Teacher, -, Ireland, 497, 497, ABB. In HH of Shepard G. Cowan m 40 Superintendent of the Leth School.James Martin is Teacher at Lithe School.

MARTIN, JAMES, 45, M, Farmer, -, Ireland, 664, 668, AND.

MARTIN, JAS., 75, M, Boot maker, -, Ireland, 25, 25, LANC.

MARTIN, JOHN, 26, M, Laborer, -, Ireland, 712, 704, CHAS%. In HH of John Steckeley m 40 born Germany.

MARTIN, JOSEPH, 13, M, None listed, -, Ireland, 664, 668, AND. In HH of James Martin

m 45 born Ireland.

MARTIN, MARTHA, 53, F, None listed, -, Ireland, 1629, 1629, ABB. In HH of James H. Marton m 50 born SC.

MARTIN, MARY, 19, F, None listed, -, Ireland, 796, 754, CHAS+. In HH of Eliza Martin f 25 born Ireland.

MARTIN, MARY, 62, F, None listed, -, Ireland, 155, 157, AND. In HH of Samuel Martin m 66 born VA.

MARTIN, MARY, 68, F, None listed, -, Ireland, 331, 331, FAIR. In HH of Robert Martin m 73 born SC.

MARTIN, MARY, 80, F, None listed, -, Ireland, 20, 20, FAIR. In HH of John A. Martin m 56 born SC.

MARTIN, MARY ANN, 16, F, None listed, -, Ireland, 992, 971, CHAS-. In HH of S.B. Bernard m 38 born France.

MARTIN, NANCY, 23, F, None listed, -, Ireland, 498, 498, ABB.

MARTIN, SARAH J., 15, F, None listed, -, Ireland, 498, 498, ABB. In HH of Nancy Martin f 23 born Ireland.

MARTIN, WILLIAM, 13, M, None listed, -, Ireland, 664, 668, AND. In HH of James Martin m 45 born Ireland.

MASSETT, M.J., 20, F, None listed, -, Ireland, 1003, 981, CHAS-. In HH of L. Watts f 32

born England.

MASTERSON, N., 30, F, None listed, -, Ireland, 47, 43, CHAS$. In HH of John Ewing m 50 born MA.

MATCHET, JOHN, 72, M, Planter, -, Ireland, 1187, 1188, FAIR.

MATCHET, RICHARD, 34, M, None listed, -, Ireland, 1187, 1188, FAIR. In HH of John Matchet m 72 born Ireland.

MATCHET, SUSANNA, 70, F, None listed, -, Ireland, 1187, 1188, FAIR. In HH of John Matchet m 72 born Ireland.

MATTAHAN, TIMOTHY, 30, M, Laborer, -, Ireland, 166, 148, CHAS. In HH of John Jenkins m 25 born England.

MATTHEWS, ELIZA, 25, F, None listed, -, Ireland, 513, 479, CHAS*. In HH of Sarah Dehon f 53 born SC.

MATTHEWS, HUGH, 60, M, Saddler, -, Ireland, 1998, 2001, EDGE. In HH of M.L. Georty m 46 born Ireland.

MATTHEWS, MARY A., 32, F, None listed, -, Ireland, 684, 685, FAIR. In HH of G.P. Matthews m 32 born KY.

MATTISON, EDWARD, 40, M, Laborer, -, Ireland, 337, 311, CHAS. In HH of William H. Fowler m 38 running Boarding house born England.

MAXWELL, HAMILTON, 72, M, Farmer, -, Ireland, 998,

998, CHES.

MAY, JOHN, 30, M, Clerk, -, Ireland, 110, 102, CHAS+.

MAY, MARGARET, 25, F, None listed, -, Ireland, 110, 102, CHAS+. In HH of John May m 30 born Ireland.

MAYER, H.A., 45, M, Laborer, -, Ireland, 748, 706, CHAS+.

MAYER, HONORA, 45, F, None listed, -, Ireland, 748, 706, CHAS+. In HH of H.A. Mayer m 45 born Ireland.

MAYER, JOHN, 30, M, Laborer, -, Ireland, 166, 148, CHAS. In HH of John Jenkins m 25 born England.

MAYHART, DANIEL, 34, M, Laborer, -, Ireland, 411, 372, CHAS.

MAYHART, JAMES, 4, M, None listed, -, Ireland, 411, 372, CHAS. In HH of Daniel Mayhart m 34 born Ireland.

MAYHART, MARGARET, 36, F, None listed, -, Ireland, 411, 372, CHAS. In HH of Daniel Mayhart m 34 born Ireland.

MAYLOVE, EDWARD, 29, M, Engineer, -, Ireland, 1136, 1115, CHAS%. In HH of Maria Carpenter f 52 born Ireland.

MAYLOVE, MICHAEL, 26, M, Painter, -, Ireland, 1136, 1115, CHAS%. In HH of Maria Carpenter f 52 born Ireland.

MAYPOWDER, EDWARD, 38, M, Taner & courser, -, Ireland, 1997, 2003, EDGE. Note; out of order after fam. No. 2000. In HH of James Gearty m 44 born Ireland.

MAZYCK, WILLIAM, 40, M, Planter, -, Ireland, 409, 407, CHAS%. In HH of Emeline Hayne f 60 born Ireland.

MCAFEE, JANE, 14, F, None listed, -, Ireland, 573, 573, CHES. In HH of J.T. M. McAfie m 42 born SC, Hotel Keeper.

MCAFFERTY, MARY, 71, F, None listed, -, Ireland, 898, 898, CHES.

MCALISTER, JAS., 35, M, Clerk, -, Ireland, 426, 426, DARL. In HH of Wm. M. Melton m 30 born SC.

MCALLISTER, A., 50, M, Farmer, -, Ireland, 1542, 1542, SPART.

MCALLISTER, ELIZA JANE, 15, F, None listed, -, Ireland, 1003, 981, CHAS-. In HH of L. Watts f 32 born England.

MCALLISTER, JOHN, 37, M, Store keeper, -, Ireland, 752, 732, CHAS-.

MCALLISTER, JOHN, 55, M, Farmer, -, Ireland, 670, 674, AND.

MCALLISTER, NATHAN, 68, M, Farmer, -, Ireland, 658,

662, AND.

MCALPIN, M.E., 39, F, None listed, -, Ireland, 1020, 1020, CHES. In HH of J.A. Walker m 34 born Ireland.

MCANDLEISH, J., 24, M, Engineer, -, Ireland, 86, 78, CHAS+. In Boarding house.

MCANDREW, ELLEN, 32, F, None listed, -, Ireland, 2, 2, CHAS*. In HH of James McAndrew m 29 born Ireland.

MCANDREW, JAMES, 29, M, Grocer, -, Ireland, 2, 2, CHAS*.

MCANDREW, JAMES, 48, M, Merchant, -, Ireland, 183, 187, RICH. Date 1849 by name of James McAndrew.

MCANDREW, JOHN, 16, M, Clerk, -, Ireland, 183, 187, RICH. In HH of James McAndrew m 48 born Ireland.

MCANDREW, MARY, 34, F, None listed, -, Ireland, 183, 187, RICH. In HH of James McAndrew m 48 born Ireland.

MCAVENEY, PHILIP, 27, M, Grocer, -, Ireland, 32, 28, CHAS$. In HH of Patrick Rahall m 28 born Ireland.

MCBRIDE, JOHN, 46, M, Farmer, -, Ireland, 158, 158, ABB.

MCBRIDE, M., 32, M, Broker, -, Ireland, 180, 163, CHAS.

MCBRIDE, PATRICK, 27, M, None listed, -, Ireland, 714,

674, CHAS+. In HH of John McManus m 30 born Ireland.

MCBURNIE, ELIZA, 33, F, None listed, -, Ireland, 1064, 1041, CHAS-. In HH of William Mc Burnie m 44 born Ireland.

MCBURNIE, WILLIAM, 44, M, Merchant, -, Ireland, 1064, 1041, CHAS-.

MCCAFFER, ELIZABETH, 20, F, None listed, -, Ireland, 787, 767, CHAS-. In HH of John McCaffer m 24 born Ireland.

MCCAFFER, JOHN, 24, M, Shoe dealer, -, Ireland, 787, 767, CHAS-.

MCCAFFREY, JAMES, 32, M, Merchant, -, Ireland, 299, 305, RICH.

MCCAIN, JOHN, 56, M, None, -, Ireland, 1329, 1329, CHES. In HH of Perry Ferguson m 39 born VA.

MCCAIRN, MARGARET, 43, F, None listed, -, Ireland, 988, 965, CHAS%. In HH of James Fitzpatrick m 40 born Ireland.

MCCAIRN, WM., 20, M, None listed, -, Ireland, 988, 965, CHAS%. In HH of James Fitzpatrick m 40 born Ireland.

MCCALEA, NANCY, 25, F, Servant, -, Ireland, 35, 35, CHAS*. In HH of Ann P. Smith f 65 born SC.

MCCAMMON, JOHN, 32,

M, Clerk, -, Ireland, 631, 649, RICH.

MCCAMRIEL, CELINA, 17, F, None listed, -, Ireland, 9, 9, CHAS-. In HH of William McCormriel m 40 born Ireland.

MCCAMRIEL, ELEANOR, 30, F, None listed, -, Ireland, 9, 9, CHAS-. In HH of William McCormriel m 40 born Ireland.

MCCAMRIEL, MARTHA, 19, F, None listed, -, Ireland, 9, 9, CHAS-. In HH of William McCormriel m 40 born Ireland.

MCCÁMRIEL, NANCY, 20, F, None listed, -, Ireland, 9, 9, CHAS-. In HH of William McCormriel m 40 born Ireland.

MCCAMRIEL, WILLIAM, 40, M, Bricklayer, -, Ireland, 9, 9, CHAS-.

MCCANDLESS, ELIZA-BETH, 50, F, None listed, -, Ireland, 889, 889, CHES. In HH of William McCandless m 48 born Ireland.

MCCANDLESS, WILLIAM, 48, M, Farmer, -, Ireland, 889, 889, CHES.

MCCANGHEY, JAMES, 48, M, Farmer, -, Ireland, 598, 598, UNION.

MCCANOL, W.J., 53, M, Farmer, -, Ireland, 588, 588, CHES.

MCCANTS, ALICE, 17, F, None listed, -, Ireland, 848, 828, CHAS-. In HH of B. Figeroux m 42 born West

Indies.

MCCANTS, ANN, 20, F, None listed, -, Ireland, 848, 828, CHAS-. In HH of B. Figeroux m 42 born West Indies.

MCCARATHY, DENNIS, 24, M, Laborer, -, Ireland, 1197, 1176, CHAS%. In Boarding house.

MCCAREY, CATHERINE, 30, F, None listed, -, Ireland, 496, 489, CHAS%. In HH of James McCarey m 28 born Ireland.

MCCAREY, JAMES, 28, M, Tallow Chandler, -, Ireland, 496, 489, CHAS%.

MCCAREY, PATRICK, 19, M, Tallow Chandler, -, Ireland, 496, 489, CHAS%. In HH of James McCarey m 28 born Ireland.

MCCARLEY, AGNES, 2, F, None listed, -, Ireland, 668, 669, FAIR. In HH of James Mc Carley m 38 born Ireland.

MCCARLEY, ELIZABETH W., 36, F, None listed, -, Ireland, 668, 669, FAIR. In HH of James McCarley m 38 born Ireland.

MCCARLEY, HUGH, 6, M, None listed, -, Ireland, 668, 669, FAIR. In HH of James Mc Carley m 38 born Ireland.

MCCARLEY, JAMES, 38, M, Planter, -, Ireland, 668, 669, FAIR.

MCCARLEY, JANE, 10, F, None listed, -, Ireland, 252, 252, FAIR. In HH of Robert McCarley m 30 born Ireland.

MCCARLEY, JOHN, 6, M, None listed, -, Ireland, 668, 669, FAIR. In HH of James Mc Carley m 38 born Ireland.

MCCARLEY, JOHN, 12, M, None listed, -, Ireland, 668, 669, FAIR. In HH of James Mc Carley m 38 born Ireland.

MCCARLEY, JOHN, 23, M, None listed, -, Ireland, 651, 651, CHES. In HH of Sarah McAliley m (sic) 50 born SC.

MCCARLEY, M., 30, F, None listed, -, Ireland, 461, 461, CHES. In HH of M. English f 66 born Ireland.

MCCARLEY, MARGARET, 30, F, None listed, -, Ireland, 252, 252, FAIR. In HH of Robert McCarley m 30 born Ireland.

MCCARLEY, MARY, 14, F, None listed, -, Ireland, 668, 669, FAIR. In HH of James Mc Carley m 38 born Ireland.

MCCARLEY, ROBERT, 30, M, Planter, -, Ireland, 252, 252, FAIR.

MCCARNS, JOHN, 26, M, None listed, -, Ireland, 328, 328, YORK. In HH of Owen Matthews m 41 born Lancester Dist., SC.

MCCARREL, JAMES, 25, M, Bricklayer, -, Ireland, 10,

9, CHAS-.

MCCARROL, MARTHA, 18, F, None listed, -, Ireland, 225, 212, CHAS+. In HH of J.B. Adger m 40 born SC.

MCCARTER, ANDREW SR., 80, M, Farmer, -, Ireland, 240, 240, YORK*.

MCCARTER, JANE, 70, F, None listed, -, Ireland, 240, 240, YORK*. In HH of Andrew McCarter Sr. m 80 born Ireland.

MCCARTER, THOMAS, 31, M, Farmer, -, Ireland, 1151, 1152, AND*.

MCCARTHY, ADELINE, 20, F, None listed, -, Ireland, 821, 804, CHAS%. In HH of James McCarthy m 49 born Ireland.

MCCARTHY, ANN, 25, F, None listed, -, Ireland, 22, 27, CHAS. In HH of Michael McCarthy m 24 born Ireland.

MCCARTHY, CATEY, 8, F, None listed, -, Ireland, 525, 475, CHAS. In HH of Dennis McCarthy m 35 born Ireland.

MCCARTHY, CATEY, 30, F, None listed, -, Ireland, 525, 475, CHAS. In HH of Dennis McCarthy m 35 born Ireland.

MCCARTHY, CATH- ERINE, 47, F, None listed, -, Ireland, 821, 804, CHAS%. In HH of James McCarthy m 49 born Ireland.

MCCARTHY, CORNELIUS, 40, M, Clerk, -, Ireland, 167, 158, CHAS+. In Boarding house.

MCCARTHY, D.L., 30, M, Shop keeper, -, Ireland, 76, 68, CHAS+.

MCCARTHY, DAN, 44, M, Laborer, -, Ireland, 348, 310, CHAS+. In HH of Dennis McCarthy m 70 born Ireland.

MCCARTHY, DANL., 35, M, Laborer, -, Ireland, 322, 297, CHAS. In Boarding house.

MCCARTHY, DENNIS, 10, M, None listed, -, Ireland, 525, 475, CHAS. In HH of Dennis McCarthy m 35 born Ireland.

MCCARTHY, DENNIS, 35, M, Laborer, -, Ireland, 525, 475, CHAS.

MCCARTHY, DENNIS, 70, M, Laborer, -, Ireland, 348, 310, CHAS+.

MCCARTHY, ELLEN, 15, F, None listed, -, Ireland, 373, 340, CHAS. In HH of Eliza Jervais f 35 born SC.

MCCARTHY, HETTY, 16, F, None listed, -, Ireland, 525, 475, CHAS. In HH of Dennis McCarthy m 35 born Ireland.

MCCARTHY, HONORE, 24, F, None listed, -, Ireland, 206, 184, CHAS. In HH of John Hurley m 27 born Ireland.

MCCARTHY, JACOB, 12, M, None listed, -, Ireland, 525, 475, CHAS. In HH of Dennis McCarthy m 35 born Ireland.

MCCARTHY, JAMES, 28, M, Mariner, -, Ireland, 337, 311, CHAS. In HH of William H. Fowler m 38 running Boarding house born England.

MCCARTHY, JAMES, 49, M, Laborer, -, Ireland, 821, 804, CHAS%.

MCCARTHY, JANE, 17, F, None listed, -, Ireland, 821, 804, CHAS%. In HH of James McCarthy m 49 born Ireland.

MCCARTHY, LAURENCE, 25, M, Laborer, -, Ireland, 351, 324, CHAS. In Boarding house.

MCCARTHY, MARGARET, 11, F, None listed, -, Ireland, 821, 804, CHAS%. In HH of James McCarthy m 49 born Ireland.

MCCARTHY, MARGERY, 64, F, None listed, -, Ireland, 348, 310, CHAS+. In HH of Dennis McCarthy m 70 born Ireland.

MCCARTHY, MICHAEL, 24, M, Stone cutter, -, Ireland, 22, 27, CHAS.

MCCARTHY, NANCY, 20, F, None listed, -, Ireland, 348, 310, CHAS+. In HH of Dennis McCarthy m 70 born Ireland.

MCCARTHY, PATRICK, 14, M, None listed, -, Ireland, 525, 475, CHAS. In HH of Dennis McCarthy m 35 born Ireland.

MCCARTHY, PATRICK, 22, M, Stone cutter, -, Ireland, 348, 310, CHAS+. In HH of

Dennis McCarthy m 70 born Ireland.

MCCARTHY, PETER, 14, M, None listed, -, Ireland, 821, 804, CHAS%. In HH of James McCarthy m 49 born Ireland.

MCCARTHY, POLLY, 40, F, None listed, -, Ireland, 348, 310, CHAS+. In HH of Dennis McCarthy m 70 born Ireland.

MCCARTHY, SUSAN, 8, F, None listed, -, Ireland, 821, 804, CHAS%. In HH of James McCarthy m 49 born Ireland.

MCCARTNY, MARY, 70, F, None listed, -, Ireland, 602, 602, ABB.

MCCARTY, JOHN, 45, M, Ditcher, -, Ireland, 265, 265, Beau+.

MCCARY, MARY, 25, F, None listed, -, Ireland, 1424, 1424, GREE. In HH of Robert McCary m 28 born Ireland.

MCCARY, ROBERT, 28, M, Laborer, -, Ireland, 1424, 1424, GREE.

MCCAUGHRIN, LETITIA, 40, F, None listed, -, Ireland, 319, 325, RICH. In HH of Thomas McCaughrin m 45 born Ireland.

MCCAUGHRIN, MARTHA, 17, F, None listed, -, Ireland, 319, 325, RICH. In HH of Thomas McCaughrin m 45 born Ireland.

MCCAUGHRIN, NANCY, 19, F, None listed, -, Ireland, 319, 325, RICH. In HH of Thomas McCaughrin m 45 born Ireland.

MCCAUGHRIN, ROBERT, 15, M, None listed, -, Ireland, 319, 325, RICH. In HH of Thomas McCaughrin m 45 born Ireland.

MCCAUGHRIN, SAMUEL, 25, M, Clerk, -, Ireland, 319, 325, RICH. In HH of Thomas McCaughrin m 45 born Ireland.

MCCAUGHRIN, THOMAS, 45, M, Merchant, -, Ireland, 319, 325, RICH.

MCCAURTLY, DANIEL, 21, M, Laborer, -, Ireland, 2007, 2013, EDGE. In HH of William Herbert m 37 born Ireland.

MCCAVE, JAMES, 48, M, Engineer, -, Ireland, 359, 321, CHAS+.

MCCLAIN, MARTHA, 42, F, None listed, -, Ireland, 656, 656, ABB. In HH of Andrew McClain m 55 born SC.

MCCLARKEY, JOHN, 50, M, City Police, -, Ireland, 124, 115, CHAS+. In Boarding house.

MCCLARKEY, PATRICK, 26, M, Clerk, -, Ireland, 124, 115, CHAS+. In Boarding house.

MCCLARKEY, THOMAS, 20, M, Student, -, Ireland, 124, 115, CHAS+. In Boarding house.

MCCLELLAND, JOHN, 80, M, None, -, Ireland, 28, 28, KERS.

MCCLINTOCK, E., 85, F, None listed, -, Ireland, 236, 236, CHES.

MCCLINTOCK, JOHN, 68, M, Farmer, -, Ireland, 803, 803, CHES. In HH of W.R. McClintock m 44 born SC.

MCCLINTON, MATHEW, 75, M, Farmer, -, Ireland, 228,

228, ABB.

MCCLINTON, PEGG, 73, F, None listed, -, Ireland, 228, 228, ABB. In HH of Mathew McClinton m 75 born Ireland.

MCCLINTON, SARAH, 80, F, None listed, -, Ireland, 210, 210, ABB. In HH of Samuel B. McClinton m 35 born SC.

MCCLUNEY, W.J., 45, M, Shoemaker, -, Ireland, 535, 535, CHES. In HH of J.L. Houerton m 35 born VA.

MCCLURE, EMILY, 23, F, None listed, -, Ireland, 277, 277, CHAS%. In HH of William McClure m 60 born Ireland.

MCCLURE, ESTHER, 95, F, None listed, -, Ireland, 112, 112, PICK+. In HH of John Price m 58 born NC.

MCCLURE, J.B., 30, M, Broker, -, Ireland, 707, 665, CHAS+.

MCCLURE, JAMES, 28, M, Tanner, -, Ireland, 1209, 1188, CHAS%.

MCCLURE, JANE, 58, F, None listed, -, Ireland, 277, 277, CHAS%. In HH of William McClure mm 60 born Ireland.

MCCLURE, MARY ANN, 35, F, None listed, -, Ireland, 367, 337, CHAS. In HH of Tho. H. McClure m 45 born Ireland.

MCCLURE, ROBERT, 19, M, Clerk, -, Ireland, 277, 277, CHAS%. In HH of William McClure mm 60 born Ireland.

MCCLURE, ROBERT, 62, M, Farmer, -, Ireland, 1397, 1397, YORK.

MCCLURE, SARAH ANN, 19, F, None listed, -, Ireland, 367, 337, CHAS. In HH of Tho. H. McClure m 45 born Ireland.

MCCLURE, T., 20, M, Carpenter, -, Ireland, 390, 354, CHAS. In HH of Hugh ONeile m 30 born Ireland.

MCCLURE, THO. H., 45, M, Shoemaker, -, Ireland, 367, 337, CHAS.

MCCLURE, WILLIAM, 21, M, Clerk, -, Ireland, 277, 277, CHAS%. In HH of William McClure mm 60 born Ireland.

MCCLURE, WILLIAM, 60, M, Chemist, -, Ireland, 277, 277, CHAS%.

MCCOBB, ELIZABETH, 25, F, Servant, -, Ireland, 514, 464, CHAS. In HH of John Flinn m 45 born NY.

MCCOBB, MARY ANN, 14, F, None listed, -, Ireland, 983, 962, CHAS-. In HH of James Grady m 40 born SC.

MCCOLLOUGH, MICHAEL, 34, M, Laborer, -, Ireland, 82, 74, CHAS+. In HH of Joseph Pattena m 41 born Italy.

MCCOMB, HANNAH, 65, F, None listed, -, Ireland, 1553, 1553, ABB.

MCCOMB, MARY, 28, F, None listed, -, Ireland, 473, 473, ABB. In HH of Robert McComb 45 m born SC.

MCCONNELL, MARY, 65, F, None listed, -, Ireland, 882, 892, RICH+. In HH of James Simms m 55 born SC.

MCCOONE, JAMES, 38, M,

Laborer, -, Ireland, 605, 563, CHAS+.

MCCOONE, JOHN, 14, M, None listed, -, Ireland, 605, 563, CHAS+. In HH of James McCoone m 38 born Ireland.

MCCOONE, SUSAN, 30, F, None listed, -, Ireland, 605, 563, CHAS+. In HH of James McCoone m 38 born Ireland.

MCCORD, HENRY, 33, M, Shoemaker, -, Ireland, 553, 553, CHES. In HH of Mary Gill m 44 born SC.

MCCORMICK, JAMES, 31, M, Laborer, -, Ireland, 331, 298, CHAS+.

MCCORMICK, JAMES, 33, M, Laborer, -, Ireland, 1090, 1068, CHAS%.

MCCORMICK, JANE, 27, F, None listed, -, Ireland, 248, 233, CHAS+. In HH of William McCormick m 36 born Ireland.

MCCORMICK, JANE, 30, F, None listed, -, Ireland, 1199, 1199, YORK. In HH of Joseph McElneagle m 45 born Ireland.

MCCORMICK, JANET, 9, F, None listed, -, Ireland, 1090, 1068, CHAS%. In HH of James McCormick m 33 born Ireland.

MCCORMICK, JOHN, 30, M, Laborer, -, Ireland, 2052, 2058, EDGE. In HH of Jas. Linch m 28 born Ireland.

MCCORMICK, JOHN, 40, M, Laborer, -, Ireland, 272, 252, CHAS+.

MCCORMICK, MARGARET, 29, F, None listed, -, Ireland, 1090, 1068, CHAS%.

In HH of James McCormick m 33 born Ireland.

MCCORMICK, MARY, 34, F, None listed, -, Ireland, 331, 298, CHAS+. In HH of James McCormick m 31 born Ireland.

MCCORMICK, MARY, 45, F, None listed, -, Ireland, 457, 457, CHES. In HH of Sam McCormick m 60 born Ireland.

MCCORMICK, MICHAEL, 27, M, Shoe maker, -, Ireland, 753, 754, FAIR. In HH of Jeremiah Cockrel m 48 born SC.

MCCORMICK, SAM, 60, M, Farmer, -, Ireland, 457, 457, CHES.

MCCORMICK, WILLIAM, 36, M, Pavor, -, Ireland, 248, 233, CHAS+.

MCCOTHERN, JAS., 25, M, Farmer, -, Ireland, 967, 967, CHES. In HH of Henry J. Culp m 41 born SC.

MCCOY, ALEXANDER, 29, M, Farmer, -, Ireland, 824, 824, ABB. In HH of Elizabeath McCoy f 30 born Ireland.

MCCOY, ELIZABETH, 30, F, None listed, -, Ireland, 824, 824, ABB.

MCCOY, ISABELLA, 25, F, None listed, -, Ireland, 824, 824, ABB. In HH of Elizabeath McCoy f 30 born Ireland.

MCCRADY, SARAH, 20, F, None listed, -, Ireland, 446, 413, CHAS*.

MCCRATE, CHARLOTTE, 14, F, None listed, -, Ireland, 133, 124, CHAS+. In HH of John McCrale m 30 born Canada. {may be McCrate}

MCCRATE, JAMES, 21, M,

Baker, -, Ireland, 132, 124, CHAS+. In HH of John McCrale {McCrate} m 30 born Canada.

MCCREE, JAMES, 67, M, Farmer, -, Ireland, 1606, 1606, ABB.

MCCREIGHT, JAMES, 51, M, Gin maker, -, Ireland, 544, 544, FAIR.

MCCULLOUGH, ANN, 60, F, None listed, -, Ireland, 1150, 1150, CHES. In HH of A. McCullough m 60 born SC.

MCCULLOUGH, ANN, 70, F, None listed, -, Ireland, 108, 108, FAIR. In HH of Robert McCullough m 76 born Ireland.

MCCULLOUGH, ANN J., 23, F, None listed, -, Ireland, 108, 108, FAIR. In HH of Robert McCullough m 76 born Ireland.

MCCULLOUGH, C.B., 5, M, None listed, -, Ireland, 88, 88, CHES. In HH of Mary McCullough f 24 born Ireland.

MCCULLOUGH, E., 46, F, None listed, -, Ireland, 88, 88, CHES. In HH of Mary McCullough f 24 born Ireland.

MCCULLOUGH, GRACE, 17, F, None listed, -, Ireland, 88, 88, CHES. In HH of Mary McCullough f 24 born Ireland.

MCCULLOUGH, JANE, 55, F, None listed, -, Ireland, 1457, 1457, GREE. In HH of Wm. McCullough m 87 born Ireland.

MCCULLOUGH, JAS., 11, M, None listed, -, Ireland, 88, 88, CHES. In HH of Mary McCullough f 24 born Ireland.

MCCULLOUGH, JOHN, 18, M, Laborer, -, Ireland, 675, 676, FAIR. In HH of Robert

MCCULLOUGH, JOHN, 19, M, Farmer, -, Ireland, 88, 88, CHES. In HH of Mary McCullough f 24 born Ireland.

MCCULLOUGH, JOHN, 47, M, Farmer, -, Ireland, 88, 88, CHES. In HH of Mary McCullough f 24 born Ireland.

MCCULLOUGH, JOSEPH, 71, M, Farmer, -, Ireland, 1420, 1420, GREE.

MCCULLOUGH, MARY, 24, F, None listed, -, Ireland, 88, 88, CHES.

MCCULLOUGH, ROBERT, 14, M, None listed, -, Ireland, 88, 88, CHES. In HH of Mary McCullough f 24 born Ireland.

MCCULLOUGH, ROBERT, 76, M, Tailor, -, Ireland, 108, 108, FAIR.

MCCULLOUGH, WM., 21, M, Farmer, -, Ireland, 88, 88, CHES. In HH of Mary McCullough f 24 born Ireland.

MCCULLOUGH, WM., 87, M, Farmer, -, Ireland, 1457, 1457, GREE.

MCCULLY, SARAH, 83, F, None listed, -, Ireland, 465, 465, CHES. In HH of Thomas Torbit m 46 born SC.

MCCULLY, STEPHEN, 50, M, Merchant, -, Ireland, 491, 493, AND.

MCCUSKER, E., 25, M, Shoemaker, -, Ireland, 560, 560, CHES.

MCDAVID, JOHN, 35, M, Brick maker, -, Ireland, 1817, 1823, EDGE.

MCDAVID, PENELOPE, 84, F, None listed, -, Ireland, 1385,

1385, GREE. In HH of Allen McDavid m 47 born SC.

MCDERMOT, JOHN, 30, M, None, -, Ireland, 520, 520, BARN.

MCDERMOT, JOHN, 30, M, Laborer, -, Ireland, 338, 303, CHAS+. In HH of Bernard Sweeney m 37 born Ireland.

MCDILL, MARY, 38, F, None listed, -, Ireland, 708, 709, FAIR.

MCDONALD, ANN, 25, F, Servant, -, Ireland, 508, 458, CHAS. In HH of James Robertson m 50 born Scotland.

MCDONALD, EDWD., 34, M, Painter, -, Ireland, 391, 355, CHAS. In HH of F.W. Theus m 28 born Germany.

MCDONALD, HENRY., 38, M, Painter, -, Ireland, 55, 55, COLL. In HH of Charles B. Farmer m 27 born SC.

MCDONALD, JANE, 12, F, Servant, -, Ireland, 508, 458, CHAS. In HH of James Robertson m 50 born Scotland.

MCDONALD, JOHN, 34, M, Conductor RR, -, Ireland, 491, 506, RICH.

MCDONALD, MARGARET, 18, F, None listed, -, Ireland, 33, 33, CHAS!. In HH of Margaret McDonald f 50 born Ireland.

MCDONALD, MARGARET, 50, F, None listed, -, Ireland, 122, 114, CHAS*.

MCDONALD, MARGARET, 50, F, None listed, -, Ireland, 33, 33, CHAS!.

MCDONALD, PATRICK,

45, M, Clerk, -, Ireland, 261, 244, CHAS+. In HH of Hugh McNamara m 28 born Ireland.

MCDONALD, PETER, 19, M, Clerk, -, Ireland, 317, 291, CHAS+. In HH of Tim Kennedy m 71 born Ireland.

MCDONALD, ROBERT, 75, M, Farmer, -, Ireland, 544, 544, ABB.

MCDONALD, THOS., 26, M, Painter, -, Ireland, 346, 308, CHAS+. In Boarding house.

MCDONALD, THOS., 28, M, Painter, -, Ireland, 391, 355, CHAS. In HH of F.W. Theus m 28 born Germany.

MCDONNAGH, ANN, 18, F, None listed, -, Ireland, 145, 136, CHAS+. In HH of John McDonnagh m 50 born Ireland.

MCDONNAGH, ANN, 44, F, None listed, -, Ireland, 145, 136, CHAS+. In HH of John McDonnagh m 50 born Ireland.

MCDONNAGH, CATHERINE, 7, F, None listed, -, Ireland, 145, 136, CHAS+. In HH of John McDonnagh m 50 born Ireland.

MCDONNAGH, JOHN, 12, M, None listed, -, Ireland, 145, 136, CHAS+. In HH of John McDonnagh m 50 born Ireland.

MCDONNAGH, JOHN, 50, M, Laborer, -, Ireland, 145, 136, CHAS+.

MCDONNAGH, JULIA, 14, F, None listed, -, Ireland, 145, 136, CHAS+. In HH of John McDonnagh m 50 born Ireland.

MCDONNAGH, MARY, 20, F, None listed, -, Ireland, 145, 136, CHAS+. In HH of John

McDonnagh m 50 born Ireland.

MCDOWEL, ESTHER, 90, F, None listed, -, Ireland, 421, 422, AND*. In HH of George W. McDowel m 28 born SC.

MCDOWEL, JOHN, 35, M, Overseer, -, Ireland, 757, 757, ABB. In HH of Thomas B. Dandy m 31 MD, born SC.

MCDOWELL, ANGHERY, 62, M, Planter, -, Ireland, 266, 266, FAIR.

MCDOWELL, DAVID, 55, M, Lawyer, -, Ireland, 504, 504, FAIR. In HH of J.F. Gamble m 42, hotel keeper, born NC. At the WinnsboroHotel.

MCDOWELL, JAMES, 36, M, Farmer, -, Ireland, 1577, 1577, YORK.

MCDOWELL, JOHN, 46, M, Farmer, -, Ireland, 1141, 1141, CHES.

MCDOWELL, JOHN, 46, M, Planter, -, Ireland, 1150, 1151, FAIR.

MCDOWELL, JOHN, 70, M, Planter, -, Ireland, 378, 378, FAIR.

MCDOWELL, THOMAS, 76, M, None listed, -, Ireland, 1144, 1144, CHES. In HH of Francis Hardin 30 born SC. Note: Listed as in Poor House.

MCDOWELL, WILLIAM, 38, M, Clerk, -, Ireland, 512, 427, RICH.

MCDURMET, BRIDGET, 18, F, None listed, -, Ireland, 965, 942, CHAS%. In HH of James Dunning m 34 born SC.

MCELHENEY, W., 30, M, Laborer, -, Ireland, 271, 252, CHAS+. In HH of Mary

Campbell f 49 born Ireland.

MCELHERAN, ANN, 41, F, None listed, -, Ireland, 227, 227, BEAU. In HH of David McElheran m 50 born Ireland.

MCELHERNA, RACHEL, 26, F, None listed, -, Ireland, 770, 728, CHAS+. In HH of W.C. McElheran m 31 born Ireland.

MCELHERNA, W.C., 31, M, Blacksmith, -, Ireland, 770, 728, CHAS+.

MCELLERON, CHARLES, 30, M, Artist, -, Ireland, 984, 963, CHAS-.

MCELLERON, ELLEN, 28, F, None listed, -, Ireland, 984, 963, CHAS-. In HH of Charles McElleron m 30 born Ireland.

MCELMOYL, HARRIET E., 18, F, None listed, -, Ireland, 1496, 1496, YORK. In HH of John D. Boyd m 45 born York Dist., SC.

MCELNEAGLE, JOSEPH, 45, M, Laborer, -, Ireland, 1199, 1199, YORK.

MCELNOYLE, DANIEL, 50, M, Farmer, -, Ireland, 619, 619, YORK.

MCELRONE, CATHERINE, 13, F, None listed, -, Ireland, 500, 515, RICH. In HH of Hugh McElrone m 42 born Ireland.

MCELRONE, HUGH, 42, M, Laborer, -, Ireland, 500, 515, RICH.

MCELRONE, JAMES, 10, M, None listed, -, Ireland, 500, 515, RICH. In HH of Hugh McElrone m 42 born Ireland.

MCELRONE, MARY, 17, F,

None listed, -, Ireland, 500, 515, RICH. In HH of Hugh McElrone m 42 born Ireland.

MCELRONE, MARY, 20, F, None listed, -, Ireland, 542, 557, RICH. In Lunatic Asylum.

MCELRONE, SUSAN, 15, F, None listed, -, Ireland, 500, 515, RICH. In HH of Hugh McElrone m 42 born Ireland.

MCELROY, JOHN, 30, M, Laborer, -, Ireland, 237, 222, CHAS-.Poor House.

MCELROY, M.J., 22, F, None listed, -, Ireland, 1003, 981, CHAS-. In HH of L. Watts f 32 born England.

MCELROY, ROBERT, 30, M, Tailor, -, Ireland, 693, 694, FAIR. In HH of Robert Brice m 58 born SC.

MCELROY, SARAH, 66, F, None listed, -, Ireland, 478, 478, CHES. In HH of James Barr m 37 born Ireland.

MCELVONE, MICHAEL, 19, M, Attendant, -, Ireland, 542, 557, RICH.At Lunatic Asylum.

MCELWAIN, CHARLES, 67, M, Farmer, -, Ireland, 100, 100, YORK.

MCELWAIN, DAVID, 69, M, None listed, -, Ireland, 77, 77, YORK. In HH of Charles McElwain m 99 born York Dist., SC.

MCELWEE, WILLIAM, 60, M, Farmer, -, Ireland, 889, 889, YORK.

MCESPAY?, PATRICK, 27, M, Farmer, -, Ireland, 1658, 1658, EDGE.

MCEVOY, WILLIAM, 40, M, Shoe/bootmaker, -, Ireland, 44, 44, EDGE.

MCFADDEN, MARY, 24, F, Servant, -, Ireland, 882, 840, CHAS+. In Charleston Hotel.

MCFEEK, JAS., 19, M, Clerk, -, Ireland, 775, 733, CHAS+. In Boarding house

MCFEELY, BARNARD, 45, M, None listed, -, Ireland, 237, 222, CHAS-. In Poor House.

MCGANN, MARY, 32, F, None listed, -, Ireland, 640, 599, CHAS+. In HH of Michael Keenan m 44 born Ireland.

MCGANN, PATRICK, 24, M, Laborer, -, Ireland, 640, 599, CHAS+. In HH of Michael Keenan m 44 born Ireland.

MCGANN, PETER, 36, M, Laborer, -, Ireland, 640, 599, CHAS+. In HH of Michael Keenan m 44 born Ireland.

MCGANN, RICHARD, 28, M, Laborer, -, Ireland, 640, 599, CHAS+. In HH of Michael Keenan m 44 born Ireland.

MCGARTHY, WM., 20, M, Laborer, -, Ireland, 338, 303, CHAS+. In HH of Bernard Sweeney m 37 born Ireland.

MCGARY, EDWARD, 7, M, None listed, -, Ireland, 445, 428, CHAS-. In HH of Patrick McGary m 38 born Ireland.

MCGARY, JAMES, 15, M, None listed, -, Ireland, 22, 25, CHAS. In HH of Patrick McGary m 40 born Ireland.

MCGARY, JOHN, 24, M, Laborer, -, Ireland, 445, 428, CHAS-. In HH of Patrick McGary m 38 born Ireland.

MCGARY, MARGERY, 26, F, None listed, -, Ireland, 445, 428, CHAS-. In HH of Patrick McGary m 38 born Ireland.

MCGARY, MARY, 4, F, None listed, -, Ireland, 445, 428, CHAS-. In HH of Patrick McGary m 38 born Ireland.

MCGARY, MARY, 36, F, None listed, -, Ireland, 445, 428, CHAS-. In HH of Patrick McGary m 38 born Ireland.

MCGARY, PATRICK, 38, M, Mason, -, Ireland, 445, 428, CHAS-.

MCGARY, PATRICK, 40, M, Shoemaker, -, Ireland, 22, 25, CHAS.

MCGENTY, JANE, 13, F, None listed, -, Ireland, 248, 233, CHAS+. In HH of William McCormick m 36 born Ireland.

MCGENTY, MARY, 15, F, None listed, -, Ireland, 248, 233, CHAS+. In HH of William McCormick m 36 born Ireland.

MCGENTY, TERRANCE, 40, M, Laborer, -, Ireland, 248, 233, CHAS+. In HH of William McCormick m 36 born Ireland.

MCGERMAN, HANNAH, 36, F, None listed, -, Ireland, 133, 125, CHAS+. In HH of John McGerman m 44 born Ireland.

MCGERMAN, JOHN, 44, M, Laborer, -, Ireland, 133, 125, CHAS+.

MCGHEE, CHARLOTTE, 25, F, None listed, -, Ireland, 643, 661, RICH. In Poor House.

MCGILL, ESTHER, 47, F, None listed, -, Ireland, 420, 420, CHES. In HH of J.B. McGill m 49 born Ireland.

MCGILL, J.B., 49, M, Farmer, -, Ireland, 420, 420, CHES.

MCGILL, JAMES, 27, M, Shoemaker, -, Ireland, 231, 231, ABB.

MCGILL, JAMES H., 29, M, Planter, -, Ireland, 458, 458, FAIR.

MCGILL, SARAH, 76, F, None listed, -, Ireland, 979, 979, YORK. In HH of Mary Henry f 78 born Ireland.

MCGILL, THOMAS, 26, M, Planter, -, Ireland, 118, 118, FAIR. In HH of John Asheford m 42 born SC.

MCGILL, WILLIAM, 25, M, Shoemaker, -, Ireland, 230, 230, ABB.

MCGINNIS, JOHN, 27, M, Drayman, -, Ireland, 853, 811, CHAS+. In HH of Bernard Carrol m 45 born Ireland.

MCGINNIS, MARY, 21, F, None listed, -, Ireland, 296, 280, CHAS-. In HH of J. Moise f 45 born SC.

MCGLADNEY, MARY, 35, F, None listed, -, Ireland, 355, 355, FAIR. In HH of William McGladney m 30 born SC.

MCGLENN, HANNAH, 30, F, None listed, -, Ireland, 207, 211, RICH. In HH of Jeremiah J. O'Connell m 30 born Ireland.

MCGONAN, JOHN, 45, M, Physician, -, Ireland, 639, 639, YORK.

MCGONAN, MARGARET, 24, F, None listed, -, Ireland, 639, 639, YORK. In HH of

John McGonan m 45 born Ireland.

MCGOORLY, ELLEN, 25, F, None listed, -, Ireland, 531, 490, CHAS+. In HH of H.W. Kuhtmann m 35 born Germany.

MCGOVERN, JAMES, 30, M, Laborer, -, Ireland, 67, 68, RICH. In HH of William Sally m 35 born Ireland.

MCGOWAN, THOMAS, 23, M, Laborer, -, Ireland, 389, 351, CHAS+. In HH of Edward Collins m 40 born Ireland.

MCGOWEN, WILLIAM, 60, M, Farmer, -, Ireland, 285, 285, LAU.

MCGRANAGAN, ESTHER, 20, F, None listed, -, Ireland, 1025, 1002, CHAS-. In HH of Charles Seyle m 32 born SC.

MCGRATH, DAVID, 25, M, Laborer, -, Ireland, 272, 252, CHAS+. In HH of John McCormick m 40 born Ireland.

MCGRATH, JERRY, 35, M, Laborer, -, Ireland, 268, 249, CHAS+. In HH of Thomas Morrison m 36 born Ireland.

MCGRATH, MICHAEL, 34, M, Overseer, -, Ireland, 87, 87, ABB.

MCGRATH, RODOLPHUS, 45, M, Laborer, -, Ireland, 88, 80, CHAS+. In HH of Michael Welch m 35 born Ireland.

MCGRAW, ANN, 25, F, None listed, -, Ireland, 675, 667, CHAS%. In HH of Michael Mc Graw m 25 born Ireland.

MCGRAW, JAMES, 40, M, Stone cutter, -, Ireland, 542, 557, RICH. Date 1842 by name. In Lunatic Asylum.

MCGRAW, MATHEW, 47, M, Welldigger, -, Ireland, 214, 214, Lex. In HH of George W. Lorick m 24 born SC.

MCGRAW, MICHAEL, 25, M, Laborer, -, Ireland, 675, 667, CHAS%.

MCGRIFFIN, ANDREW, 60, M, Farmer, -, Ireland, 803, 842, PICK.

MCGUINNIS, CATH-ERINE, 44, F, None listed, -, Ireland, 332, 338, RICH. In HH of William McGuinnis m 45 born Ireland.

MCGUINNIS, WILLIAM, 45, M, Merchant, -, Ireland, 332, 338, RICH.

MCGUIRE, DANIEL, 40, M, Shop keeper, -, Ireland, 781, 761, CHAS-.

MCGUIRE, ELLEN, 18, F, None listed, -, Ireland, 224, 200, CHAS*. In HH of Vincent Odes m 27 born GA.

MCGUIRE, HENRY, 35, M, Laborer, -, Ireland, 292, 292, CHAS%.

MCGUIRE, JAMES, 25, M, Laborer, -, Ireland, 338, 303, CHAS+. In HH of Bernard Sweeney m 37 born Ireland.

MCGUIRE, JAMES, 29, M, Coal passer, -, Ireland, 326, 301, CHAS. In HH of William Rollins m 40 born {-}. In crew of the Steam Ship Isabel.

MCGUIRE, JOANA, 28, F, None listed, -, Ireland, 781, 761, CHAS-. In HH of Daniel Mc Guire m 40 born Ireland.

MCGUIRE, ROSANA, 23, F, None listed, -, Ireland, 48, 48, CHAS*. In HH of W.C. Gatewood m 43 born VA.

MCGUIRY, CATHERINE, 23, F, None listed, -, Ireland, 551, 543, CHAS%. In HH of James Mc Guiry m 25 born Ireland.

MCGUIRY, JAMES, 25, M, Laborer, -, Ireland, 551, 543, CHAS%.

MCHENTY, JOSEPH, 23, M, Hireling, -, Ireland, 673, 673, ABB.

MCHENY, G., 65, M, Farmer, -, Ireland, 92, 92, CHES.

MCHILL, ELEANOR, 70, F, None listed, -, Ireland, 2282, 2282, ABB.

MCHUALLY, JAS., 23, M, Laborer, -, Ireland, 2057, 2060, EDGE. In HH of Michael Corner m 27 born Ireland.

MCHUGH, BRIGET, 43, F, None listed, -, Ireland, 901, 881, CHAS-. In HH of Philip McHugh m 47 born Ireland.

MCHUGH, CATHERINE, 10, F, None listed, -, Ireland, 901, 881, CHAS-. In HH of Philip McHugh m 47 born Ireland.

MCHUGH, JOHN, 12, M, None listed, -, Ireland, 901, 881, CHAS-. In HH of Philip McHugh m 47 born Ireland.

MCHUGH, MARY, 17, F, None listed, -, Ireland, 901, 881, CHAS-. In HH of Philip McHugh m 47 born Ireland.

MCHUGH, MARY, 46, F, None listed, -, Ireland, 392, 375, CHAS-.

MCHUGH, PHILIP, 47, M, Laborer, -, Ireland, 901, 881, CHAS-.

MCILWAIN, JANE, 53, F, None listed, -, Ireland, 2234, 2234, ABB.

MCILWAIN, JOHN, 49, M, Brick mason, -, Ireland, 549, 549, UNION.

MCILWAIN, MARTHA, 49, F, None listed, -, Ireland, 549, 549, UNION. In HH of John McIlwain m 49 born Ireland.

MCILWAIN, WILLIAM, 56, M, Farmer, -, Ireland, 1584, 1584, ABB.

MCINNERNY, JOHANNA, 34, F, None listed, -, Ireland, 17, 16, CHAS$. In HH of Michael McInnerny m 45 born Ireland.

MCINNERNY, MICHAEL, 45, M, Laborer, -, Ireland, 17, 16, CHAS$.

MCINNIS, JOHN, 29, M, Laborer, -, Ireland, 31, 27, CHAS$. In HH of E. Reynolds m 33 mulatto born Ireland.

MCINTIRE, JOHN, 47, M, Clerk, -, Ireland, 76, 68, CHAS+. In HH of D.L. McCarthy m 30 born Ireland.

MCINTOSH, DONALD, 38, M, Merchant, -, Ireland, 509, 502, CHAS%.

MCINTOSH, MARGARET, 40, F, None listed, -, Ireland, 509, 502, CHAS%. In HH of Donald McIntosh m 38 born Ireland.

MCIVER, JANE, 68, F, None listed, -, Ireland, 785, 765, CHAS-. In HH of Miles Drake m 42 born Ireland.

MCKANE, JOHN, 26, M,

Laborer, -, Ireland, 292, 269, CHAS+. In HH of Michael McMurray m 50 born Ireland.

MCKAY, DERMOT, 22, M, Laborer, -, Ireland, 1197, 1176, CHAS%. In Boarding house.

MCKAY, EDWARD, 18, M, Laborer, -, Ireland, 1197, 1176, CHAS%. In Boarding house.

MCKEAN, M.G., 65, F, Teacher, -, Ireland, 159, 159, BEAU.

MCKEE, ARCHIBALD, 80, M, Farmer, -, Ireland, 631, 635, AND.

MCKEE, JOHN, 62, M, Merchant, -, Ireland, 533, 533, CHES.

MCKEEGAN, ANN, 45, F, None listed, -, Ireland, 885, 843, CHAS+. In HH of John McKeegan m 55 born Ireland.

MCKEEGAN, ANN, 50, F, None listed, -, Ireland, 872, 830, CHAS+. In HH of John McKeegan m 50 born Ireland.

MCKEEGAN, JOHN, 50, M, Blacksmith, -, Ireland, 872, 830, CHAS+.

MCKEEGAN, JOHN, 55, M, Blacksmith, -, Ireland, 885, 843, CHAS+.

MCKENNA, EDWARD, 25, M, None listed, -, Ireland, 30, 30, LANC. In HH of Wm. McKenna m 60 born Ireland.

MCKENNA, PATRICK, 30, M, None listed, -, Ireland, 30, 30, LANC. In HH of Wm. McKenna m 60 born Ireland.

MCKENNA, WM., 60, M, Farmer, -, Ireland, 30, 30, LANC.

MCKENNOR, ELIZA, 21, F,

None listed, -, Ireland, 67, 68, RICH. In HH of William Sally m 35 born Ireland.

MCKENNY, ELIZA, 30, F, None listed, -, Ireland, 118, 112, CHAS*. In HH of Thomas Moore m 30 born Ireland.

MCKENSIE, ARCHIBALD, 38, M, Sadler, -, Ireland, 478, 436, CHAS. In HH of R.B. McKensie m 30 born Ireland.

MCKENSIE, ELIZA, 32, F, None listed, -, Ireland, 478, 436, CHAS. In HH of R.B. McKensie m 30 born Ireland.

MCKENSIE, MARGARET, 60, F, None listed, -, Ireland, 478, 436, CHAS. In HH of R.B. McKensie m 30 born Ireland.

MCKENSIE, R.B., 30, M, Sadler, -, Ireland, 478, 436, CHAS.

MCKENSIE, ROSE, 62, F, None listed, -, Ireland, 478, 436, CHAS. In HH of R.B. McKensie m 30 born Ireland.

MCKEOWAN, JOHN, 50, M, Planter, -, Ireland, 772, 773, FAIR.

MCKEOWN, CATHARINE, 80, F, None listed, -, Ireland, 2284, 2284, ABB.

MCKEOWN, MARY, 74, F, None listed, -, Ireland, 727, 727, CHES. In HH of H.C. McKeown m 37 born SC.

MCKEOWN, MOSES SR., 70, M, Farmer, -, Ireland, 804, 804, CHES.

MCKERNRY, SAMUEL, 27, M, Shoemaker, -, Ireland, 770, 728, CHAS+. In HH of W.C. McElheran m 31 born Ireland.

MCKETRIC, BENJAMIN, 52, M, Farmer, -, Ireland, 504, 504, ABB.

MCKINLEY, MICHAEL, 47, M, Planter, -, Ireland, 819, 820, FAIR.

MCKINNEY, CHARLES, 24, M, None, -, Ireland, 1883, 1883, SUMT. In Hotel.

MCKINNEY, JAMES, 69, M, Farmer, -, Ireland, 1046, 1047, AND*.

MCKINNEY, JAS. C., 30, M, None, -, Ireland, 1883, 1883, SUMT. In Hotel.

MCKINNEY, JOHN, 47, M, Farmer, -, Ireland, 565, 565, NEWB.

MCKUON, MARY, 40, F, None listed, -, Ireland, 38, 34, CHAS$.

MCLARNON, B., MRS., 50, F, None listed, -, Ireland, 26, 26, LANC.

MCLARRY, JANE, 12, F, None listed, -, Ireland, 496, 454, CHAS+. In HH of Thomas McLarry m 49 born Ireland.

MCLARRY, KATEY, 34, F, None listed, -, Ireland, 496, 454, CHAS+. In HH of Thomas McLarry m 49 born Ireland.

MCLARRY, MARY, 19, F, None listed, -, Ireland, 496, 454, CHAS+. In HH of Thomas McLarry m 49 born Ireland.

MCLARRY, THOMAS, 40, M, Plasterer, -, Ireland, 496, 454, CHAS+.

MCLAUCHLIN, SAML., 12, M, None listed, -, Ireland, 914,
914, CHES. In HH of Jane McLuchlin m 30 {sic} born SC.

MCLAUGHLIN, DANIEL, 26, M, Farmer, -, Ireland, 1613, 1613, SPART.

MCLAUGHLIN, EDWD., 23, M, Laborer, -, Ireland, 326, 295, CHAS+.

MCLAUGHLIN, MARY, 38, F, None listed, -, Ireland, 542, 557, RICH. In Lunatic Asylum.

MCLAUGHLIN, W., 29, M, Harness maker, -, Ireland, 88, 88, SPART. In HH of R.C. Poole m 48 born SC.

MCLESTERE, ALEXANDER, 58, M, Farmer, -, Ireland, 237, 237, CHES.

MCLESTERE, MARY, 58, F, None listed, -, Ireland, 237, 237, CHES. In HH of Alexander McLestere

MCLOSH, JOSEPH, 65, M, Clerk, -, Ireland, 1158, 1158, YORK.

MCLOSH, MARY, 53, F, None listed, -, Ireland, 1158, 1158, YORK. In HH of Joseph McLosh m 65 born Ireland.

MCLURE, M., 80, F, None listed, -, Ireland, 89, 89, CHES.

MCMAHAN, MARY, 77, F, None listed, -, Ireland, 740, 744, AND. In HH of Samuel McMahan m 62 born Ireland.

MCMAHAN, MICHAEL, 30, M, Laborer, -, Ireland, 389, 351, CHAS+. In HH of Edward Collins m 40 born Ireland.

MCMAHAN, SAMUEL, 62, M, Farmer, -, Ireland, 740, 744, AND.

MCMAHON, JAMES, 58, M, Cotton weigher, -, Ireland, 445, 457, RICH.

MCMAHON, JAMES S., 20, M, Clerk, -, Ireland, 445, 457, RICH. In HH of James McMahon m 58 born Ireland.

MCMAHON, MARY, 48, F, None listed, -, Ireland, 445, 457, RICH. In HH of James McMahon m 58 born Ireland.

MCMAHON, THOMAS, 30, M, Carriage maker, -, Ireland, 347, 353, RICH. In HH of Jane E. Reeder f 37 born MA.

MCMANIS, MARY, 38, F, None listed, -, Ireland, 4, 4, CHAS$.

MCMANUS, ANN, 32, F, None listed, -, Ireland, 22, 22, CHAS*. In HH of F.F. McManus m 40 born Ireland.

MCMANUS, CATHERINE, 22, F, None listed, -, Ireland, 714, 674, CHAS+. In HH of John McManus m 30 born Ireland.

MCMANUS, F.F., 40, M, Grocer, -, Ireland, 22, 22, CHAS*.

MCMANUS, JOHN, 30, M, Drayman, -, Ireland, 714, 674, CHAS+.

MCMASTER, JOHN, 63, M, P. Master, -, Ireland, 495, 495, FAIR. Occupation: P. Master & Merchant.

MCMELLAN, MARY, 28, F, None listed, -, Ireland, 78, 70, CHAS+. In HH of Thomas McMellan m 46 born Ireland.

MCMILLAN, ANN, 29, F, None listed, -, Ireland, 351, 351, CHES. In HH of Mary Thomas f 35 born Ireland.

MCMILLAN, JAS., 37, M, None, -, Ireland, 348, 348, CHES.

MCMILLAN, MARY, 29, F, None listed, -, Ireland, 50, 50, CHAS!. In HH of Thos. McMillan m 44 born Scotland.

MCMILLAN, WILLIAM G., 16, M, None listed, -, Ireland, 50, 50, CHAS!. In HH of Thos. McMillan m 44 born Scotland.

MCMILLAN, WM. B., 26, M, Mechanic, -, Ireland, 351, 351, CHES. In HH of Mary Thomas f 35 born Ireland.

MCMUKIN, ANDREW, 62, M, Planter, -, Ireland, 53, 53, FAIR.

MCMULLAN, WILLIAM, 44, M, Farmer, -, Ireland, 923, 923, LANC*.

MCMULLEN, PATRICK, 26, M, Laborer, -, Ireland, 237, 222, CHAS-. In Poor House.

MCMURRAY, MICHAEL, 50, M, Laborer, -, Ireland, 292, 269, CHAS+.

MCMURRY, MARY, 60, F, None listed, -, Ireland, 501, 501, SPART. In HH of R. McMurry m 63 born Ireland.

MCMURRY, R., 63, M, Farmer, -, Ireland, 501, 501, SPART.

MCNABB, HENRY, 21, M, Laborer, -, Ireland, 199, 182, CHAS*. In HH of John Kirk m 30 born Ireland.

MCNABB, WILLIAM, 17, M, Laborer, -, Ireland, 199, 182, CHAS*. In HH of John Kirk m 30 born Ireland.

MCNAMARA, CATH-
ERINE, 20, F, None listed, -,
Ireland, 422, 405, CHAS-. In
HH of A. Fogartie m 30 born
SC.

MCNAMARA, HANNAH,
50, F, Servant, -, Ireland, 103,
101, CHAS*. In HH of R.B.
Hayne f 55 born SC.

MCNAMARA, HUGH, 28,
M, Clerk, -, Ireland, 261, 244,
CHAS+.

MCNAMARA, MARIA, 24,
F, None listed, -, Ireland, 777,
760, CHAS%. In HH of Mary
Ann McGinnis f 56 born SC.

MCNAMARA, MARY, 38, F,
None listed, -, Ireland, 167,
158, CHAS+. In Boarding
house.

MCNAMARA, MICHAEL,
38, M, Laborer, -, Ireland, 777,
760, CHAS%. In HH of Mary
Ann McGinnis f 56 born SC.

MCNAMARRON, CATH-
ARINE, 5, F, None listed, -,
Ireland, 552, 544, CHAS%. In
HH of Michael McNamarron m
38 born Ireland.

MCNAMARRON, CATH-
ERINE, 36, F, None listed, -,
Ireland, 552, 544, CHAS%. In
HH of Michael McNamarron m
38 born Ireland.

MCNAMARRON, DANIEL,
12, M, None listed, -, Ireland,
552, 544, CHAS%. In HH of
Michael McNamarron m 38
born Ireland.

MCNAMARRON,EDMUND,
7, M, None listed, -, Ireland,
552, 544, CHAS%. In HH of
Michael McNamarron m 38
born Ireland.

MCNAMARRON, JOHN, 14,
M, None listed, -, Ireland, 552,
544, CHAS%. In HH of
Michael McNamarron m 38
born Ireland.

MCNAMARRON,
MICHAEL, 38, M, Laborer, -,
Ireland, 552, 544, CHAS%.

MCNAMARRON,
TIMOTHY, 3, F, None listed,
-, Ireland, 552, 544, CHAS%.
In HH of Michael McNamarron
m 38 born Ireland.

MCNAMEE, SUSAN E., 38,
F, None listed, -, Ireland, 329,
335, RICH.

MCNANCE, JOHN, 24, M,
Baker, -, Ireland, 40, 37,
CHAS-.Listed as prisoner, Date
1850.

MCNANLEY, PATRICK, 35,
M, Laborer, -, Ireland, 346, 308,
CHAS+. In Boarding house.

MCNEIL, ALEX., 34, M,
Farmer, -, Ireland, 814, 814,
CHES. In HH of Grace McNeil
f 67 born Ireland.

MCNEIL, ANN, 30, F, None
listed, -, Ireland, 814, 814,
CHES. In HH of Grace McNeil
f 67 born Ireland.

MCNEIL, ELIZA, 15, F,
None listed, -, Ireland, 814, 814,
ABB. In HH of Thomas
McNeil m 40 born Ireland.

MCNEIL, GRACE, 67, F,
None listed, -, Ireland, 814, 814,
CHES.

MCNEIL, JANE, 13, F, None
listed, -, Ireland, 814, 814,
ABB. In HH of Thomas
McNeil m 40 born Ireland.

MCNEIL, JOHN, 60, M, Planter, -, Ireland, 90, 90, FAIR.

MCNEIL, MARGAREAT, 6, F, None listed, -, Ireland, 814, 814, ABB. In HH of Thomas McNeil m 40 born Ireland.

MCNEIL, MARGARET, 36, F, None listed, -, Ireland, 814, 814, ABB. In HH of Thomas McNeil m 40 born Ireland.

MCNEIL, MARY, 26, F, None listed, -, Ireland, 814, 814, CHES. In HH of Grace McNeil f 67 born Ireland.

MCNEIL, ROBERT, 8, M, None listed, -, Ireland, 814, 814, ABB. In HH of Thomas McNeil m 40 born Ireland.

MCNEIL, SARAH, 55, F, None listed, -, Ireland, 90, 90, FAIR. In HH of John McNeil m 60 born Ireland.

MCNEIL, THOMAS, 40, M, Overseer, -, Ireland, 814, 814, ABB.

MCNEIL, WILLIAM, 10, M, None listed, -, Ireland, 814, 814, ABB. In HH of Thomas McNeil m 40 born Ireland.

MCNEILL, ARTHUR, 79, M, Planter, -, Ireland, 707, 716, RICH+.

MCNEILL, GEORGE, 40, M, Farmer, -, Ireland, 789, 789, CHES.

MCNEILL, MARGARET, 21, F, None listed, -, Ireland, 236, 211, CHAS*. In HH of Robert McNeill m 23 born England.

MCNEILL, MARY, 68, F, None listed, -, Ireland, 707, 716, RICH+. In HH of Arthur McNeill m 79 born Ireland.

MCNELLAGE, ELIZA-BETH, 22, F, Servant, -, Ireland, 285, 262, CHAS. In Planters Hotel.

MCNERVEY, ELLEN, 34, F, None listed, -, Ireland, 732, 723, CHAS%. In HH of Hugh Winters m 40 born Ireland.

MCNERVEY, JULIA, 12, F, None listed, -, Ireland, 732, 723, CHAS%. In HH of Hugh Winters m 40 born Ireland.

MCNERVEY, MICHAEL, 37, M, Laborer, -, Ireland, 732, 723, CHAS%. In HH of Hugh Winters m 40 born Ireland.

MCNETTY, MARGARET, 35, F, None listed, -, Ireland, 1003, 980, CHAS%. In HH of Timothy McNetty m 35 born Ireland.

MCNETTY, TIMOTHY, 35, M, Laborer, -, Ireland, 1003, 980, CHAS%.

MCNICHOLS, BRIDGET, 35, F, None listed, -, Ireland, 542, 557, RICH. Date 1844 by name. In Lunatic Asylum.

MCNINCH, J., 55, F, None listed, -, Ireland, 537, 537, CHES. In HH of Robert McNinch m 52 born Ireland.

MCNINCH, JAMES, 50, M, Farmer, -, Ireland, 434, 434, LAU.

MCNINCH, JOHN, 50, M, Farmer, -, Ireland, 796, 796, CHES.

MCNINCH, ROBERT., 52, M, Mechanic, -, Ireland, 537, 537, CHES.

MCNINCH, SAMUEL, 45, M, Stone cutter, -, Ireland, 780,

780, CHES.

MCOWEN, P., 70, M, Merchant, -, Ireland, 234, 219, CHAS-.

MCOWEN, PATRICK, 24, M, Laborer, -, Ireland, 1197, 1176, CHAS%. In Boarding house.

MCPHERSON, SARAH, 30, F, None listed, -, Ireland, 2299, 2299, GREE. In HH of James McPherson m 37 born Scotland.

MCQUISTON, ELIZA-BETH, 64, F, None listed, -, Ireland, 708, 708, CHES. In HH of Wm. McQuiston m 62 born SC.

MCRAE, ELLEN, 25, F, None listed, -, Ireland, 37, 37, CHAS*. In HH of Sarah M. Pringle f 45 born SC.

MCWHORTER, JANE, 40, F, None listed, -, Ireland, 287, 287, PICK+.

MCWILLIAMS, ALEX-ANDRE, 52, M, Farmer, -, Ireland, 271, 271, LAU.

MCWILLIAMS, DAVID, 60, M, Farmer, -, Ireland, 1574, 1574, ABB.

MCWILLIAMS, JANE A., 51, F, None listed, -, Ireland, 634, 634, ABB. In HH of Abasolam Gray m 39 born SC.

MCWILLIE, THO. W., 25, M, Clerk, -, Ireland, 753, 733, CHAS-. In HH of John McAllister m 37 born Ireland. In American Hotel.

MEIGHAN, JOHN, 21, M, Merchant, -, Ireland, 197, 201, RICH. In HH of Gouveneur M. Thompson m 48 born CT.

MELDON, JAMES, 23, M, Wheel right, -, Ireland, 128, 128, Beau+. In HH of Michael Doyle m 30 born Ireland. Elizabeth 4/12 mo.

MENOSTHON, JAMES, 41, M, Male spinner, -, Ireland, 1624, 1624, EDGE.

MENOSTHON, SARAH, 21, F, None listed, -, Ireland, 1624, 1624, EDGE. In HH of James Menosthon m 41 born Ireland.

MERAN, CATHERINE, 23, F, None listed, -, Ireland, 380, 345, CHAS. In HH of Patrick Meran m 26 born Ireland.

MERAN, FRANCIS, 27, M, Taylor, -, Ireland, 380, 345, CHAS. In HH of Patrick Meran m 26 born Ireland.

MERAN, JOHN, 21, M, Cooper, -, Ireland, 380, 345, CHAS. In HH of Patrick Meran m 26 born Ireland.

MERAN, PATRICK, 26, M, Clerk, -, Ireland, 380, 345, CHAS.

MEREDITH, ELIZA, 30, F, None listed, -, Ireland, 803, 786, CHAS%. In HH of R. Meredith m 35 born Ireland.

MEREDITH, R., 35, M, Shop keeper, -, Ireland, 803, 786, CHAS%.

MERRISON, CATHARINE, 5, F, None listed, -, Ireland, 687, 688, FAIR. In HH of Chesnut Merrison m 35 born Ireland.

MERRISON, CHESNUT, 35, M, Shoe maker, -, Ireland, 687, 688, FAIR.

MERRISON, MARGARET, 25, F, None listed, -, Ireland, 687, 688, FAIR. In HH of Chesnut Merrison m 35 born

Ireland.

METZLER, JOHN, 35, M, Laborer, -, Ireland, 481, 438, CHAS. In HH of George Belton m 50 born England.

MEYRS, BRIGET, 22, F, None listed, -, Ireland, 396, 358, CHAS+. In HH of J.J. Meyrs m 27 born England.

MICHOUALLY, WILLIAM, 34, M, Mariner, -, Ireland, 337, 311, CHAS. In HH of William H. Fowler m 38 running Boarding house born England.

MILAN, ELIZABETH, 28, F, None listed, -, Ireland, 278, 258, CHAS+. In HH of John Milan m 30 born Ireland.

MILAN, HENRY, 12, M, None listed, -, Ireland, 278, 258, CHAS+. In HH of John Milan m 30 born Ireland.

MILAN, JOHN, 30, M, Laborer, -, Ireland, 278, 258, CHAS+.

MILLAR, ROBERT, 18, M, Mariner, -, Ireland, 237, 222, CHAS-.Poor House.

MILLER, ANN, 32, F, None listed, -, Ireland, 643, 602, CHAS+. In HH of John Miller m 47 born Ireland.

MILLER, ANN, 60, F, None listed, -, Ireland, 332, 315, CHAS-. In HH of Samuel Duffy m 40 born Ireland.

MILLER, DANIEL, 9, M, None listed, -, Ireland, 643, 602, CHAS+. In HH of John Miller m 47 born Ireland.

MILLER, GEORGE, 20, M, Bricklayer, -, Ireland, 214, 192, CHAS. In HH of J.H. Miller m 28 born Ireland.

MILLER, J.H., 28, M, Bricklayer, -, Ireland, 214, 192, CHAS.

MILLER, JAMES, 34, M, Driver, -, Ireland, 592, 550, CHAS+.

MILLER, JANE, 32, F, None listed, -, Ireland, 592, 550, CHAS+. In HH of James Miller m 34 born Ireland.

MILLER, JANE, 35, F, None listed, -, Ireland, 109, 122, CHAS. In HH of John Miller m 59 born Germany.

MILLER, JOHN, 47, M, Caster, -, Ireland, 643, 602, CHAS+.

MILLER, JOHN, 63, M, Farmer, -, Ireland, 2269, 2269, ABB.

MILLER, MARTHA, 13, F, None listed, -, Ireland, 592, 550, CHAS+. In HH of James Miller m 34 born Ireland.

MILLER, PIERCE, 40, M, Cabinet maker, -, Ireland, 40, 37, CHAS-. Listed as prisoner.

MILLER, R.A., 60, F, None listed, -, Ireland, 78, 88, CHAS. In HH of Otis Mills m 53 born MA.

MILLER, ROBERT, 78, M, Planter, -, Ireland, 634, 643, RICH+.

MILLER, SARAH, 15, F, None listed, -, Ireland, 643, 602, CHAS+. In HH of John Miller m 47 born Ireland.

MILLER, SARAH J., 8, F, None listed, -, Ireland, 592, 550, CHAS+. In HH of James Miller m 34 born Ireland.

MILLER, THOMAS, 12, M, None listed, -, Ireland, 643, 602, CHAS+. In HH of John Miller

m 47 born Ireland.

MILLER, THOMAS, 24, M, Laborer, -, Ireland, 1197, 1176, CHAS%. In Boarding house.

MILLER, WILSON, 30, M, Stone cutter, -, Ireland, 63, 63, FAIR. In HH of Adna Johnson m 53 born CT.

MILLIGAN, JOHN, 30, M, Laborer, -, Ireland, 212, 199, CHAS+.

MILLIGAN, MARY, 27, F, None listed, -, Ireland, 212, 199, CHAS+. In HH of John Milligan m 30 born Ireland.

MILLIKIN, THOMAS, 70, M, Planter, -, Ireland, 864, 822, CHAS+.

MILLING, DAVID, 52, M, Planter, -, Ireland, 268, 268, FAIR.

MILLING, ELIZABETH, 50, F, None listed, -, Ireland, 306, 306, FAIR. In HH of Thomas Milling m 56 born Ireland.

MILLING, JAMES, 23, M, Clerk, -, Ireland, 313, 318, RICH. In HH of Robert Cathcart m 35 born Ireland.

MILLING, JOHN, 25, M, Planter, -, Ireland, 268, 268, FAIR. In HH of David Milling m 52 born Ireland.

MILLING, MARGARET, 26, F, None listed, -, Ireland, 306, 306, FAIR. In HH of Thomas Milling m 56 born Ireland.

MILLING, MARGARET, 26, F, None listed, -, Ireland, 306, 306, FAIR. In HH of Thomas Milling m 56 born Ireland.

MILLING, THOMAS, 56, M, Planter, -, Ireland, 306, 306, FAIR.

MINNIS, ROBERT, 28, M, Laborer, -, Ireland, 21, 24, CHAS.

MOFFATT, SAML., 83, M, None, -, Ireland, 60, 60, CHES.

MOLLOY, JAMES B., 53, M, Teaching school, -, Ireland, 1658, 1658, LAU.

MONOHON, THOS., 23, M, Taylor, -, Ireland, 1842, 1842, SUMT. In Hotel.

MONROE, MARGARET, 45, F, None listed, -, Ireland, 41, 41, YORK+. In HH of Robert Monroe m 68 born Chester Dist., SC.

MONTGOMERY, ANDREW, 56, M, Watch maker, -, Ireland, 1065, 1042, CHAS-.

MONTGOMERY, ANN, 22, F, None listed, -, Ireland, 11, 11, NEWB. In HH of James Cranford 38 m stone mason born SC.

MONTGOMERY, NANCY, 68, F, None listed, -, Ireland, 845, 846, FAIR.

MONTGOMERY, SAML., 53, M, Planter, -, Ireland, 264, 264, SUMT.

MOONEY, DENNIS, 54, M, Merchant, -, Ireland, 882, 840, CHAS+. In Charleston Hotel.

MOONEY, JOHN, 35, M, Laborer, -, Ireland, 464, 461, CHAS%. In HH of Thomas Cantwell m 45 born Ireland.

MOONEY, MARY, 64, F, None listed, -, Ireland, 460, 417, CHAS. In HH of Dinah Caldwell f 62 born SC.

MOONEY, PATRICK, 28,

M, Laborer, -, Ireland, 144, 135, CHAS+. In HH of Daniel Larry m 30 born Ireland.

MOONEY, PATRICK, 35, M, Laborer, -, Ireland, 202, 190, CHAS+. In Boarding house.

MOONEY, WILLIAM, 35, M, None, -, Ireland, 303, 309, RICH.

MOOR, THOMAS, 35, M, Farmer, -, Ireland, 1096, 1096, LAU.

MOORE, ANDREW, 39, M, Blacksmith, -, Ireland, 580, 580, YORK.

MOORE, BRIDGET, 25, F, Servant, -, Ireland, 273, 250, CHAS.

MOORE, CATHERINE, 11, F, None listed, -, Ireland, 123, 115, CHAS*. In HH of Mary Moore f 50 born Ireland.

MOORE, CATHERINE, 29, F, Servant, -, Ireland, 273, 250, CHAS. In HH of Bridget Moore m 25 born Ireland.

MOORE, DAVID, 31, M, Mason, -, Ireland, 1415, 1415, ABB.

MOORE, ELIZABETH, 63, F, None listed, -, Ireland, 580, 580, YORK. In HH of Andrew Moore m 39 born Ireland.

MOORE, JAMES, 20, M, Laborer, -, Ireland, 123, 115, CHAS*. In HH of Mary More f 50 born Ireland.

MOORE, JANE, 86, F, None listed, -, Ireland, 1415, 1415, ABB. In HH of David Moore m 37 born Ireland.

MOORE, JANNET, 32, F, None listed, -, Ireland, 1415, 1415, ABB. In HH of David Moore m 37 born Ireland.

MOORE, JENNY, 22, F, None listed, -, Ireland, 1416, 1416, ABB. In HH of Mary Moore f 66 born Ireland.

MOORE, JERRY, 33, M, Sailor, -, Ireland, 542, 557, RICH. Date 1850 by name. In Lunatic Asylum.

MOORE, JOHN, 17, M, Student, -, Ireland, 480, 446, CHAS*. In HH of Rt. Revd. Jgn. A. Reynolds m 51 born KY.

MOORE, JOHN, 50, M, Farmer, -, Ireland, 1483, 1483, ABB.

MOORE, JOHN A., 31, M, Lawyer, -, Ireland, 813, 823, RICH+.

MOORE, JULIA, 40, F, None listed, -, Ireland, 118, 112, CHAS*. In HH of Thomas Moore m 30 born Ireland.

MOORE, MARY, 26, F, None listed, -, Ireland, 1416, 1416, ABB. In HH of Mary Moore f 66 born Ireland.

MOORE, MARY, 50, F, None listed, -, Ireland, 123, 115, CHAS*.

MOORE, MARY, 66, F, None listed, -, Ireland, 1416, 1416, ABB.

MOORE, NANCY, 60, F, None listed, -, Ireland, 385, 385, ABB. In HH of John Workman m 28 born Ireland.

MOORE, PATRICK, 20, M, Laborer, -, Ireland, 118, 112, CHAS*. In HH of Thomas Moore m 30 born Ireland.

MOORE, PATRICK, 40, M, Merchant, -, Ireland, 189, 189, EDGE.

MOORE, ROSANNA, 81, F, None listed, -, Ireland, 1326,

1326, NEWB.

MOORE, SAMUEL J., 18, M, None listed, -, Ireland, 1416, 1416, ABB. In HH of Mary Moore f 66 born Ireland.

MOORE, THOMAS, 22, M, Carpenter, -, Ireland, 123, 115, CHAS*. In HH of Mary More f 50 born Ireland.

MOORE, THOMAS, 30, M, Laborer, -, Ireland, 118, 112, CHAS*.

MOORE, THOMAS, 96, M, Rev. Pensioner, -, Ireland, 2193, 2193, ABB.

MOORE, VAHALA, 26, F, None listed, -, Ireland, 580, 580, YORK. In HH of Andrew Moore m 39 born Ireland

MOORHEAD, JAMES, 50, M, Grocer, -, Ireland, 2, 2, CHAS-.

MOORING, ANN, 27, F, None listed, -, Ireland, 319, 303, CHAS-. In HH of C.Y. Richardson m 35 born England.

MORAN, ELIZA, 35, F, None listed, -, Ireland, 168, 168, CHAS%. In HH of William Moran m 30 born Ireland.

MORAN, JOHN A., 34, M, Carpenter, -, Ireland, 220, 207, CHAS+. In HH of Daraby Lyon m 40 born Ireland.

MORAN, MARY, 28, F, None listed, -, Ireland, 220, 207, CHAS+. In HH of Darby Lyon m 40 born Ireland.

MORAN, MICHAEL, 40, M, None listed, -, Ireland, 257, 257, CHAS%.

MORAN, WILLIAM, 30, M, Drayman, -, Ireland, 168, 168,

CHAS%.

MOREEN, JOHN, 35, M, Carpenter, -, Ireland, 635, 593, CHAS+.

MOREEN, MARY, 26, F, None listed, -, Ireland, 635, 593, CHAS+. In HH of John Moreen m 35 born Ireland.

MORELAND, ANDREW, 50, M, Merchant, -, Ireland, 3, 3, CHAS*.

MORGAN, MARY, 23, F, None listed, -, Ireland, 476, 459, CHAS-. In HH of George Black m 37 born Ireland.

MORRESON, ROBERT, 25, M, Laborer, -, Ireland, 54, 49, CHAS-. In HH of Robert Leckia m 28 born Ireland.

MORRIS, ELLEN, 23, F, None listed, -, Ireland, 166, 148, CHAS. In HH of John Jenkins m 25 born England.

MORRIS, JAMES, 9, M, None listed, -, Ireland, 174, 164, CHAS+. In HH of Richard Hogan m 36 born Ireland.

MORRIS, JAMES., 29, M, Tailor, -, Ireland, 14, 14, BEAU+.

MORRIS, JOANA, 4, F, None listed, -, Ireland, 174, 164, CHAS+. In HH of Richard Hogan m 36 born Ireland.

MORRIS, JOHN, 14, M, None listed, -, Ireland, 174, 164, CHAS+. In HH of Richard Hogan m 36 born Ireland.

MORRIS, MARGARET, 34, F, None listed, -, Ireland, 174, 164, CHAS+. In HH of Richard Hogan m 36 born Ireland.

MORRIS, PATRICK, 7, M, None listed, -, Ireland, 174, 164,

CHAS+. In HH of Richard Hogan m 36 born Ireland.

MORRIS, PATRICK, 40, M, Laborer, -, Ireland, 174, 164, CHAS+. In HH of Richard Hogan m 36 born Ireland.

MORRIS, RICHARD, 12, M, None listed, -, Ireland, 174, 164, CHAS+. In HH of Richard Hogan m 36 born Ireland.

MORRIS, ROBERT, 24, M, Stick maker, -, Ireland, 678, 658, CHAS-. In HH of Samuel S. Gammer m 30 born Ireland.

MORRIS, THOMAS, 16, M, None listed, -, Ireland, 174, 164, CHAS+. In HH of Richard Hogan m 36 born Ireland.

MORRIS, THOMAS, 18, M, Ordinance man, -, Ireland, 1005, 982, CHAS%.Under command of Major P. Hagnes, Comg. Off. U.S. Arnsel.

MORRIS, WILLIAM, 21, M, Laborer, -, Ireland, 166, 148, CHAS. In HH of John Jenkins m 25 born England.

MORRISON, ELIZA, 30, F, None listed, -, Ireland, 268, 249, CHAS+. In HH of Thomas Morrison m 36 born Ireland.

MORRISON, GRACE, 63, F, None listed, -, Ireland, 191, 179, CHAS-. In HH of Patrick OConnel m 35 born Ireland.

MORRISON, NANCY, 65, F, None listed, -, Ireland, 1589, 1589, ABB. In HH of William Morrison m 65 born Ireland.

MORRISON, S., 30, M, Bar Keeper, -, Ireland, 185, 168, CHAS.

MORRISON, THOMAS, 36, M, Laborer, -, Ireland, 268, 249, CHAS+.

MORRISON, WILLIAM, 65, M, Farmer, -, Ireland, 1589, 1589, ABB.

MORRISSON, ROBT., 21, M, None listed, -, Ireland, 687, 687, BARN. In HH of Nat. Ashley m 23 born SC.

MOSS, HUGH, 28, M, Coalpasser, -, Ireland, 326, 301, CHAS. In HH of William Rollins m 40 born {-}. In crew of the Steam Ship Isabel.

MOTEN, MARGARET, 45, F, None listed, -, Ireland, 279, 279, GEOR*.

MOUTTON, ELLENOR, 52, F, None listed, -, Ireland, 1005, 1005, CHES. In HH of Saml. L. Mutton m 63 born MA.

MULCKEY, CHARLES, 56, M, Miller, -, Ireland, 237, 222, CHAS-.Poor House.

MULHOLLAND, AGNES, 58, F, None listed, -, Ireland, 662, 662, UNION. In HH of Hamilton Mulholland m 56 born Ireland.

MULHOLLAND, HAMILTON, 56, M, Laborer, -, Ireland, 662, 662, UNION.

MULHOLLAND, ROBERT, 9, M, None listed, -, Ireland, 662, 662, UNION. In HH of Hamilton Mulholland m 56 born Ireland.

MULLERY, WILLIAM, 30, M, Clerk, -, Ireland, 259, 243, CHAS+. In HH of T.L. Quackenbush m 35 born NY.

MULLIGEN, CHARLES, 23, M, Laborer, -, Ireland, 921, 898, CHAS%. In HH of John Dewley m 32 born Ireland.

MULLIN, MATHEW C., 12, M, None listed, -, Ireland, 1106, 1083, CHAS-. In Charleston Orphan House.

MULLIN, NOLAND, 11, M, None listed, -, Ireland, 1106, 1083, CHAS-. In Charleston Orphan House.

MULLINS, C.P., 45, M, None listed, -, Ireland, 162, 145, CHAS. In HH of A.R. Tash m 23 born SC.

MULLINS, C.P., 45, M, None listed, -, Ireland, 162, 145, CHAS. In HH of A.R. Tash0 born St. Domingo.

MULLINS, JOHN, 68, M, Gardner, -, Ireland, 682, 662, CHAS-. In HH of James Gamble f 50 born Ireland.

MULLINS, SARAH, 45, F, None listed, -, Ireland, 122, 114, CHAS*. In HH of Margaret McDonald f 50 born Ireland.

MUNDLE, SAMUEL, 38, M, Planter, -, Ireland, 340, 340, FAIR.

MURDOCK, JAMES, 84, M, None listed, -, Ireland, 1272, 1272, ABB.

MURDOCK, PETER, 35, M, Laborer, -, Ireland, 40, 37, CHAS-.Listed as prisioner.

MURPHEY, CATHERINE, 28, F, None listed, -, Ireland, 16, 19, CHAS.

MURPHEY, CATHERINE, 28, F, None listed, -, Ireland, 884, 842, CHAS+. In HH of C.C. Pritchard m 40 born SC.

MURPHEY, ELIZA, 28, F, None listed, -, Ireland, 617, 609, CHAS%. In HH of James Murphey m 27 born Ireland.

MURPHEY, JAMES, 27, M, Clerk, -, Ireland, 617, 609, CHAS%.

MURPHEY, JAMES, 58, M, Laborer, -, Ireland, 36, 31, CHAS+.

MURPHEY, JOHN, 14, M, None listed, -, Ireland, 36, 31, CHAS+. In HH of James Murphey m 58 born Ireland.

MURPHEY, MARGARET, 35, F, None listed, -, Ireland, 168, 159, CHAS+. In HH of Thomas Murphey m 35 born Ireland.

MURPHEY, MARGARET, 36, F, None listed, -, Ireland, 395, 393, CHAS%. In HH of Thomas Murphey m 38 born Ireland.

MURPHEY, MARY, 28, F, None listed, -, Ireland, 575, 533, CHAS+. In HH of Richard Butler m 28 born NC.

MURPHEY, MICHAEL, 12, M, None listed, -, Ireland, 395, 393, CHAS%. In HH of Thomas Murphey m 38 born Ireland.

MURPHEY, PATRICK, 7, M, None listed, -, Ireland, 617, 609, CHAS%. In HH of James Murphey m 27 born Ireland.

MURPHEY, THOMAS, 31, M, Laborer, -, Ireland, 36, 31, CHAS+. In HH of James Murphey m 58 born Ireland.

MURPHEY, THOMAS, 35, M, Clerk, -, Ireland, 168, 159,

MURPHEY, THOMAS, 38, M, Bricklayer, -, Ireland, 395, 393, CHAS%.

MURPHY, CATHARIN, 29, F, None listed, -, Ireland, 915, 892, CHAS%. In HH of Samuel Page m 22 born SC.

MURPHY, EDMUND, 27, M, Merchant, -, Ireland, 182, 186, RICH.

MURPHY, JAMES, 62, M, None listed, -, Ireland, 659, 659, UNION.

MURPHY, JOHN, 16, M, Sadler, -, Ireland, 161, 148, CHAS*.

MURPHY, JOHN, 26, M, Laborer, -, Ireland, 388, 350, CHAS+. In HH of Andrew Bryan m 25 born Ireland.

MURPHY, JOHN, 66, M, Tailor, -, Ireland, 721, 722, FAIR. In poor house.

MURPHY, PETER, 34, M, Laborer, -, Ireland, 160, 147, CHAS*. In HH of George Walker m 45 born NH.

MURPHY, WILLIAM, 3, M, None listed, -, Ireland, 16, 19, CHAS. In HH of Catherine Murphy 28 f born Ireland.

MURPHY, WILLIAM, 17, M, Clerk, -, Ireland, 317, 291, CHAS+. In HH of Tim Kennedy m 71 born Ireland.

MURRAY, AGNESS, 23, F, None listed, -, Ireland, 190, 178, CHAS+. In HH of James Murray m 30 born Ireland.

MURRAY, ANN, 19, F, None listed, -, Ireland, 578, 561, CHAS-. In HH of Edward C. Jones m 38 born SC.

MURRAY, BARNEY, 37, M, Laborer, -, Ireland, 241, 227, CHAS+. In HH of James Kennedy m 30 born Ireland.

MURRAY, CHARLOTTE, 38, F, None listed, -, Ireland, 223, 201, CHAS.

MURRAY, DINAH, 3, F, None listed, -, Ireland, 340, 304, CHAS+. In HH of Patrick Murray m 30 born Ireland.

MURRAY, JAMES, 7, M, None listed, -, Ireland, 340, 304, CHAS+. In HH of Patrick Murray m 30 born Ireland.

MURRAY, JAMES, 16, F, None listed, -, Ireland, 209, 283, CHAS*. In HH of Joseph Murray m 38 born Ireland.

MURRAY, JAMES, 30, M, Laborer, -, Ireland, 190, 178, CHAS+.

MURRAY, JAMES, 34, M, Stone cutter, -, Ireland, 63, 63, FAIR. In HH of Adna Johnson m 53 born CT.

MURRAY, JAMES, 34, M, Stone cutter, -, Ireland, 147, 151, RICH. In HH out of order, follows 185/189.

MURRAY, JOSEPH, 6, M, None listed, -, Ireland, 209, 283, CHAS*. In HH of Joseph Murray m 38 born Ireland.

MURRAY, JOSEPH, 38, M, Sexton, -, Ireland, 209, 283, CHAS*.Occupation: Sexton St. Finburs Church.

MURRAY, MARY, 28, F, None listed, -, Ireland, 340, 304, CHAS+. In HH of Patrick Murray m 30 born Ireland.

MURRAY, MARY ANN, 5, F, None listed, -, Ireland, 209,

283, CHAS*. In HH of Joseph
Murray m 38 born Ireland.

MURRAY, MARY ANN, 26,
F, None listed, -, Ireland, 209,
283, CHAS*. In HH of Joseph
Murray m 38 born Ireland.

MURRAY, MARY ANN, 45,
F, None listed, -, Ireland, 279,
263, CHAS-. In HH of Ann
Guerard f 50 born SC.

MURRAY, MICHAEL, 11,
M, None listed, -, Ireland, 209,
283, CHAS*. In HH of Joseph
Murray m 38 born Ireland.

MURRAY, PATRICK, 30,
M, Laborer, -, Ireland, 340,
304, CHAS+.

MURRAY, PATRICK, 34,
M, Fireman, -, Ireland, 326,
301, CHAS. In HH of William
Rollins m 40 born {-}.

MURRAY, PATRICK, 35,
M, Laborer, -, Ireland, 118,
112, CHAS*. In HH of
Thomas Moore m 30 born
Ireland.

MURREY, BRIGET, 28, F,
None listed, -, Ireland, 379,
362, CHAS-. In HH of S.
Moury, Jr. m 50 born RI.

MURREY, MICHAEL, 32,
M, Ordinance man, -, Ireland,
1005, 982, CHAS%.Under
command of Major P. Hagnes,
Comg. Off. U.S. Arnsel.

MURRY, CATHERINE, 34,
F, None listed, -, Ireland, 2300,
2300, GREE. In HH of
Thomas Murry m 40 born
Ireland.

MURRY, THOMAS, 40, M,
Boot maker, -, Ireland, 2300,
2300, GREE.

NABORS, JANE, 70, F, None
listed, -, Ireland, 1170, 1170,
NEWB.

NAGLE, DENNIS, 30, M,
Clerk, -, Ireland, 253, 238,
CHAS+. In HH of John Dunn
m 32 born Ireland.

NAGLE, ELLEN, 2, F, None
listed, -, Ireland, 253, 238,
CHAS+. In HH of John Dunn
m 32 born Ireland.

NAGLE, ELLEN, 27, F, None
listed, -, Ireland, 214, 201,
CHAS+.

NAGLE, J., 21, F, None listed,
-, Ireland, 253, 238, CHAS+. In
HH of John Dunn m 32 born
Ireland.

NAGLE, JOANA, 1, F, None
listed, -, Ireland, 253, 238,
CHAS+. In HH of John Dunn
m 32 born Ireland.

NAGLE, LAWRENCE, 34,
M, Laborer, -, Ireland, 214, 201,
CHAS+. In HH of Ellen Nagle
f 27 born Ireland.

NEAL, ELIZABETH, 75, F,
None listed, -, Ireland, 1584,
1584, ABB. In HH of William
McIlwain m 56 born Ireland.

NEAL, HAIGH, 71, M,
Farmer, -, Ireland, 64, 64,
EDGE*.

NEIL, CATHARINE, 39, F,
None listed, -, Ireland, 1160,
1161, FAIR. In HH of James C.
Neil m 43 born SC.

NELSON, FRANK, 34, M,
Farmer, -, Ireland, 767, 767,
CHES.

NELSON, ISABELLA, 66, F,
None listed, -, Ireland, 792, 792,

CHES. In HH of Robt. Nelson m 68 born Ireland.

NELSON, JANE, 16, F, None listed, -, Ireland, 1541, 1541, CHES. In HH of John Nelson m 44 born Ireland.

NELSON, JAS., 13, M, None listed, -, Ireland, 1541, 1541, CHES. In HH of John Nelson m 44 born Ireland.

NELSON, JOHN, 9, M, None listed, -, Ireland, 1541, 1541, CHES. In HH of John Nelson m 44 born Ireland.

NELSON, JOHN, 9, M, None listed, -, Ireland, 1541, 1541, CHES. In HH of John Nelson m 44 born Ireland.

NELSON, JOHN, 44, M, Hatter, -, Ireland, 1541, 1541, CHES.

NELSON, MARGARET, 11, F, None listed, -, Ireland, 1541, 1541, CHES. In HH of John Nelson m 44 born Ireland.

NELSON, ROBT., 68, M, Farmer, -, Ireland, 792, 792, CHES.

NESBIT, ROBERT, 64, M, Farmer, -, Ireland, 685, 685, YORK.

NEVIN, PATRICK, 30, M, Butcher, -, Ireland, 496, 489, CHAS%. In HH of James McCarey m 28 born Ireland.

NEWCOMB, JOHN, 31, M, Laborer, -, Ireland, 237, 222, CHAS-.Poor House.

NEWMAN, SARAH ANN, 19, F, None listed, -, Ireland, 585, 585, UNION. In HH of Thomas Newman m 22 born SC.

NEWSTEAD, THOMAS, 28,

M, Laborer, -, Ireland, 237, 222, CHAS-.Poor House.

NICHOLSON, DORCAS, 25, F, None listed, -, Ireland, 189, 177, CHAS-. In HH of Ann Schine f 30 born Ireland.

NICKLIN, WM., 24, M, Painter, -, Ireland, 124, 115, CHAS+. In Boarding house.

NIELAND, P., 19, M, Priv. U.S.A., -, Ireland, 47, 43, CHAS$. In HH of John Ewing m 50 born MA.

NIPPERS, MARY, 8, F, None listed, -, Ireland, 553, 519, CHAS*. In Catholic Seminary.

NOLAN, JOHN, 35, M, Laborer, -, Ireland, 11, 10, CHAS-.

NOLAND, ISABELLA, 32, F, None listed, -, Ireland, 187, 170, CHAS. In HH of Thomas Noland m 40 born Ireland.

NOLAND, JOHN, 45, M, Wheelwright, -, Ireland, 338, 303, CHAS+. In HH of Bernard Sweeney m 37 born Ireland.

NOLAND, JOHN JR., 16, M, Blacksmith, -, Ireland, 338, 303, CHAS+. In HH of Bernard Sweeney m 37 born Ireland.

NOLAND, MARY, 50, F, None listed, -, Ireland, 754, 712, CHAS+. In HH of F.M. Robertson m 40 born SC.

NOLAND, ROSANA, 25, F, None listed, -, Ireland, 803, 786, CHAS%. In HH of R. Meredith m 35 born Ireland.

NOLAND, THOMAS, 28, M, Laborer, -, Ireland, 322, 294, CHAS+. In HH of John Dowling m 34 born Ireland.

NOLAND, THOMAS, 40, M,

Stevedore, -, Ireland, 187, 170, CHAS.

NORRIS, JANE, 24, F, None listed, -, Ireland, 788, 746, CHAS+. In HH of William Norris m 28 born Ireland.

NORRIS, MARY, 19, F, None listed, -, Ireland, 788, 746, CHAS+. In HH of William Norris m 28 born Ireland.

NORRIS, NANCY, 50, F, None listed, -, Ireland, 788, 746, CHAS+. In HH of William Norris m 28 born Ireland.

NORRIS, WILLIAM, 28, M, None listed, -, Ireland, 788, 746, CHAS+.

NORTON, CATHERINE, 50, F, None listed, -, Ireland, 471, 486, RICH. In HH of George Boland m 33 born Ireland.

NORTON, JOHN JOHNSON, 55, M, Tailor, -, Ireland, 1500, 1500, ABB. In HH of William Norton m 27 born SC.

NUGENT, FRANCES, 23, F, None listed, -, Ireland, 821, 801, CHAS-. In HH of August Pelerun m 31 born France.

NUGENT, HENRY M., 4, M, None listed, -, Ireland, 121, 113, CHAS*. In HH of P. Nugent f 30 born Ireland.

NUGENT, MARGARET ANN, 9, F, None listed, -, Ireland, 121, 113, CHAS*. In HH of P. Nugent f 30 born Ireland.

NUGENT, MARY JANE, 7, F, None listed, -, Ireland, 121,

113, CHAS*. In HH of P. Nugent f 30 born Ireland.

NUGENT, P., 30, F, None listed, -, Ireland, 121, 113, CHAS*.

NUNAN, BRIDGET, 30, F, None listed, -, Ireland, 131, 123, CHAS*. In HH of William Nunan m 39 born Ireland.

NUNAN, CATHERINE, 23, F, None listed, -, Ireland, 1220, 1199, CHAS%. In HH of George Nunan m 35 born Ireland.

NUNAN, GEORGE, 35, M, Farmer, -, Ireland, 1220, 1199, CHAS%.

NUNAN, WILLIAM, 39, M, Laborer, -, Ireland, 131, 123, CHAS*.

O

O CALLAGHAM, PATRICK, 40, M, Laborer, -, Ireland, 245, 223, CHAS.

O CONNELL, JOHN, 39, M, Laborer, -, Ireland, 351, 324, CHAS. In Boarding house.

O'BRIAN, JAMES, 36, M, Laborer, -, Ireland, 412, 372, CHAS. In HH of Christopher King m 23 born Ireland.

O'BRIAN, MARGARET, 30, F, None listed, -, Ireland, 412, 372, CHAS. In HH of Christopher King m 23 born Ireland.

O'BRYAN, JOHN, 22, M, Laborer, -, Ireland, 921, 898, CHAS%. In HH of John Dewley m 32 born Ireland.

O'CALLAGHAN, DENNIS, 10, M, None listed, -, Ireland,

690, 682, CHAS%. In HH of Dennis O'Callaghan m 38 born Ireland.

O'CALLAGHAN, DENNIS, 38, M, Bricklayer, -, Ireland, 690, 682, CHAS%.

O'CALLAGHAN, MARY ANN, 12, F, None listed, -, Ireland, 690, 682, CHAS%. In HH of Dennis O'Callaghan m 38 born Ireland.

O'CALLAGHAN, SABINA, 34, F, None listed, -, Ireland, 690, 682, CHAS%. In HH of Dennis O'Callaghan m 38 born Ireland.

O'CONNELL, ELLEN, 23, F, None listed, -, Ireland, 79, 77, CHAS*. In HH of John Mahoney m 40 born Ireland.

O'CONNELL, JEREMIAH J., 30, M, R.C. Clergyman, -, Ireland, 207, 211, RICH.

O'CONNELL, LAURENCE P., 24, M, R.C. Clergyman, -, Ireland, 207, 211, RICH. In HH of Jeremiah J. O'Connell m 30 born Ireland.

O'CONNELL, PATRICK O., 65, M, None, -, Ireland, 207, 211, RICH. In HH of Jeremiah J. O'Connell m 30 born Ireland.

O'CONNER, ANN, 22, F, None listed, -, Ireland, 1874, 1874, SUMT. In HH of John O'Conner m 26 born Ireland.

O'CONNER, F., 60, M, Farmer, -, Ireland, 205, 205, EDGE.

O'CONNER, JOHN, 17, M, Blacksmith, -, Ireland, 1908, 1908, SUMT. In HH of T.J. Coughlan m 45 born NC.

O'CONNER, JOHN, 26, M,

Baker, -, Ireland, 1874, 1874, SUMT.

O'CONNER, MICHAEL, 57, M, Store Keeper, -, Ireland, 145, 145, BEAU.

O'CONNOR, WM., 45, M, Tailor, -, Ireland, 23, 23, NEWB. In HH of J. Wilson 33 m Hotel Keeper born SC.

O'CONORON, BARNEY, 35, M, Attendant, -, Ireland, 542, 557, RICH. In Lunatic Asylum.

O'DONNEL, EMMA, 40, F, None listed, -, Ireland, 394, 392, CHAS%. In HH of John O'Connel m 45 born Ireland.

O'DONNEL, JOHN, 45, M, Plasterer, -, Ireland, 394, 392, CHAS%.

O'DONNEL, THOMAS, 15, M, None listed, -, Ireland, 394, 392, CHAS%. In HH of John O'Connel m 45 born Ireland.

O'DONNEL, THOMAS, 34, M, Stone cutter, -, Ireland, 461, 461, NEWB. In HH of Hugh Wilson, 60 m born SC.

O'FARREL, CATHERINE, 32, F, None listed, -, Ireland, 89, 89, YORK+. In HH of Thomas O'Farrel m 38 born Ireland.

O'FARREL, THOMAS, 38, M, Stonemason, -, Ireland, 89, 89, YORK+.

O'FERRIL, PATRICK, 57, M, Merchant, -, Ireland, 89, 89, NEWB.

O'HARMAN, TERRENCE, 90, M, Merchant, -, Ireland, 511, 511, FAIR.

O'KEFE, CORNELIUS, 24, M, Clerk, -, Ireland, 63, 64, RICH.

O'MALLARY, JOHN, 23, M, Journeyman, -, Ireland, 520, 520, FAIR. In HH of David Cremer m 49 born NJ.

O'NEAL, CATHARINE, 49, F, None listed, -, Ireland, 458, 458, DARL. In HH of Griffin O'Neal m 60 born Ireland.

O'NEAL, GRIFFIN, 60, M, Farmer, -, Ireland, 458, 458, DARL.

O'NEAL, MAXWELL, 70, M, Farmer, -, Ireland, 460, 460, DARL.

O'NEAL, MICHAEL, 34, M, Wheelwright, -, Ireland, 203, 203, CHAS%.

O'NEALL, BARNEY, 59, M, Farmer, -, Ireland, 841, 841, UNION.

O'NEIL, SINEY, 57, F, None listed, -, Ireland, 668, 668, NEWB. In HH of Piercy Slattery f 28 born SC.

O'WEN, G.D., 47, F, None listed, -, Ireland, 465, 422, CHAS. In HH of Leslie O'Wen m 47 born Ireland.

O'WEN, LESLIE, 47, M, Dentist, -, Ireland, 465, 422, CHAS. In HH of Leslie O'Wen m 47 born Ireland.

O.MARA, JAMES, 35, M, Laborer, -, Ireland, 166, 148, CHAS. In HH of John Jenkins m 25 born England.

OBRIAN, ALICE, 30, F, None listed, -, Ireland, 125, 116, CHAS+.

OBRIAN, ALLMONG, 40, F, None listed, -, Ireland, 419, 377, CHAS. In HH of Thomas OBrian m 39 born Ireland.

OBRIAN, AMELILA, 14, F, None listed, -, Ireland, 448, 405, CHAS. In HH of Dan OBrian m 54 born Ireland.

OBRIAN, ANN, 18, F, None listed, -, Ireland, 992, 971, CHAS-. In HH of S.B. Bernard m 38 born France.

OBRIAN, BRIGET, 17, F, None listed, -, Ireland, 719, 699, CHAS-. In HH of Teddy OBrian m 36 born Ireland.

OBRIAN, CATHARINE, 14, F, None listed, -, Ireland, 1655, 1655, EDGE. In HH of Micheal Obrian m 36 born Ireland.

OBRIAN, DAN, 54, M, Laborer, -, Ireland, 448, 405, CHAS.

OBRIAN, DAN., 18, M, Gass fitter, -, Ireland, 448, 405, CHAS. In HH of Dan OBrian m 54 born Ireland.

OBRIAN, DENNIS, 30, M, Laborer, -, Ireland, 326, 295, CHAS+. In HH of Edwd McLaughlin m 23 born Ireland.

OBRIAN, ELLEN, 12, F, None listed, -, Ireland, 1655, 1655, EDGE. In HH of Micheal Obrian m 36 born Ireland.

OBRIAN, ELLEN, 35, F, None listed, -, Ireland, 419, 377, CHAS. In HH of Thomas OBrian m 39 born Ireland.

OBRIAN, HONORE, 20, F, None listed, -, Ireland, 992, 971, CHAS-. In HH of S.B. Bernard m 38 born France.

OBRIAN, JOHN, 9, M, None listed, -, Ireland, 448, 405, CHAS. In HH of Dan OBrian m 54 born Ireland.

OBRIAN, JOHN, 36, M, Laborer, -, Ireland, 326, 295, CHAS+. In HH of Edwd McLaughlin m 23 born Ireland.

OBRIAN, KATE, 30, F, None listed, -, Ireland, 719, 699, CHAS-. In HH of Teddy OBrian m 36 born Ireland.

OBRIAN, MARGARET, 48, F, None listed, -, Ireland, 448, 405, CHAS. In HH of Dan OBrian m 54 born Ireland.

OBRIAN, MARY, 40, F, None listed, -, Ireland, 1655, 1655, EDGE. In HH of Micheal Obrian m 36 born Ireland.

OBRIAN, MAURICE, 21, M, Laborer, -, Ireland, 719, 699, CHAS-. In HH of Teddy OBrian m 36 born Ireland.

OBRIAN, MICHEAL, 36, M, Laborer, -, Ireland, 1655, 1655, EDGE.

OBRIAN, PATRICK, 30, M, Laborer, -, Ireland, 326, 295, CHAS+. In HH of Edwd McLaughlin m 23 born Ireland.

OBRIAN, SARAH, 12, F, None listed, -, Ireland, 448, 405, CHAS. In HH of Dan OBrian m 54 born Ireland.

OBRIAN, SARAH, 19, F, None listed, -, Ireland, 553, 519, CHAS*. In Catholic Seminary.

OBRIAN, SUSAN, 37, M, None listed, -, Ireland, 448, 405, CHAS. In HH of Dan OBrian m 54 born Ireland.

OBRIAN, TEDDY, 36, M, Laborer, -, Ireland, 719, 699, CHAS-.

OBRIAN, TERRANCE, 34, M, Gass fitter, -, Ireland, 448, 405, CHAS. In HH of Dan OBrian m 54 born Ireland.

OBRIAN, THOMAS, 39, M, Stable keeper, -, Ireland, 419, 377, CHAS.

OBRIEN, BRIGET, 25, F, None listed, -, Ireland, 266, 249, CHAS+. In HH of Timothy OBrien m 27 born Ireland.

OBRIEN, EDWARD, 24, M, Carpenter, -, Ireland, 190, 174, CHAS*. In HH of William Edward m 30 born NY.

OBRIEN, TIMOTHY, 27, M, Laborer, -, Ireland, 266, 249, CHAS+.

OBRYAN, JOHN, 32, M, Laborer, -, Ireland, 292, 269, CHAS+. In HH of Michael McMurray m 50 born Ireland.

OCALLAGHAM, BRIDGET, 18, F, None listed, -, Ireland, 245, 223, CHAS. In HH of Patrick OCallagham m 49 born Ireland.

OCALLAGHAM, BRIGET, 25, F, Servant, -, Ireland, 882, 840, CHAS+. In Charleston Hotel.

OCALLAGHAM, CAM-ETTA, 38, F, None listed, -, Ireland, 245, 223, CHAS. In HH of Patrick OCallagham m 49 born Ireland.

OCALLAGHAM, CON-STANCE, 14, F, None listed, -, Ireland, 245, 223, CHAS. In HH of Patrick OCallagham m 49 born Ireland.

OCALLAGHAM, DORCAS, 9, F, None listed, -, Ireland, 245, 223, CHAS. In HH of Patrick OCallagham m 49 born Ireland.

OCALLAGHAM, ED-WARD, 24, M, None listed, -, Ireland, 245, 223, CHAS. In HH of Patrick OCallagham m 49 born Ireland.

OCALLAGHAM, MARY, 22, F, None listed, -, Ireland, 245, 223, CHAS. In HH of Patrick OCallagham m 49 born Ireland.

OCALLAGHAN, DENNIS, 31, M, Laborer, -, Ireland, 259, 243, CHAS+. In HH of T.L. Quackenbush m 35 born NY.

OCALLAGHAN, JOHN, 21, M, Laborer, -, Ireland, 1197, 1176, CHAS%. In Boarding house.

OCANE, GELNDELL, 25, M, Clerk, -, Ireland, 94, 86, CHAS+. In HH of Bernard ONeill m 28 born Ireland.

OCANE, PATRICK, 22, M, Clerk, -, Ireland, 94, 86, CHAS+. In HH of Bernard ONeill m 28 born Ireland.

OCONNEL, JOHN, 30, M, Laborer, -, Ireland, 871, 829, CHAS+. In HH of John H. Margarat m 68 born SC.

OCONNEL, MARGARET, 30, F, None listed, -, Ireland, 191, 179, CHAS-. In HH of Patrick OConnel m 35 born Ireland.

OCONNEL, MARGARET, 30, F, None listed, -, Ireland, 871, 829, CHAS+. In HH of John H. Margarat m 68 born SC.

OCONNEL, PATRICK, 35, M, Laborer, -, Ireland, 191, 179, CHAS-.

OCONNELL, JOSEPH, 17, M, Student, -, Ireland, 480, 446, CHAS*. In HH of Rt. Revd. Jgn. A. Reynolds m 51 born KY.

OCONNER, BRIGET, 11, F, None listed, -, Ireland, 604, 562, CHAS+. In HH of Pat. OConner m 40 born Ireland.

OCONNER, BRIGET, 30, F, None listed, -, Ireland, 839, 797, CHAS+. In HH of George B. Locke m 52 born MA.

OCONNER, CATHERINE, 20, F, None listed, -, Ireland, 604, 562, CHAS+. In HH of Pat. OConner m 40 born Ireland.

OCONNER, D., 22, M, Gunsmith, -, Ireland, 784, 764, CHAS-.

OCONNER, DENNIS, 40, M, Laborer, -, Ireland, 188, 177, CHAS+. In HH of Mary OConner f 30 born Ireland.

OCONNER, ELLEN, 7, F, None listed, -, Ireland, 188, 177, CHAS+. In HH of Mary OConner f 30 born Ireland.

OCONNER, JULIA, 17, F, None listed, -, Ireland, 604, 562, CHAS+. In HH of Pat. OConner m 40 born Ireland.

OCONNER, MARY, 19, F, None listed, -, Ireland, 784, 764, CHAS-. In HH of D. OConner m 22 born Ireland.

OCONNER, MARY, 30, F, None listed, -, Ireland, 188, 177, CHAS+.

OCONNER, MARY, 38, F, None listed, -, Ireland, 604, 562, CHAS+. In HH of Pat. OConner m 40 born Ireland.

OCONNER, PAT., 40, M,

Laborer, -, Ireland, 604, 562, CHAS+.

OCONNER, PATRICK, 30, M, Clerk, -, Ireland, 124, 115, CHAS+. In Boarding house.

OCONNER, TIMOTHY, 15, M, None listed, -, Ireland, 604, 562, CHAS+. In HH of Pat. OConner m 40 born Ireland.

ODONNAHOUGH, MARY, 22, F, Servant, -, Ireland, 882, 840, CHAS+. In Charleston Hotel.

ODONNELL, CATHERINE, 38, F, None listed, -, Ireland, 292, 269, CHAS+. In HH of Michael McMurray m 50 born Ireland.

ODONNELL, JAMES, 27, M, Laborer, -, Ireland, 292, 269, CHAS+. In HH of Michael McMurray m 50 born Ireland.

ODONNELL, WILLIAM, 25, M, 3nd Cook, -, Ireland, 326, 301, CHAS. In HH of William Rollins m 40 born {-}.

OFLAHERTY, BRIGET, 32, F, Servant, -, Ireland, 882, 840, CHAS+. In Charleston Hotel.

OFLAHERTY, BRIGET, 35, F, None listed, -, Ireland, 531, 490, CHAS+. In HH of H.W. Kuhtmann m 35 born Germany.

OGLEGY, DANIL., 30, M, Farmer, -, Ireland, 246, 246, CHES. In HH of Wm. Omelveney m 46 born SC.

OGLESLY, JOHN, 48, M, Farmer, -, Ireland, 1611, 1611, SPART.

OGRADY, MARY, 41, F, None listed, -, Ireland, 1119, 1096, CHAS-. In HH of W.P. Finley m 47 born SC.

OGRE, JEREMIAH, 37, M, Clerk, -, Ireland, 415, 373, CHAS. In HH of Mary Eugene Ogre f 30 born Ireland.

OGRE, MARY EUGENE, 30, F, None listed, -, Ireland, 415, 373, CHAS.

OHARA, DANIEL, 45, M, Mariner, -, Ireland, 183, 172, CHAS+. In HH of W. Vironee m 50 born SC.

OHARA, JAMES, 13, M, None listed, -, Ireland, 885, 865, CHAS-. In HH of Richard Baker m 44 born Ireland.

OHARA, WM. P., 23, M, Clerk, -, Ireland, 520, 479, CHAS+. In HH of William Mathiepen m born SC.

OHEAREY, ROSE A., 39, F, None listed, -, Ireland, 63, 63, YORK+.

OKEEFE, DAVID, 30, M, Laborer, -, Ireland, 222, 209, CHAS+. In HH of John Donnahugh m 22 born Ireland.

OKEEFE, MICHAEL, 30, M, City Police, -, Ireland, 124, 115, CHAS+. In Boarding house.

OKEEFFE, MICHEAL, 37, M, Merchant, -, Ireland, 2008, 2014, EDGE.

OLIVER, BRIGET, 43, F, None listed, -, Ireland, 74, 72, CHAS*. In HH of Joseph H. Oliver m 50 born England.

OLIVER, MARGARET, 40, F, None listed, -, Ireland, 1005, 982, CHAS%.Under command of Major P. Hagnes, Comg. Off. U.S. Arnsel.

OMARA, JAMES, 5, M, None listed, -, Ireland, 636, 594, CHAS+. In HH of Simon OMara m 40 born Ireland.

OMARA, JOHN, 35, M, Shop keeper, -, Ireland, 86, 80, CHAS-.

OMARA, MAGDELINE, 9, F, None listed, -, Ireland, 636, 594, CHAS+. In HH of Simon OMara m 40 born Ireland.

OMARA, MARGARET, 35, F, None listed, -, Ireland, 636, 594, CHAS+. In HH of Simon OMara m 40 born Ireland.

OMARA, SIMON, 40, M, Laborer, -, Ireland, 636, 594, CHAS+.

OMARA, THEODORE, 12, M, None listed, -, Ireland, 636, 594, CHAS+. In HH of Simon OMara m 40 born Ireland.

OMARA, URSULINE, 7, F, None listed, -, Ireland, 636, 594, CHAS+. In HH of Simon OMara m 40 born Ireland.

OMELVENEY, HUGH, 56, M, Farmer, -, Ireland, 246, 246, CHES. In HH of Wm. Omelveney m 46 born SC.

OMELVENEY, SARAH, 38, F, None listed, -, Ireland, 246, 246, CHES. In HH of Wm. Omelveney m 46 born SC.

OMENE, EDWARD, 32, M, Clerk, -, Ireland, 94, 86, CHAS+. In HH of Bernard ONeill m 28 born Ireland.

ONEAL, BERTHA, 31, F, None listed, -, Ireland, 637, 595, CHAS+. In HH of James ONeal m 39 born Ireland.

ONEAL, ELLEN, 20, F, None listed, -, Ireland, 240, 226, CHAS+. In HH of William Farley m 38 born Ireland.

ONEAL, J., 40, M, Laborer, -, Ireland, 165, 156, CHAS+. In

HH of F. Schecter f 50 born Germany.

ONEAL, JAMES, 15, M, None, -, Ireland, 209, 189, CHAS*. In HH of John ONeal m 34 born Ireland.

ONEAL, JAMES, 39, M, None listed, -, Ireland, 637, 595, CHAS+.

ONEAL, JAMES, 43, M, Shoemaker, -, Ireland, 23, 19, CHAS+.

ONEAL, JOHN, 34, M, Police, -, Ireland, 209, 189, CHAS*.

ONEAL, JOHN, 34, M, Laborer, -, Ireland, 1197, 1176, CHAS%. In Boarding house.

ONEAL, MARY, 14, F, None listed, -, Ireland, 637, 595, CHAS+. In HH of James ONeal m 39 born Ireland.

ONEAL, PATRICK, 25, M, Laborer, -, Ireland, 240, 226, CHAS+. In HH of William Farley m 38 born Ireland.

ONEAL, PATRICK, 59, M, Planter, -, Ireland, 1079, 1057, CHAS%.

ONEAL, SUSAN, 35, F, None listed, -, Ireland, 165, 156, CHAS+. In HH of F. Schecter f 50 born Germany.

ONEAL, THOMAS, 50, M, Shoemaker, -, Ireland, 23, 19, CHAS+. In HH of James ONeal m 43 born Ireland.

ONEALE, JAMES, 51, M, Carpenter, -, Ireland, 76, 70, CHAS-.

ONEALE, JOHN, 20, M, Laborer, -, Ireland, 332, 298, CHAS+. In HH of Joseph Fowler m 28 born England.

ONEALE, SARAH E., 50, F, None listed, -, Ireland, 76, 70, CHAS-. In HH of James ONeale m 51 born Ireland.

ONEALE, THOMAS B., 21, M, Clerk, -, Ireland, 76, 70, CHAS-. In HH of James ONeale m 51 born Ireland.

ONEALE, WILLIAM T., 17, M, Clerk, -, Ireland, 76, 70, CHAS-. In HH of James ONeale m 51 born Ireland.

ONEIL, DENNIS, 60, M, Laborer, -, Ireland, 817, 827, RICH+.

ONEILE, EDMUND, 60, M, None, -, Ireland, 793, 776, CHAS%. In HH of B. Burghman m 48 born Germany.

ONEILE, ELIRA, 30, F, None listed, -, Ireland, 390, 354, CHAS. In HH of Hugh ONeile m 30 born Ireland.

ONEILE, HUGH, 30, M, Sadler, -, Ireland, 390, 354, CHAS.

ONEILL, ANASTACIA, 24, F, None listed, -, Ireland, 1098, 1075, CHAS-. In HH of P. ONeill m 37 born Ireland.

ONEILL, BERNARD, 28, M, Merchant, -, Ireland, 94, 86, CHAS+.

ONEILL, ELIZA, 18, F, None listed, -, Ireland, 1098, 1075, CHAS-. In HH of P. ONeill m 37 born Ireland.

ONEILL, ELIZABETH, 23, F, None listed, -, Ireland, 94, 86, CHAS+. In HH of Bernard ONeill m 28 born Ireland.

ONEILL, FRANCES, 32, M, Laborer, -, Ireland, 322, 297, CHAS. In Boarding house.

ONEILL, JAMES, 14, M, None listed, -, Ireland, 237, 222, CHAS-.Poor House.

ONEILL, P., 37, M, Cath. Priest, -, Ireland, 1098, 1075, CHAS-.

ORR, THOMAS, 45, M, Farmer, -, Ireland, 678, 678, CHES.

ORR, THOMAS, 67, M, Farmer, -, Ireland, 1045, 1046, AND*.

ORR, WILLIAM SENR., 62, M, Farmer, -, Ireland, 796, 797, AND*.

OSBORN, F., 34, M, Priv. U.S.A., -, Ireland, 47, 43, CHAS$. In HH of John Ewing m 50 born MA.

OSULLIVAN, ABIGAIL, 68, F, None listed, -, Ireland, 200, 188, CHAS+. In HH of Benj. B. Becaise m 37 born SC.

OSULLIVAN, BERNARD, 38, M, Laborer, -, Ireland, 497, 455, CHAS+.

OSULLIVAN, IVANA, 17, F, None listed, -, Ireland, 497, 455, CHAS+. In HH of Bernard OSullivan m 38 born Ireland.

OSULLIVAN, MIRA, 39, F, None listed, -, Ireland, 497, 455, CHAS+. In HH of Bernard OSullivan m 38 born Ireland.

OSULLIVAN, TERESA, 14, F, None listed, -, Ireland, 497, 455, CHAS+. In HH of Bernard OSullivan m 38 born Ireland.

OWENS, ALENDER, 35, M, Butcher, -, Ireland, 1141, 1120, CHAS%.

OWENS, CATHERINE, 36, F, None listed, -, Ireland, 338, 321, CHAS-. In HH of P.

Owens m 40 born Ireland.

OWENS, CATHERINE, 38, F, None listed, -, Ireland, 515, 498, CHAS-. In HH of Patrick Owens m 42 born Ireland.

OWENS, DENNIS, 8, M, None listed, -, Ireland, 1085, 1107, CHAS%. In HH of Joseph Owens m 47 born Ireland.

OWENS, ELIZA, 42, F, None listed, -, Ireland, 785, 765, CHAS-. In HH of Miles Drake m 42 born Ireland.

OWENS, JANE, 10, F, None listed, -, Ireland, 1085, 1107, CHAS%. In HH of Joseph Owens m 47 born Ireland.

OWENS, JOHN, 12, M, None listed, -, Ireland, 338, 321, CHAS-. In HH of P. Owens m 40 born Ireland.

OWENS, JOSEPH, 47, M, Carpenter, -, Ireland, 1085, 1107, CHAS%.

OWENS, MAGDELINE, 16, F, None listed, -, Ireland, 515, 498, CHAS-. In HH of Patrick Owens m 42 born Ireland.

OWENS, MARY, 16, F, None listed, -, Ireland, 338, 321, CHAS-. In HH of P. Owens m 40 born Ireland.

OWENS, MARY, 40, F, None listed, -, Ireland, 27, 27, CHAS%. In HH of Stephen Owens m 45 born Ireland.

OWENS, MARY, 41, F, None listed, -, Ireland, 1085, 1107, CHAS%. In HH of Joseph Owens m 47 born Ireland.

OWENS, P., 40, M, Drayman, -, Ireland, 338, 321, CHAS-.

OWENS, PATRICK, 22, M, Tailor, -, Ireland, 743, 743, ABB. In HH of Samuel A. Hodges m 43 Innkeeper born SC.

OWENS, PATRICK, 42, M, Laborer, -, Ireland, 515, 498, CHAS-.

OWENS, STEPHEN, 45, M, Clerk, -, Ireland, 27, 27, CHAS%.

OWENS, TIMOTHY, 12, M, None listed, -, Ireland, 1085, 1107, CHAS%. In HH of Joseph Owens m 47 born Ireland.

OWENS, WM., 50, M, Farmer, -, Ireland, 435, 435, CHES.

P

PALMER, THOMAS, 51, M, Shoemaker, -, Ireland, 77, 77, YORK+.

PARDON, PATRICK, 22, M, Laborer, -, Ireland, 401, 384, CHAS-.

PATRICK, CATHERINE, 18, F, Servant, -, Ireland, 241, 219, CHAS. In HH of William Lloyd m 45 born SC.

PATRICK, ISABELLA, 75, F, None listed, -, Ireland, 702, 702, UNION.

PATRICK, SARAH, 68, F, None listed, -, Ireland, 709, 709, UNION.

PATTERSON, ARMAR-INTHA, 12, F, None listed, -, Ireland, 410, 408, CHAS%. In HH of Jones Patterson m 40 born Ireland.

PATTERSON, CAROLINE, 80, F, None listed, -, Ireland, 410, 408, CHAS%. In HH of Jones Patterson m 40 born Ireland.

PATTERSON, CLEMENT, 6, M, None listed, -, Ireland, 410, 408, CHAS%. In HH of Jones Patterson m 40 born Ireland.

PATTERSON, ELODIA, 8, F, None listed, -, Ireland, 410, 408, CHAS%. In HH of Jones Patterson m 40 born Ireland.

PATTERSON, JAMES, 10, M, None listed, -, Ireland, 410, 408, CHAS%. In HH of Jones Patterson m 40 born Ireland.

PATTERSON, JONATHAN, 3, M, None listed, -, Ireland, 410, 408, CHAS%. In HH of Jones Patterson m 40 born Ireland.

PATTERSON, JONES, 40, M, Clerk, -, Ireland, 410, 408, CHAS%.

PATTERSON, LUCY, 14, F, None listed, -, Ireland, 410, 408, CHAS%. In HH of Jones Patterson m 40 born Ireland.

PATTERSON, MARY, 37, F, None listed, -, Ireland, 410, 408, CHAS%. In HH of Jones Patterson m 40 born Ireland.

PATTERSON, THOS., 22, M, Teacher, -, Ireland, 291, 291, DARL. In HH of James W. Hill m 51 born SC.

PATTON, DAVIS, 77, M, Farmer, -, Ireland, 50, 50, CHES.

PATTON, NANCY, 78, F, None listed, -, Ireland, 50, 50, CHES. In HH of Davis Patton m 77 born Ireland.

PAUL, MARY, 51, F, None listed, -, Ireland, 573, 590, RICH.

PEARCE, ISABEL, 68, F, None listed, -, Ireland, 149, 149, BEAU.

PEARSON, JOSEPH, 45, M, Planter, -, Ireland, 893, 893, UNION.

PEASE, ELLEN, 30, F, None listed, -, Ireland, 36, 32, CHAS$. In HH of J.F. Pease m 29 born ME.

PELLEGREW, MATTHEW, 38, M, Planter, -, Ireland, 60, 60, FAIR.

PEMPLE, J.B., 50, M, Merchant, -, Ireland, 286, 263, CHAS. In Carolina Hotel.

PENDERGRASS, M., 54, M, Clerk, -, Ireland, 286, 263, CHAS. In Carolina Hotel.

PENDERGRAST, M., 48, M, Clerk, -, Ireland, 211, 190, CHAS*.

PENDLE, THOMAS, 38, M, Farmer, -, Ireland, 197, 198, AND*.

PENNEL, ELLEN, 46, F, None listed, -, Ireland, 808, 808, ABB. In HH of William Pennel m 50 born Ireland.

PENNEL, ESTHER, 22, F, None listed, -, Ireland, 688, 688, ABB. In HH of Esther Pennel f 40 born Ireland.

PENNEL, ESTHER, 40, F, None listed, -, Ireland, 688, 688, ABB.

PENNEL, JANE, 48, F, None listed, -, Ireland, 372, 372, ABB.

PENNEL, WILLIAM, 50, M,

Manager, -, Ireland, 808, 808, ABB.

PERKENS, ELLAN, 45, F, None listed, -, Ireland, 1106, 1083, CHAS-. In Charleston Orphan House.

PERRY, MARGARET, 76, F, None listed, -, Ireland, 111, 111, FAIR. In HH of Daniel B. Kirland m 41 born SC.

PERRY, NANCY, 63, F, None listed, -, Ireland, 1276, 1277, FAIR.

PERSELL, JAMES, 28, M, Laborer, -, Ireland, 2007, 2013, EDGE. In HH of William Herbert m 37 born Ireland.

PERVZ, M., MRS., 60, F, None listed, -, Ireland, 14, 14, LANC. In HH of A.M. Cruise f 25 born England.

PETERS, MARY, 80, F, None listed, -, Ireland, 367, 367, YORK*. In HH of David F. Jackson m 39 born York Dist., SC.

PHILLIPS, JAMES, 23, M, Clerk, -, Ireland, 445, 456, RICH. In HH of Robert Agnew m 27 born Ireland.

PHILLIPS, JOHN, 30, M, R.R. Laborer, -, Ireland, 987, 964, CHAS%. In Boarding house.

PHILLIPS, JOHN, 40, M, Carpenter, -, Ireland, 492, 492, FAIR.

PHILLIPS, MARY, 35, F, None listed, -, Ireland, 492, 492, FAIR. In HH of John Phillips m 40 born Ireland.

PIERCE, MARY, 45, F, None listed, -, Ireland, 1000, 977, CHAS%. In HH of Thos.

Baker m 35 born Ireland.

PIERCE, MATHEW, 26, M, Clerk, -, Ireland, 804, 784, CHAS-. In HH of John Daly m 30 born Ireland.

PIRSON, JAMES, 35, M, Farmer, -, Ireland, 560, 560, HORR.

PLUNKETT, BERNARD, 19, M, Student, -, Ireland, 480, 446, CHAS*. In HH of Rt. Revd. Jgn. A. Reynolds m 51 born KY.

POLAND, LEWIS, 30, M, Ditcher, -, Ireland, 1846, 1846, ABB. In HH of Christopher W. Mants m 57 born SC.

POLLEY, CATHARINE, 55, F, None listed, -, Ireland, 787, 788, FAIR.

PORCHER, WILLIAM S., 40, M, Ditcher, -, Ireland, 542, 557, RICH. Date 1845 by name. In Lunatic Asylum.

PORTER, EDWARD J., 27, M, Lawyer, -, Ireland, 707, 707, Will. In HH of Thomas M. Mouzon m 23 born SC.

POWELL, MARY, 53, F, None listed, -, Ireland, 2304, 2304, GREE. In HH of Joseph Powell m 50 born TN.

POWER, JAMES, 35, M, Ship carpenter, -, Ireland, 522, 515, CHAS%.

POWER, JOANA, 40, F, None listed, -, Ireland, 522, 515, CHAS%. In HH of James Power m 35 born Ireland.

POWER, MARGARET, 11, F, None listed, -, Ireland, 522, 515, CHAS%. In HH of James Power m 35 born Ireland.

POWER, PATRICK, 5, M, None listed, -, Ireland, 522, 515, CHAS%. In HH of James

Power m 35 born Ireland.

POWERS, EDWARD, 24, M, Laborer, -, Ireland, 316, 291, CHAS+. In HH of Owen Sweeny m 33 born Ireland.

POWERS, HONVIA, 18, F, None listed, -, Ireland, 281, 261, CHAS+. In HH of John Cahill m 45 born Ireland.

POWERS, MARY, 22, F, None listed, -, Ireland, 316, 291, CHAS+. In HH of Owen Sweeny m 33 born Ireland.

POWERS, MARY, 30, F, None listed, -, Ireland, 700, 692, CHAS%. In HH of William Powers m 34 born Ireland.

POWERS, PAT., 50, M, Laborer, -, Ireland, 629, 587, CHAS+.

POWERS, PATRICK, 30, M, Laborer, -, Ireland, 292, 292, CHAS%. In HH of Henry McGuire m 35 born Ireland.

POWERS, PETER, 25, M, Laborer, -, Ireland, 629, 587, CHAS+. In HH of Pat. Powers m 50 born Ireland.

POWERS, SARAH, 21, F, None listed, -, Ireland, 673, 653, CHAS-. In HH of J.G. Newcomb m 27 born NY.

POWERS, WILLIAM, 34, M, Laborer, -, Ireland, 700, 692, CHAS%.

PRAG, JOHN, 63, M, Farmer, -, Ireland, 1062, 1062, CHES.

PRESTON, ANN, 42, F, None listed, -, Ireland, 146, 137, CHAS+. In HH of James Preston m 50 born Ireland.

PRESTON, ANNA, 15, F, None listed, -, Ireland, 477,

435, CHAS. In HH of John Preston m 50 born Ireland.

PRESTON, JAMES, 50, M, Merchant, -, Ireland, 146, 137, CHAS+.

PRESTON, JOHN, 50, M, Store keeper, -, Ireland, 477, 435, CHAS.

PRESTON, ROSE, 45, F, None listed, -, Ireland, 477, 435, CHAS. In HH of John Preston m 50 born Ireland.

PRICE, MARY Y., 39, F, None listed, -, Ireland, 527, 527, FAIR.

PRICE, PATRICK, 24, M, Laborer, -, Ireland, 2057, 2060, EDGE. In HH of Michael Corner m 27 born Ireland.

PRIOR, BERNARDRINE, 24, M, Clerk, -, Ireland, 315, 291, CHAS+. In HH of Edward Henry m 42 born Ireland.

PROUT, ELLEN, 29, F, None listed, -, Ireland, 219, 206, CHAS+. In HH of John Prout m 38 born Ireland.

PROUT, JOHN, 38, M, Laborer, -, Ireland, 219, 206, CHAS+.

PROUT, MICHAEL, 4, M, None listed, -, Ireland, 219, 206, CHAS+. In HH of John Prout m 38 born Ireland.

PRYOR, ELIZABETH, 28, F, None listed, -, Ireland, 565, 523, CHAS+. In HH of John Pryor m 45 born Ireland.

PRYOR, JOHN, 45, M, Porter, -, Ireland, 565, 523, CHAS+.

PURCELL, JAMES, 60, M, Planter, -, Ireland, 18, 18, COLL.

PURSE, MILLEY, 30, F, None listed, -, Ireland, 988, 967, CHAS-. In HH of Eliza Dallwig f 23 born MD.

Q

QUACKENBUSH, NORA, 30, F, None listed, -, Ireland, 259, 243, CHAS+. In HH of T.L. Quackenbush m 35 born NY.

QUAIL, JOHN, 27, M, Clerk, -, Ireland, 749, 729, CHAS-. In HH of Margaret Quail f 24 born England.

QUAY, CATHARINE, 99, F, None listed, -, Ireland, 1, 1, UNN+. In HH of C.S. Sims m 52 born SC.

QUIGLEY, THOMAS, 21, M, Cath. Minister, -, Ireland, 885, 865, CHAS-. In HH of Richard Baker m 44 born Ireland.

QUIGLY, CHARLES, 35, M, Shoe Store, M, Ireland, 455, 412, CHAS.

QUIN, ANN, 24, F, None listed, -, Ireland, 2106, 2106, BARN. In HH of Patrick Quinn m 30 born Ireland.

QUIN, ANN, 46, F, None listed, -, Ireland, 123, 115, CHAS*. In HH of Mary Moore f 50 born Ireland.

QUIN, CATHERINE, 26, F, None listed, -, Ireland, 277, 257, CHAS+. In HH of A. Gilbert m 40 born MA.

QUIN, GEORGIA, 34, M, Laborer, -, Ireland, 123, 115, CHAS*. In HH of Mary Moore f 50 born Ireland.

QUIN, JOHN, 34, M, Laborer, -, Ireland, 746, 732, CHAS%.

QUIN, JOSEPH, 21, M, Stone mason, -, Ireland, 322, 297, CHAS. In Boarding house.

QUIN, MARY, 26, F, None listed, -, Ireland, 238, 224, CHAS+. In HH of Thomas Quin m 30 born Ireland.

QUIN, MARY, 30, F, None listed, -, Ireland, 746, 732, CHAS%. In HH of John Quin m 34 born Ireland.

QUIN, PATRICK, 30, M, Schoolmaster, -, Ireland, 2106, 2106, BARN.

QUIN, PATRICK, 38, M, Laborer, -, Ireland, 277, 257, CHAS+. In HH of A. Gilbert m 40 born MA.

QUIN, PHILIP, 24, M, Laborer, -, Ireland, 746, 732, CHAS%. In HH of John Quin m 34 born Ireland.

QUIN, THOMAS, 30, M, Laborer, -, Ireland, 238, 224, CHAS+.

QUIN, THOMAS, 55, M, Planter, -, Ireland, 658, 658, BARN.

QUINLAY, C. MARY JANE, 7, F, None listed, -, Ireland, 201, 181, CHAS. In HH of Michael Quinlay m 38 born Ireland.

QUINLAY, CHARLES, 10, M, None listed, -, Ireland, 201, 181, CHAS. In HH of Michael Quinlay m 38 born Ireland.

QUINLAY, FRANCES, 28, M, None listed, -, Ireland, 201, 181, CHAS. In HH of Michael Quinlay m 38 born Ireland.

QUINLAY, MICHAEL, 38,

M, Bricklayer, -, Ireland, 201, 181, CHAS.

QUINLAY, WILLIAM, 12, M, None listed, -, Ireland, 201, 181, CHAS. In HH of Michael Quinlay m 38 born Ireland.

QUINN, CATHERINE, 30, F, None listed, -, Ireland, 634, 592, CHAS+. In HH of Daniel Quinn m 32 born Ireland.

QUINN, DANIEL, 32, M, Wheelwright, -, Ireland, 634, 592, CHAS+.

QUINN, JAMES, 16, M, Wheelwright, -, Ireland, 634, 592, CHAS+. In HH of Daniel Quinn m 32 born Ireland.

QUINN, JOHN, 11, M, None listed, -, Ireland, 634, 592, CHAS+. In HH of Daniel Quinn m 32 born Ireland.

QUINN, KATE, 20, F, None listed, -, Ireland, 322, 297, CHAS. In HH of Michael Quinn m 23 born England.

QUINN, MARY, 30, F, None listed, -, Ireland, 933, 910, CHAS%. In HH of Thomas Quinn m 35 born Ireland.

QUINN, MICHAEL, 28, M, Laborer, -, Ireland, 401, 384, CHAS-. In HH of Patrick Pardon m 22 born Ireland.

QUINN, RICHARD, 9, M, None listed, -, Ireland, 634, 592, CHAS+. In HH of Daniel Quinn m 32 born Ireland.

QUINN, THOMAS, 35, M, Laborer, -, Ireland, 933, 910, CHAS%.

QUIRKS, BRIDGET, 19, F, None listed, -, Ireland, 480, 438, CHAS. In HH of Dennis Quirks m 23 born Ireland.

QUIRKS, DENNIS, 23, M, Laborer, -, Ireland, 480, 438, CHAS.

R

RADY, BRIGET, 31, F, None listed, -, Ireland, 237, 222, CHAS-.Poor House.

RAHAL, JAMES, 25, M, Carpenter, -, Ireland, 38, 34, CHAS$. In HH of Mary McKuon f 40 born Ireland.

RAHALL, PATRICK, 28, M, Grocer, -, Ireland, 32, 28, CHAS$.

RAHAN, BRIGET, 34, F, None listed, -, Ireland, 635, 593, CHAS+. In HH of John Moreen m 35 born Ireland.

RAHAN, JANE, 30, F, None listed, -, Ireland, 635, 593, CHAS+. In HH of John Moreen m 35 born Ireland.

RAHAN, MARY, 7, F, None listed, -, Ireland, 635, 593, CHAS+. In HH of John Moreen m 35 born Ireland.

RAHAN, R.P., 37, M, Laborer, -, Ireland, 635, 593, CHAS+. In HH of John Moreen m 35 born Ireland.

RAHAN, RICHARD, 9, M, None listed, -, Ireland, 635, 593, CHAS+. In HH of John Moreen m 35 born Ireland.

RAINEY, ISABELLA, 70, F, None listed, -, Ireland, 6, 6, YORK. In HH of Jonas M. Rainey m 34 born Chester Co., SC.

RAINING, CLARK, 25, M, Stevedore, -, Ireland, 322, 297, CHAS. In Boarding house.

RAMSEY, JANE, 60, F, None listed, -, Ireland, 1695, 1695,

GREE. In HH of Samuel Ramsey m 54 born Ireland.

RAMSEY, SAMUEL, 54, M, Farmer, -, Ireland, 1695, 1695, GREE.

RANDALLS, THOS., 40, M, Tavern Keeper, -, Ireland, 87, 79, CHAS+.

RANSON, WILLIAM, 62, M, Farmer, -, Ireland, 732, 736, AND.

RATCHFORD, ELISA, 22, F, None listed, -, Ireland, 546, 546, YORK. In HH of Robert W. Ratchford m 36 born York Dist., SC.

RATCHFORD, MAR-GARET, 65, F, None listed, -, Ireland, 542, 542, YORK. In HH of George Ratchford m 75 born York Dist., SC.

RAY, PATRICK, 46, M, Laborer, -, Ireland, 237, 222, CHAS-.Poor House.

REABSON, MARY A., 35, F, None listed, -, Ireland, 2315, 2315, ABB. In HH ob Thomas Reabson m 38 born Ireland.

REABSON, THOMAS, 38, M, Tailor, -, Ireland, 2315, 2315, ABB.

READ, BARBARA, 47, F, None listed, -, Ireland, 465, 422, CHAS. In HH of Leslie O'Wen m 47 born Ireland.

REDD, JAMES, 82, M, Farmer, -, Ireland, 562, 562, NEWB.

REDDEN, MICHAEL, 40, M, Laborer, -, Ireland, 675, 667, CHAS%. In HH of Michael McGraw m 25 born Ireland.

REDDON, CHARLES, 40, M, Laborer, -, Ireland, 338, 303, CHAS+. In HH of

Bernard Sweeney m 37 born Ireland.

REDFERN, BRIGET, 40, F, None listed, -, Ireland, 192, 180, CHAS+. In HH of John Cowan m 55 born MA.

REDFERN, JOHN, 40, M, None listed, -, Ireland, 192, 180, CHAS+. In HH of John Cowan m 55 born MA.

REDMOND, GEORGE, 26, M, Shop keeper, -, Ireland, 410, 372, CHAS.

REDMOND, MARY ANN, 23, F, None listed, -, Ireland, 410, 372, CHAS. In HH of George Redmond m 26 born Ireland.

REED, ALLICE MURRAY, 26, F, None listed, -, Ireland, 1002, 979, CHAS%. In HH of Gilbert Reed m 32 born RI.

REED, CAROLINE, 30, F, None listed, -, Ireland, 486, 482, CHAS%. In HH of John P. Reed m 36 born Ireland.

REED, ELIZA, 82, F, None listed, -, Ireland, 618, 618, CHES.

REED, HUGH, 65, M, Planter, -, Ireland, 2225, 2225, BARN.

REED, JAMES, 45, M, Silver Smith, -, Ireland, 1420, 1420, GREE. In HH of Joseph McCullough m 71 born Ireland.

REED, JOHN P., 36, M, Store keeper, -, Ireland, 486, 482, CHAS%.

REED, WM., 37, M, Farmer, -, Ireland, 1467, 1467, CHES.

REEDY, CATHERINE, 25, F, None listed, -, Ireland, 393, 366, CHAS*. In HH of James J.B. Heyward m 35 born SC.

REEDY, CATHERINE, 25, F, None listed, -, Ireland, 251, 236, CHAS-. In HH of William B. Thompson m 40 born England.

REEDY, JAMES, 20, M, Clerk, -, Ireland, 35, 35, CHAS%. In HH of Henry Zerbet m 31 born Germany.

REEDY, MARY, 48, F, None listed, -, Ireland, 150, 141, CHAS+.

REEGAN, TIMOTHY, 29, M, Packer, -, Ireland, 322, 297, CHAS. In Boarding house.

REEVES, ELLEN, 10, F, None listed, -, Ireland, 279, 259, CHAS+. In HH of James Kenny m 43 born Ireland.

REEVES, MARY, 14, F, None listed, -, Ireland, 279, 259, CHAS+. In HH of James Kenny m 43 born Ireland.

REEVES, MARY, 35, F, None listed, -, Ireland, 279, 259, CHAS+. In HH of James Kenny m 43 born Ireland.

REEVES, P., 43, M, Laborer, -, Ireland, 279, 259, CHAS+. In HH of James Kenny m 43 born Ireland.

REID, ELIZABETH, 74, F, None listed, -, Ireland, 144, 144, LAU.

REILLY, MARY, 24, F, None listed, -, Ireland, 413, 411, CHAS%. In HH of Philip Reilly m 28 born Ireland.

REILLY, PHILIP, 28, M, Shop keeper, -, Ireland, 413, 411, CHAS%.

REILLY, R., 25, M, Clerk, -, Ireland, 150, 141, CHAS+. In Boarding house.

REMLEY, JAMES, 30, M, Laborer, -, Ireland, 346, 320, CHAS.

REMLEY, JOANE, 7, F, None listed, -, Ireland, 346, 320, CHAS. In HH of James Remley m 30 born Ireland.

REMLEY, JOANE, 25, F, None listed, -, Ireland, 346, 320, CHAS. In HH of James Remley m 30 born Ireland.

REMLEY, JOHN, 9, M, None listed, -, Ireland, 346, 320, CHAS. In HH of James Remley m 30 born Ireland.

REOBSON, ISABELLA, 28, F, None listed, -, Ireland, 2345, 2345, ABB. In HH of George Reobson m 23 born SC.

REYNOLD, SARAH, 55, F, None listed, -, Ireland, 367, 337, CHAS. In HH of Tho. H. McClure m 45 born Ireland.

REYNOLDS, ALICE, 35, F, None listed, -, Ireland, 254, 228, CHAS*. In HH of James L. Petigrw {sic} m 60 born SC.

REYNOLDS, E., 22, M, Laborer, M, Ireland, 31, 27, CHAS$.

REYNOLDS, EDWARD, 25, M, Drayman, -, Ireland, 853, 811, CHAS+. In HH of Bernard Carrol m 45 born Ireland.

REYNOLDS, HUGH, 23, M, Drayman, -, Ireland, 853, 811, CHAS+. In HH of Bernard Carrol m 45 born Ireland.

REYNOLDS, NANCY, 47, F, None listed, -, Ireland, 1821, 1821, ABB. In HH of Bennet Reynolds m 46 born SC.

REYNOLDS, SARAH, 60, F, None listed, -, Ireland, 1011,

988, CHAS-. In HH of H.D Lesesne m 40 born SC.

REYNOLDS, SOPHIA M., 13, F, None listed, -, Ireland, 632, 650, RICH. In HH of William Reynolds m 42 born Ireland.

REYNOLDS, WILLIAM, 42, M, Dentist, -, Ireland, 632, 650, RICH.

RHODUS, JANE, 62, F, None listed, -, Ireland, 116, 116, SUMT. In HH of Wm. Rhodus Sr. m 72 born SC.

RICHARDSON, JOHN, 60, M, Carpenter, -, Ireland, 1591, 1591, ABB.

RICHEE, JEANNETTE, 80, F, None listed, -, Ireland, 1040, 1040, NEWB.

RICHIE, JAMES, 22, M, Shoe Manf., -, Ireland, 671, 672, FAIR. In HH of John Brice m 48 born Ireland.

RICHIE, MARY, 30, F, None listed, -, Ireland, 671, 672, FAIR. In HH of John Brice m 48 born Ireland.

RICKENBACKER, E.V., 80, F, None listed, -, Ireland, 85, 86, ORNG+.

RIDGELL, MARY, 67, F, None listed, -, Ireland, 430, 430, SUMT. In HH of Jas. Ridgell m 65 born SC.

RILEY, ALEXANDER, 25, M, Laborer, -, Ireland, 644, 604, CHAS+.

RILEY, ANDREW, 18, M, Laborer, -, Ireland, 644, 604, CHAS+. In HH of Alexander Riley m 25 born Ireland.

RILEY, ANN, 25, F, None listed, -, Ireland, 883, 860,

CHAS%. In HH of George H. Winges m 21 born SC.

RILEY, BRIGET, 25, F, None listed, -, Ireland, 819, 777, CHAS+. In HH of James Taylor m 30 born England.

RILEY, CATHERINE, 28, F, None listed, -, Ireland, 984, 963, CHAS-. In HH of Charles McElleron m 30 born Ireland.

RILEY, HONORE, 70, F, None listed, -, Ireland, 377, 342, CHAS. In HH of Caroline Trouclue f 40 born SC.

RILEY, JOHN, 20, M, Painter, -, Ireland, 124, 115, CHAS+. In Boarding house.

RILEY, JOHN, 30, M, Carter, -, Ireland, 819, 777, CHAS+. In HH of James Taylor m 30 born England.

RILEY, JOHN, 40, M, Planter, -, Ireland, 77, 77, CHAS!.

RILEY, JOHN, 45, M, Laborer, -, Ireland, 408, 371, CHAS. In HH of J. McDonald m 50 born SC.

RILEY, JOHN, 64, M, None, -, Ireland, 987, 964, CHAS%. In Boarding house.

RILEY, JOHN P., 28, M, Stevedore, -, Ireland, 26, 31, CHAS. In HH of Moses Levy m 45 taven keeper born SC.

RILEY, MARGARET, 45, F, None listed, -, Ireland, 408, 371, CHAS. In HH of J. McDonald m 50 born SC.

RILEY, PATRICK, 46, M, Ditcher, -, Ireland, 994, 995, AND*. In HH of William Anderson m 50 born SC.

RILEY, ROSEY, 22, F, None listed, -, Ireland, 644, 604, CHAS+. In HH of Alexander Riley m 25 born Ireland.

RILEY, SABINA, 22, F, None listed, -, Ireland, 39, 35, CHAS$. In HH of John Kenney m 27 born Ireland.

RILEY, WILLIAM J., 22, M, Laborer, -, Ireland, 644, 604, CHAS+. In HH of Alexander Riley m 25 born Ireland.

RILY, PATRICK, 60, M, None listed, -, Ireland, 536, 528, CHAS%.

RITCHIE, ANDREW, 3, M, None listed, -, Ireland, 688, 689, FAIR. In HH of John Ritchie m 52 born Ireland.

RITCHIE, JANE, 20, F, None listed, -, Ireland, 688, 689, FAIR. In HH of John Ritchie m 52 born Ireland.

RITCHIE, JOHN, 18, M, Shoe maker, -, Ireland, 688, 689, FAIR. In HH of John Ritchie m 52 born Ireland.

RITCHIE, JOHN, 52, M, Shoe maker, -, Ireland, 688, 689, FAIR.

RITCHIE, MARTHA, 40, F, None listed, -, Ireland, 688, 689, FAIR. In HH of John Ritchie m 52 born Ireland.

RITCHIE, MATILDA, 13, F, None listed, -, Ireland, 688, 689, FAIR. In HH of John Ritchie m 52 born Ireland.

RITCHIE, WILLIAM, 8, M, None listed, -, Ireland, 688, 689, FAIR. In HH of John Ritchie m 52 born Ireland.

ROACH, JOHN, 39, M, Merchant, -, Ireland, 282, 288,

RICH.

ROACH, MARIA, 30, F, None listed, -, Ireland, 282, 288, RICH. In HH of John Roach m 39 born Ireland.

ROACH, MAURICE, 13, M, None listed, -, Ireland, 282, 288, RICH. In HH of John Roach m 39 born Ireland.

ROACH, MORRIS, 35, M, Bootmaker, -, Ireland, 619, 619, ABB.

ROACH, REDMOND, 10, M, None listed, -, Ireland, 282, 288, RICH. In HH of John Roach m 39 born Ireland.

ROACH, WILLIAM, 37, M, None, -, Ireland, 282, 288, RICH. In HH of John Roach m 39 born Ireland.

ROAM, JAMES, 30, M, Laborer, -, Ireland, 199, 181, CHAS.

ROBBINSON, CHAR-LOTTE, 40, F, None listed, -, Ireland, 1091, 1092, AND*. In HH of David Robbinson m 52 born SC.

ROBERTS, J.S., 30, M, Blacksmith, -, Ireland, 775, 775, BARN.

ROBERTS, JACOB, 52, M, Farmer, -, Ireland, 1355, 1355, GREE.

ROBERTSON, JANE, 35, F, None listed, -, Ireland, 2239, 2239, ABB. In HH of Jane Robertson f 67 born Ireland.

ROBERTSON, JANE, 67, F, None listed, -, Ireland, 2239, 2239, ABB.

ROBERTSON, WM., 43, M, Farmer, -, Ireland, 8, 8, LANC.

ROBESON, DAVID, 54, M, Farmer, -, Ireland, 2237, 2237, ABB.

ROBESON, JANE M., 30, F, None listed, -, Ireland, 2237, 2237, ABB. In HH of David Robeson m 54 born Ireland.

ROBESON, RACHEL, 50, F, None listed, -, Ireland, 2237, 2237, ABB. In HH of David Robeson m 54 born Ireland.

ROBINSON, EDWARD, 20, M, Farmer, -, Ireland, 1555, 1555, ABB. In HH of Samuel Robinson m 66 born Ireland.

ROBINSON, JANE, 65, F, None listed, -, Ireland, 1555, 1555, ABB. In HH of Samuel Robinson m 66 born Ireland.

ROBINSON, JAS., 47, M, Farmer, -, Ireland, 244, 244, CHES.

ROBINSON, JOHN, 10, M, None listed, -, Ireland, 1555, 1555, ABB. In HH of Samuel Robinson m 66 born Ireland.

ROBINSON, JOHN, 28, M, Farmer, -, Ireland, 1555, 1555, ABB. In HH of Samuel Robinson m 66 born Ireland.

ROBINSON, M.A., 42, F, None listed, -, Ireland, 244, 244, CHES. In HH of Jas. Robinson m 47 born Ireland.

ROBINSON, MARY, 22, F, None listed, -, Ireland, 1555, 1555, ABB. In HH of Samuel Robinson m 66 born Ireland.

ROBINSON, MARY, 54, F, None listed, -, Ireland, 145, 145, ABB.

ROBINSON, RANDALL, 60, M, None, -, Ireland, 85, 85, CHAS%.

ROBINSON, SAMUEL, 66, M, Farmer, -, Ireland, 1555, 1555, ABB.

ROCHE, JOHN, 40, M, Attendant, -, Ireland, 542, 557, RICH.At Lunatic Asylum.

ROCHE, MARGARET, 18, F, None listed, -, Ireland, 804, 787, CHAS%. In HH of John Berry m 35 born Ireland.

RODDY, MARTIN, 30, M, Shop keeper, -, Ireland, 427, 425, CHAS%.

RODDY, MARY, 60, F, None listed, -, Ireland, 228, 214, CHAS-.

RODDY, MARY JANE, 8, F, None listed, -, Ireland, 427, 425, CHAS%. In HH of Martin Roddy m 30 born Ireland.

RODDY, ROSA A., 26, F, None listed, -, Ireland, 427, 425, CHAS%. In HH of Martin Roddy m 30 born Ireland.

RODDY, THOMAS, 5, M, None listed, -, Ireland, 427, 425, CHAS%. In HH of Martin Roddy m 30 born Ireland.

ROGERS, MARGARET, 23, F, None listed, -, Ireland, 834, 814, CHAS-. In HH of T.W. Rogers m 30 born Ireland.

ROGERS, T.W., 30, M, Clothing store, -, Ireland, 834, 814, CHAS-.

ROONEY, ANN, 12, F, None listed, -, Ireland, 252, 237, CHAS+. In HH of Michael Lines m 30 born Ireland.

ROONEY, DAN, 11, M, None listed, -, Ireland, 302, 278, CHAS+. In HH of Patrick Rooney m 57 born Ireland.

ROONEY, DAN, 34, M,

Laborer, -, Ireland, 302, 278, CHAS+. In HH of Patrick Rooney m 57 born Ireland.

ROONEY, ELLEN, 9, F, None listed, -, Ireland, 302, 278, CHAS+. In HH of Patrick Rooney m 57 born Ireland.

ROONEY, JOHN, 21, M, Laborer, -, Ireland, 309, 285, CHAS. In HH of Paul Rooney m 44 born Ireland.

ROONEY, MARAGARET, 14, F, None listed, -, Ireland, 679, 659, CHAS-. In HH of Mary Gallaway f 26 born NY.

ROONEY, MARGARET, 7, F, None listed, -, Ireland, 252, 237, CHAS+. In HH of Michael Lines m 30 born Ireland.

ROONEY, MARGARET, 38, F, None listed, -, Ireland, 309, 285, CHAS. In HH of Paul Rooney m 44 born Ireland.

ROONEY, MARY, 23, F, None listed, -, Ireland, 309, 285, CHAS. In HH of Paul Rooney m 44 born Ireland.

ROONEY, MARY, 50, F, None listed, -, Ireland, 302, 278, CHAS+. In HH of Patrick Rooney m 57 born Ireland.

ROONEY, NANCY, 29, F, None listed, -, Ireland, 302, 278, CHAS+. In HH of Patrick Rooney m 57 born Ireland.

ROONEY, PATRICK, 14, F, None listed, -, Ireland, 302, 278, CHAS+. In HH of Patrick Rooney m 57 born Ireland.

ROONEY, PATRICK, 57, M, Laborer, -, Ireland, 302, 278, CHAS+.

ROONEY, PAUL, 44, M, Mason, -, Ireland, 309, 285, CHAS.

ROSE, MARY, 20, F, None listed, -, Ireland, 12, 12, CHAS+. In HH of Caroline Douglas f 30 born GA.

ROSE, MARY, 22, F, None listed, -, Ireland, 418, 390, CHAS*. In HH of John L. Smith m 28 born Ireland.

ROSS, HUGH, 84, M, Farmer, -, Ireland, 643, 643, CHES.

ROSS, JANE, 66, F, None listed, -, Ireland, 508, 508, CHES.

ROSS, JOHN, 42, M, Overseer, -, Ireland, 425, 425, DARL.

ROWAN, WILLIAM, 42, M, Clerk, -, Ireland, 477, 492, RICH.

RULLY, BERNARD, 55, M, Merchant, -, Ireland, 435, 446, RICH.

RUNAN, SARAH, 30, F, None listed, -, Ireland, 1067, 1067, CHES.

RUNNETT, EMMA, 21, F, None listed, -, Ireland, 389, 351, CHAS+. In HH of Edward Collins m 40 born Ireland.

RUNNETT, WILLIAM, 23, M, Laborer, -, Ireland, 389, 351, CHAS+. In HH of Edward Collins m 40 born Ireland.

RUSH, NANCY, 49, F, None listed, -, Ireland, 923, 923, LANC*. In HH of William McMullan m 44 born Ireland.

RUSSEL, MARY, 40, F, None listed, -, Ireland, 354, 327, CHAS*. In HH of Paul Dunbar m 60 born Scotland.

RUSSELL, ROBERT Y., 50, M, Clergyman, -, Ireland, 1372, 1372, YORK.

RUTH, ELEANOR, 27, F, None listed, -, Ireland, 444, 411, CHAS*. In HH of James Ruth m 32 born Ireland.

RUTH, JAMES, 32, M, Laborer, -, Ireland, 444, 411, CHAS*.

RYAN, ANN, 35, F, None listed, -, Ireland, 456, 454, CHAS%. In HH of Peter Ryan m 45 born Ireland.

RYAN, ANSTICE, 60, F, None listed, -, Ireland, 463, 446, CHAS-. In HH of James Ryan m 30 born Ireland.

RYAN, CATHERINE, 13, F, None listed, -, Ireland, 78, 78, CHAS%. In HH of Maria Langlors f 59 born St. Marks, West Indies.

RYAN, CATHERINE, 28, F, None listed, -, Ireland, 364, 326, CHAS+. In HH of Archibald Dunkin m 37 born Scotland.

RYAN, CATHERINE, 50, F, None listed, -, Ireland, 111, 103, CHAS-. In HH of Thomas Ryan m 49 born Ireland.

RYAN, ELLEN, 18, F, None listed, -, Ireland, 748, 706, CHAS+. In HH of H.A. Mayer m 45 born Ireland.

RYAN, HONORA, 40, F, None listed, -, Ireland, 729, 687, CHAS+.

RYAN, JAMES, 30, M, Laborer, -, Ireland, 463, 446, CHAS-.

RYAN, JAMES, 46, M, Musician, -, Ireland, 595, 612, RICH.

RYAN, JOHN, 33, M, Mercht., -, Ireland, 21, 21, BARN.

RYAN, JOHN, 47, M, Carpenter, -, Ireland, 214, 191, CHAS*.

RYAN, JOHN S., 40, M, Broker, -, Ireland, 85, 83, CHAS*.

RYAN, JOHN S., 53, M, Carpenter, -, Ireland, 711, 703, CHAS%.

RYAN, MARY, 20, F, None listed, -, Ireland, 636, 628, CHAS%. In HH of Nicholas Bunger m 36 born Germany.

RYAN, MARY, 25, F, None listed, -, Ireland, 463, 446, CHAS-. In HH of James Ryan m 30 born Ireland.

RYAN, MARY, 35, F, None listed, -, Ireland, 1058, 1036, CHAS%. In HH of Matthew Ryan m 39 born Ireland.

RYAN, MARY, 40, F, None listed, -, Ireland, 474, 432, CHAS. In HH of William Ryan m 56 born Ireland.

RYAN, MARY, 49, F, None listed, -, Ireland, 711, 703, CHAS%. In HH of John S. Ryan m 53 born Ireland.

RYAN, MATHEW, 36, M, Clerk, -, Ireland, 375, 358, CHAS-. In HH of Thomas Dillon m 32 born Ireland.

RYAN, MATTHEW, 39, M, Carpenter, -, Ireland, 1058, 1036, CHAS%.

RYAN, MICHAEL, 54, M, Laborer, -, Ireland, 237, 222, CHAS-.Works in Poor House.

RYAN, O'LE TYNE, 36, M, Agent, -, Ireland, 754, 754, COLL.

RYAN, P., 23, M, Clerk, -, Ireland, 150, 141, CHAS+. In Boarding house.

RYAN, PETER, 25, M, R.R. Laborer, -, Ireland, 987, 964, CHAS%. In Boarding house.

RYAN, PETER, 45, M, Laborer, -, Ireland, 456, 454, CHAS%.

RYAN, THOMAS, 49, M, Broker, -, Ireland, 111, 103, CHAS-.

RYAN, WILLIAM, 12, M, None listed, -, Ireland, 1058, 1036, CHAS%. In HH of Matthew Ryan m 39 born Ireland.

RYAN, WILLIAM, 23, M, Laborer, -, Ireland, 222, 209, CHAS+. In HH of John Donnahugh m 22 born Ireland.

RYAN, WILLIAM, 56, M, Miner, -, Ireland, 474, 432, CHAS.

S

SACK, JANE, 30, F, None listed, -, Ireland, 884, 864, CHAS-. In HH of Alexander Abrahams m 30 born SC.

SALLY, ROSE, 30, F, None listed, -, Ireland, 67, 68, RICH. In HH of William Sally m 35 born Ireland.

SALLY, WILLIAM, 35, M, Bricklayer, -, Ireland, 67, 68, RICH.

SANDFORD, MATHEW, 58, M, Planter, -, Ireland, 139, 139, COLL+.

SARBRAY, MARGARET, 24, F, None listed, -, Ireland, 321, 293, CHAS+. In HH of Thomas Sarbray m 25 born Ireland.

SARBRAY, THOMAS, 25, M, Laborer, -, Ireland, 321, 293, CHAS+.

SAUNDERS, CAROLINE, 25, F, None listed, -, Ireland, 188, 192, RICH. In Hotel.

SAUNDERS, MARY, 22, F, None listed, -, Ireland, 188, 192, RICH. In Hotel.

SAUNDERS, S., 39, F, Hair Dresser, -, Ireland, 235, 213, CHAS.

SAVAGE, HENRY, 18, M, Baker, -, Ireland, 132, 124, CHAS+. In HH of John McCrale {McCrate} m 30 born Canada.

SAXON, ELIZA, 9, F, None listed, M, Ireland, 55, 50, CHAS-. In HH of Juliet Saxon f 35 mulatto born Ireland {sic}.

SAXON, ELLA, 5, F, None listed, M, Ireland, 55, 50, CHAS-. In HH of Juliet Saxon f 35 mulatto born Ireland {sic}.

SAXON, JULIA, 7, F, None listed, M, Ireland, 55, 50, CHAS-. In HH of Juliet Saxon f 35 mulatto born Ireland {sic}.

SAXON, JULIET, 35, F, None listed, M, Ireland, 55, 50, CHAS-.

SCANDLIN, JAMES, 33, M, Blacksmith, -, Ireland, 119, 110, CHAS+. In HH of William Condell m 34 born Ireland.

SCANDLIN, MARY, 28, F, None listed, -, Ireland, 119, 110, CHAS+. In HH of William

Condell m 34 born Ireland.

SCANTON, MARTIN, 22, M, RR Agent, -, Ireland, 796, 796, SUMT.

SCHINE, ANN, 30, F, None listed, -, Ireland, 189, 177, CHAS-.

SCHUBASH, MARGARET, 62, F, None listed, -, Ireland, 180, 180, EDGE*. In HH of Joseph Pealer m 35 born PA.

SCOTT, ARCHY, 3, M, None listed, -, Ireland, 1423, 1423, GREE. In HH of John Scott m 39 born Ireland.

SCOTT, HENRY, 32, M, Planter, -, Ireland, 847, 848, FAIR.

SCOTT, JAMES, 17, M, Laborer, -, Ireland, 1423, 1423, GREE. In HH of John Scott m 39 born Ireland.

SCOTT, JAMES S., 45, M, Planter, -, Ireland, 722, 731, RICH+.

SCOTT, JOHN, 7, M, None listed, -, Ireland, 1423, 1423, GREE. In HH of John Scott m 39 born Ireland.

SCOTT, JOHN, 39, M, Laborer, -, Ireland, 1423, 1423, GREE.

SCOTT, JOHN JR., 47, M, Shoemaker, -, Ireland, 894, 894, YORK.

SCOTT, JOHN S., 45, M, Merchant, -, Ireland, 229, 234, RICH.

SCOTT, JOHN SR., 76, M, Shoemaker, -, Ireland, 893, 893, YORK.

SCOTT, JOSEPH, 2, M, None listed, -, Ireland, 1423, 1423, GREE. In HH of John

Scott m 39 born Ireland.

SCOTT, MARY, 30, F, None listed, -, Ireland, 26, 23, CHAS$. In HH of William Scott m 30 born Ireland.

SCOTT, MARY, 35, F, None listed, -, Ireland, 1466, 1466, GREE. In HH of Allen Scott m 37 born Ireland.

SCOTT, MARY, 40, F, None listed, -, Ireland, 893, 893, YORK. In HH of John Scott, Sr. m 76 born Ireland.

SCOTT, MATHEW, 30, M, Overseer, -, Ireland, 504, 504, FAIR. In HH of J.F. Gamble m 42, hotel keeper, born NC. At the Winnsboro Hotel.

SCOTT, NANCY, 12, F, None listed, -, Ireland, 1423, 1423, GREE. In HH of John Scott m 39 born Ireland.

SCOTT, NANCY, 30, F, None listed, -, Ireland, 600, 617, RICH.

SCOTT, NANCY, 73, F, None listed, -, Ireland, 1138, 1138, NEWB. In HH of William Scott m 39 born SC.

SCOTT, PATRICK, 40, M, Tailor, -, Ireland, 662, 681, RICH.

SCOTT, ROBERT, 20, M, Laborer, -, Ireland, 1423, 1423, GREE. In HH of John Scott m 39 born Ireland.

SCOTT, ROSANNA, 45, F, None listed, -, Ireland, 722, 731, RICH+. In HH of James S. Scott m 45 born Ireland.

SCOTT, SARAH, 30, F, None listed, -, Ireland, 1423, 1423, GREE. In HH of John Scott m 39 born Ireland.

SCOTT, SARAH, 37, F, None listed, -, Ireland, 893, 893, YORK. In HH of John Scott, Sr. m 76 born Ireland.

SCOTT, WILLIAM, 15, M, Laborer, -, Ireland, 1423, 1423, GREE. In HH of John Scott m 39 born Ireland.

SCOTT, WILLIAM, 30, M, Laborer, -, Ireland, 26, 23, CHAS$.

SCOTT, WILLIAM, 59, M, Shoemaker, -, Ireland, 1181, 1181, YORK.

SEGEE, CAROLINE, 30, F, None listed, -, Ireland, 415, 374, CHAS+.

SEILEY, EMMA, 30, F, None listed, -, Ireland, 495, 453, CHAS+. In HH of Patrick Seiley m 39 born Ireland.

SEILEY, JANE, 13, F, None listed, -, Ireland, 495, 453, CHAS+. In HH of Patrick Seiley m 39 born Ireland.

SEILEY, PATRICK, 39, M, Laborer, -, Ireland, 495, 453, CHAS+.

SEILEY, PHILIP, 11, M, None listed, -, Ireland, 495, 453, CHAS+. In HH of Patrick Seiley m 39 born Ireland.

SEMMONS, MOSES, 96, M, None, -, Ireland, 1012, 1012, CHES.

SERA, ANN, 21, F, None listed, -, Ireland, 413, 372, CHAS+. In HH of Francsis Sera m 26 born Genoa.

SERGENT, GEORGE, 37, M, Shoe dealer, -, Ireland, 258, 243, CHAS-.

SERGENT, SARAH, 37, F, None listed, -, Ireland, 258, 243, CHAS-. In HH of George Sergent m 37 born Ireland.

SERVICE, ELIZABETH, 16, F, None listed, -, Ireland, 661, 661, UNION. In HH of Robert Service m 39 born Ireland.

SERVICE, JOHN, 18, M, Laborer, -, Ireland, 661, 661, UNION. In HH of Robert Service m 39 born Ireland.

SERVICE, JOHN, 31, M, Shoemaker, -, Ireland, 647, 647, UNION.

SERVICE, MARGARET, 48, F, None listed, -, Ireland, 642, 642, UNION.

SERVICE, MARY, 39, F, None listed, -, Ireland, 661, 661, UNION. In HH of Robert Service m 39 born Ireland.

SERVICE, ROBERT, 39, M, Laborer, -, Ireland, 661, 661, UNION.

SERVICE, THOMAS, 28, M, Peddler, -, Ireland, 642, 642, UNION. In HH of Margaret Service f 48 born Ireland.

SESSENE, HANNAH, 56, F, None listed, -, Ireland, 366, 339, CHAS*. In HH of Ann Sessene f 80 born SC.

SHALLOC, MICHAEL, 27, M, Clerk, -, Ireland, 826, 806, CHAS-. In HH of John Cummins m 29 born Ireland.

SHARLEY, JOHN, 30, M, Laborer, -, Ireland, 538, 497, CHAS+.

SHARLEYSON, JOHN, 39, M, Laborer, -, Ireland, 541, 500, CHAS+.

SHARLOCK, JAMES, 35, M, Laborer, -, Ireland, 187, 187, CHAS3.

SHARP, PETER, 45, M, Shoemaker, -, Ireland, 156, 156, PICK+.

SHAW, BRIDGET, 12, F, None listed, -, Ireland, 526, 476, CHAS. In HH of James Shaw m 40 born Ireland.

SHAW, BRIDGET, 35, F, None listed, -, Ireland, 526, 476, CHAS. In HH of James Shaw m 40 born Ireland.

SHAW, CATEY, 10, F, None listed, -, Ireland, 526, 476, CHAS. In HH of James Shaw m 40 born Ireland.

SHAW, ELIZABETH, 30, F, None listed, -, Ireland, 48, 48, AND*. In HH of Vincent Shaw m 49 born SC.

SHAW, J.W., 25, M, Watch maker, -, Ireland, 529, 529, FAIR. In HH of Grandy Parker m 36 born NC.

SHAW, JAMES, 16, M, Laborer, -, Ireland, 526, 476, CHAS. In HH of James Shaw m 40 born Ireland.

SHAW, JAMES, 40, M, Gardner, -, Ireland, 526, 476, CHAS.

SHAW, NANCY, 18, F, None listed, -, Ireland, 526, 476, CHAS. In HH of James Shaw m 40 born Ireland.

SHAW, PATRICK, 30, M, Laborer, -, Ireland, 67, 68, RICH. In HH of William Sally m 35 born Ireland.

SHAW, THOS., 30, M, Laborer, -, Ireland, 2057, 2060, EDGE. In HH of Michael Corner m 27 born Ireland.

SHEA, BARTON, 15, M, Clerk, -, Ireland, 23, 28, CHAS. In HH of Geo. Shea m 46 born Ireland.

SHEA, GEO., 46, M, Taylor, -, Ireland, 23, 28, CHAS.

SHEA, JACOB, 28, M, Laborer, -, Ireland, 409, 371, CHAS. In HH of Mary Shea f 45 born Ireland.

SHEA, MARY, 42, F, None listed, -, Ireland, 23, 28, CHAS. In HH of Geo. Shea m 46 born Ireland.

SHEA, MARY, 45, F, None listed, -, Ireland, 409, 371, CHAS.

SHEA, PATRICK, 24, M, Laborer, -, Ireland, 409, 371, CHAS. In HH of Mary Shea f 45 born Ireland.

SHEFOR, DENNIS, 22, M, None listed, -, Ireland, 910, 887, CHAS%. In HH of Patrick Courtney m 27 born Ireland.

SHEGOG, GEORGE, 40, M, Mechanic, -, Ireland, 159, 163, RICH. In HH of Elliza Fleming f 50 born Ireland.

SHELLAR, MARY, 25, F, None listed, -, Ireland, 23, 19, CHAS+. In HH of James ONeal m 43 born Ireland.

SHELNUTT, MARY, 84, F, None listed, -, Ireland, 852, 582, EDGE.

SHERIDAN, ANNETTE, 13, F, None listed, -, Ireland, 730, 721, CHAS%. In HH of Mary Sheridan f 50 born Ireland.

SHERIDAN, CATHERINE, 26, F, None listed, -, Ireland, 542, 557, RICH. Date 1850 by name. In Lunatic Asylum.

SHERIDAN, EDWARD, 29, M, Saddler, -, Ireland, 89, 90, RICH. Note: dwelling 89/Family 90 followed 43/44, apparently copied out of order.

SHERIDAN, JAMES, 25, M, Laborer, -, Ireland, 389, 351, CHAS+. In HH of Edward Collins m 40 born Ireland.

SHERIDAN, JOHN, 48, M, Laborer, -, Ireland, 730, 721, CHAS%. In HH of Mary Sheridan f 50 born Ireland.

SHERIDAN, MARY, 50, F, None listed, -, Ireland, 730, 721, CHAS%.

SHERIDAN, PATRICK, 25, M, Laborer, -, Ireland, 401, 361, CHAS+. In HH of Catherine Brady f 40 born Ireland.

SHERIDAN, PATRICK, 30, M, Shoe maker, -, Ireland, 205, 188, CHAS*.

SHERIDAN, STEPHEN, 19, M, Saddler, -, Ireland, 89, 90, RICH. Note: dwelling 89/ Family 90 followed 43/44, apparently copied out of order.

SHERIDAN, SUSAN, 25, F, None listed, -, Ireland, 839, 819, CHAS-. In HH of John S. Richards m 45 born GA.

SHERIDAN, THOMAS, 16, M, Laborer, -, Ireland, 730, 721, CHAS%. In HH of Mary Sheridan f 50 born Ireland.

SHERLOCK, THOMAS, 31, M, Ditcher, -, Ireland, 585, 586, ORNG+. In HH of F.. Keller m 29 born SC.

SHERLOCK, THOMAS, 31, M, Ditcher, -, Ireland, 585, 586, ORNG+. In HH of J. Keller m 29 born SC.

SHERRY, CATHERINE, 30, F, None listed, -, Ireland, 480, 476, CHAS%.

SHIELDS, JOHN, 23, M, Shoemaker, -, Ireland, 752, 752, ABB. In HH of Joseph T. Moore m 25 born SC.

SHIELDS, JOHN, 30, M, Painter, -, Ireland, 337, 302, CHAS+. In HH of John Lindsay m 30 born England.

SHORT, JAMES, 40, M, Clerk, -, Ireland, 463, 460, CHAS%. In HH of W.C. Leak m 35 born SC.

SILCORE, DANIEL, 11, M, None listed, -, Ireland, 75, 69, CHAS-. In HH of Daniel H. Silcore m 36 born England.

SILCORE, FERDINAND, 4, M, None listed, -, Ireland, 75, 69, CHAS-. In HH of Daniel H. Silcore m 36 born England.

SILCORE, HENRY W., 2, M, None listed, -, Ireland, 75, 69, CHAS-. In HH of Daniel H. Silcore m 36 born England.

SILCORE, JAMES, 7, M, None listed, -, Ireland, 75, 69, CHAS-. In HH of Daniel H. Silcore m 36 born England.

SILCORE, MATILDA, 5, F, None listed, -, Ireland, 75, 69, CHAS-. In HH of Daniel H. Silcore m 36 born England.

SIMONS, CHS. LOWNDES, 3, M, None listed, -, Ireland, 1146, 1125, CHAS%. In HH of Harris Simons m 43 born Ireland.

SIMONS, HARRIET H., 16, F, None listed, -, Ireland, 1146, 1125, CHAS%. In HH of

Harris Simons m 43 born Ireland.

SIMONS, HARRIS, 9, M, None listed, -, Ireland, 1146, 1125, CHAS%. In HH of Harris Simons m 43 born Ireland.

SIMONS, HARRIS, 43, M, Factor, -, Ireland, 1146, 1125, CHAS%.

SIMONS, JAMES S., 7, M, None listed, -, Ireland, 1146, 1125, CHAS%. In HH of Harris Simons m 43 born Ireland.

SIMONS, JON, 11, M, None listed, -, Ireland, 1146, 1125, CHAS%. In HH of Harris Simons m 43 born Ireland.

SIMONS, MARIE RAMSAY, 0, F, None listed, -, Ireland, 1146, 1125, CHAS% In HH of Harris Simons m 43 born Ireland. Marie Ramsay Simons age 8/12 yr.

SIMONS, MARY JON, 38, F, None listed, -, Ireland, 1146, 1125, CHAS%. In HH of Harris Simons m 43 born Ireland.

SIMONS, SAML. WRAGG, 13, M, None listed, -, Ireland, 1146, 1125, CHAS%. In HH of Harris Simons m 43 born Ireland.

SIMONS, SARAH H., 18, F, None listed, -, Ireland, 1146, 1125, CHAS%. In HH of Harris Simons m 43 born Ireland.

SIMONS, WILLIAM WRAGG, 5, M, None listed, -, Ireland, 1146, 1125, CHAS%. In HH of Harris Simons m 43

born Ireland.

SIMPSON, AMELIA, 36, F, None listed, -, Ireland, 500, 466, CHAS*. In HH of Edward Simpson m 41 born Ireland.

SIMPSON, BRIGET, 16, F, None listed, -, Ireland, 500, 466, CHAS*. In HH of Edward Simpson m 41 born Ireland.

SIMPSON, EDMUND, 29, M, Laborer, -, Ireland, 500, 466, CHAS*. In HH of Edward Simpson m 41 born Ireland.

SIMPSON, EDWARD, 41, M, Gas fitter, -, Ireland, 500, 466, CHAS*.

SIMPSON, JOHN, 27, M, Pavior, -, Ireland, 500, 466, CHAS*. In HH of Edward Simpson m 41 born Ireland.

SIMPSON, JOHN B., 68, M, Farmer, -, Ireland, 1773, 1773, LAU.

SIMPSON, JOSEPH, 25, M, Laborer, -, Ireland, 229, 229, FAIR. In HH of Col. Nicholas Peay m 39 born SC.

SIMPSON, MARTHA, 9, F, None listed, -, Ireland, 231, 231, FAIR. In HH of Robert Simpson m 39 born Ireland.

SIMPSON, MARY, 40, F, None listed, -, Ireland, 231, 231, FAIR. In HH of Robert Simpson m 39 born Ireland.

SIMPSON, MARY, 72, F, None listed, -, Ireland, 1773, 1773, LAU. In HH of John B. Simpson m 68 born Ireland.

SIMPSON, PATRICK, 78, M, None, -, Ireland, 500, 466, CHAS*. In HH of Edward Simpson m 41 born Ireland.

SIMPSON, REBECCA, 11, F,

None listed, -, Ireland, 231, 231, FAIR. In HH of Robert Simpson m 39 born Ireland.

SIMPSON, ROBERT, 39, M, Planter, -, Ireland, 231, 231, FAIR.

SIMPSON, THOS., 39, M, Tailor, -, Ireland, 86, 86, BARN.

SLAGAN, ELLEN, 24, F, None listed, -, Ireland, 635, 593, CHAS+. In HH of John Moreen m 35 born Ireland.

SLAGAN, PATRICK, 28, M, Laborer, -, Ireland, 635, 593, CHAS+. In HH of John Moreen m 35 born Ireland.

SLANET, ANN, 28, F, None listed, -, Ireland, 927, 828, FAIR

SLANTER, MARGARET, 26, F, None listed, -, Ireland, 706, 697, CHAS%. In HH of John Cornell m 38 born England.

SLANTER, STEPHEN, 29, M, Laborer, -, Ireland, 706, 697, CHAS%. In HH of John Cornell m 38 born England.

SLATTERY, CATHERINE, 25, F, None listed, -, Ireland, 243, 228, CHAS+. In HH of John Conners m 30 born Ireland.

SLATTERY, MARGARET, 50, F, None listed, -, Ireland, 476, 459, CHAS-. In HH of George Black m 37 born Ireland.

SLATTERY, THOMAS, 22, M, Waiter, -, Ireland, 326, 301, CHAS. On Steam Ship Southerner.

SLOAN, EDWARD, 20, M, Farmer, -, Ireland, 807, 807, CHES. In HH of Edward Sloan m 50 born Ireland.

SLOAN, EDWARD, 50, M, Farmer, -, Ireland, 807, 807, CHES.

SLOAN, ELIZA, 15, F, None listed, -, Ireland, 807, 807, CHES. In HH of Edward Sloan m 50 born Ireland.

SLOAN, ELIZABETH, 70, F, None listed, -, Ireland, 1995, 1995, LAU.

SLOAN, JANE, 57, F, None listed, -, Ireland, 839, 839, YORK. In HH of William A. Faris m 37 born Ireland.

SLOAN, JOHN J., 72, M, Farmer, -, Ireland, 188, 188, YORK.

SLOAN, MARGARET, 22, F, None listed, -, Ireland, 807, 807, CHES. In HH of Edward Sloan m 50 born Ireland.

SLOAN, MARGARET, 45, F, None listed, -, Ireland, 807, 807, CHES. In HH of Edward Sloan m 50 born Ireland.

SLOAN, NANCY, 18, F, None listed, -, Ireland, 807, 807, CHES. In HH of Edward Sloan m 50 born Ireland.

SLOAN, ROBT., 27, M, Farmer, -, Ireland, 807, 807, CHES. In HH of Edward Sloan m 50 born Ireland.

SLOAN, SUSAN, 25, F, None listed, -, Ireland, 807, 807, CHES. In HH of Edward Sloan m 50 born Ireland.

SMALL, ANN, 45, F, None listed, -, Ireland, 1008, 985, CHAS-.

SMALL, ELIZA, 13, F, None listed, -, Ireland, 1008, 985, CHAS-. In HH of Ann Small f 45 born Ireland.

SMALL, JOHN S., 23, M, Clerk, -, Ireland, 1008, 985, CHAS-. In HH of Ann Small f 45 born Ireland.

SMALL, MARY, 15, F, None listed, -, Ireland, 1008, 985, CHAS-. In HH of Ann Small f 45 born Ireland.

SMALL, PATRICK, 26, M, Baker, -, Ireland, 132, 124, CHAS+. In HH of John McCrale {McCrate} m 30 born Canada.

SMALL, ROBERT, 50, M, Clerk, -, Ireland, 1008, 985, CHAS-. In HH of Ann Small f 45 born Ireland.

SMITH, ANN, 30, F, Servant, -, Ireland, 54, 64, CHAS. In HH of William Ravenel m 43 born SC.

SMITH, ELIZABETH, 40, F, None listed, -, Ireland, 1183, 1183, SUMT. In HH of Jas. M. Smith m 42 born Ireland.

SMITH, ELIZABETH, 60, M, None listed, -, Ireland, 81, 81, FAIR. In HH of William Robertson m 42 born NC.

SMITH, ISABELLA J., 17, F, None listed, -, Ireland, 393, 393, YORK*. In HH of William A. Smith m 47 born Ireland.

SMITH, JANE, 60, F, None listed, -, Ireland, 706, 706, CHES. In HH of James Sterling m 49 born SC.

SMITH, JAS. M., 42, M, Teacher, -, Ireland, 1183, 1183, SUMT.

SMITH, JOHN, 34, M, Laborer, -, Ireland, 261, 244, CHAS+. In HH of Hugh McNamara m 28 born Ireland.

SMITH, JOHN, 70, M, None, -, Ireland, 77, 77, KERS.

SMITH, JOHN L., 28, M, Clerk, -, Ireland, 418, 390, CHAS*.

SMITH, MARGARET, 23, F, None listed, -, Ireland, 418, 390, CHAS*. In HH of John L. Smith m 28 born Ireland.

SMITH, MARTHA, 70, F, None listed, -, Ireland, 433, 434, AND*.

SMITH, MARY J., 15, F, None listed, -, Ireland, 393, 393, YORK*. In HH of William A. Smith m 47 born Ireland.

SMITH, MARY P., 45, F, None listed, -, Ireland, 393, 393, YORK*. In HH of William A. Smith m 47 born Ireland.

SMITH, NANCY, 70, F, None listed, -, Ireland, 1164, 1165, FAIR.

SMITH, PATRICK, 27, M, Laborer, -, Ireland, 2052, 2058, EDGE. In HH of Jas. Linch m 28 born Ireland.

SMITH, QUINTEN, 54, M, None listed, -, Ireland, 700, 658, CHAS+. In HH of R.J. Griffith m 36 born Ireland.

SMITH, SARAH, 60, F, None listed, -, Ireland, 1233, 1233, CHES.

SMITH, SARAH, 80, F, None listed, -, Ireland, 1624, 1624, YORK. In HH of Johon W. Smith m 33 born York Dist., SC.

SMITH, WILLIAM A., 47, M, Mechanic, -, Ireland, 393, 393, YORK*.

SMYTH, E., 22, M, Clerk, -, Ireland, 1092, 1069, CHAS-. In HH of Samuel Wiley m 34 born Ireland.

SMYTH, JOHN A., 65, M, Clerk, -, Ireland, 179, 183, RICH. Page out of order, follow HH 135/139. In HH of Thomas Frean m 57 born Ireland.

SMYTH, THOMAS REVD., 40, M, Episcopal Clergyman, -, Ireland, 14, 14, CHAS%.

SNARDY, SML., 56, M, Farmer, -, Ireland, 1170, 1170, CHES.

SNIDER, MARGARET, 19, F, None listed, -, Ireland, 84, 84, YORK+. In HH of James J. Snider m 30 born Yorkville, SC.

SPEARS, A., 65, F, None listed, -, Ireland, 167, 167, KERS. In HH of J.B. Lucas m 49 born VA.

SPELLAN, ANN, 19, F, None listed, -, Ireland, 1011, 988, CHAS-. In HH of H.D Lesesne m 40 born SC.

SPELLAN, IVANA, 28, F, None listed, -, Ireland, 418, 390, CHAS*. In HH of John L. Smith m 28 born Ireland.

SPENCE, SAML., 42, M, Teacher, -, Ireland, 341, 341, KERS.

SPENCER, JAMEY, 78, F, None listed, -, Ireland, 114, 114, YORK. In HH of Jackson Spencer m 61 born York Dist., SC.

SPENCER, NANCY, 28, F, None listed, -, Ireland, 14, 14, YORK. In HH of Thomas Spencer m 40 born York Co., SC.

SPROULE, RACHEL, 55, F, None listed, -, Ireland, 153, 157, RICH. HH out of order, follows 185/189.

SPROULE, THOMAS, 29, M, Stone cutter, -, Ireland, 153, 157, RICH. HH out of order, follows 185/189. In HH of Rachel Sproule f 55 born Ireland.

STANLEY, BRIGET, 13, F, None listed, -, Ireland, 315, 291, CHAS+. In HH of Edward Henry m 42 born Ireland.

STANLEY, CATHERINE, 11, F, None listed, -, Ireland, 315, 291, CHAS+. In HH of Edward Henry m 42 born Ireland.

STANLOW, CON., 30, M, Laborer, -, Ireland, 261, 244, CHAS+. In HH of Hugh McNamara m 28 born Ireland.

STANTEN, ANN DELA, 13, F, None listed, -, Ireland, 553, 519, CHAS*. In Catholic Seminary.

STANTON, ANDREW, 12, M, Porter, -, Ireland, 693, 673, CHAS-. In HH of Walter Lambert m 22 born Ireland.

STANTON, JOHN, 40, M, Porter, -, Ireland, 693, 673, CHAS-. In HH of Walter Lambert m 22 born Ireland.

STANTON, PATRICK, 20, M, Laborer, -, Ireland, 389, 351, CHAS+. In HH of Edward Collins m 40 born Ireland.

STANTON, PEGGY, 35, F, None listed, -, Ireland, 850, 808, CHAS+. In HH of Robert Lambert m 43 born Ireland.

START, CATHERINE, 30, F, None listed, -, Ireland, 65, 64, CHAS*. In HH of Charles Start m 35 born Ireland.

START, CHARLES, 35, M, Policeman, -, Ireland, 65, 64, CHAS*.

STAUNTON, JOHN, 40, M, None listed, -, Ireland, 544, 536, CHAS%. In HH of E.M. Whiting m 45 born SC.

STEALE, J., 67, M, Farmer, -, Ireland, 10, 10, LANC*.

STEELE, HANNAH, 26, F, None listed, -, Ireland, 69, 69, NEWB. In HH of Mary Graham 52 f born SC

STEELE, HENRY, 26, M, Waggon Maker, -, Ireland, 456, 458, AND.

STEELE, WILLIAM, 24, M, Painter, -, Ireland, 69, 69, NEWB. In HH of Mary Graham 52 f born SC

STEMNAN, RUTH, 19, F, None listed, -, Ireland, 877, 856, CHAS-. In HH of Rufus Fairchild m 40 born PA.

STEPHENSON, MARGARET, 80, F, None listed, -, Ireland, 779, 783, AND. In HH of George Stephenson m 37 born SC.

STERLING, SAM, 52, M, Farmer, -, Ireland, 33, 33, CHES.

STEVENS, THOMAS, 21, M, Carriage Maker, -, Ireland, 35, 35, EDGE. In HH of Charles J. Glover m 41 born SC.

STEVENS, WILLIAM, 35, M, Carpenter, -, Ireland, 305, 305, EDGE*. In HH of Nancy Runnels f 76 born SC.

STEVENSON, JAMES, 64, M, Planter, -, Ireland, 830, 831, FAIR.

STEVENSON, JEANNETTE, 92, F, None listed, -, Ireland, 695, 696, FAIR. In HH of Robert Stevenson m 50 born SC.

STEVISON, WM., 22, M, Clerk, -, Ireland, 54, 54, LANC*. In HH of B. Lizerl (?) m 50 born CT.

STEWART, ELIZABETH, 59, F, None listed, -, Ireland, 214, 214, LAU.

STEWART, ESTHER, 22, F, None listed, -, Ireland, 1138, 1138, UNION. In HH of Esther Stewart f 56 born Ireland.

STEWART, ESTHER, 56, F, None listed, -, Ireland, 1138, 1138, UNION.

STEWART, JOHN, 62, M, Farmer, -, Ireland, 681, 681, LAU.

STEWART, MARGARET, 80, F, None listed, -, Ireland, 1379, 1379, YORK.

STEWART, ROBERT, 48, M, Farmer, -, Ireland, 315, 315, YORK.

STEWART, W.K., 33, M, School teacher, -, Ireland, 760, 760, SUMT.

STEWART, WILLIAM, 63,, Farmer, -, Ireland, 1930, 1930, ABB.

STODY, JAMES, 50, M, Laborer, -, Ireland, 322, 294, CHAS+. In HH of John

Dowling m 34 born Ireland.

STOOP, HUGH, 60, M, None, -, Ireland, 139, 129, CHAS-.

STRINGER, MARY E., 35, F, None listed, -, Ireland, 719, 677, CHAS+. In HH of Phoebe Ann Ellis f 30 born PA.

STRONG, J., 30, M, None listed, -, Ireland, 518, 484, CHAS*. In HH of Briget Flannagan f 28 born Ireland.

STUART, ANN, 30, F, None listed, -, Ireland, 111, 103, CHAS-. In HH of Thomas Ryan m 49 born Ireland.

STUART, ELIZA, 25, F, None listed, -, Ireland, 744, 745, FAIR. In HH of James Stuart m 30 born Ireland.

STUART, JAMES, 23, M, Overseer, -, Ireland, 132, 132, FAIR.

STUART, JAMES, 30, M, Tailor, -, Ireland, 744, 745, FAIR.

STUART, JANE, 30, F, None listed, -, Ireland, 132, 132, FAIR. In HH of James Stuart m 23 born Ireland.

SULIVAN, DANL., 22, M, None, -, Ireland, 1879, 1879, SUMT. In HH of P.O. Sulivan m 35 born Ireland.

SULIVAN, P.O., 35, M, Merchant, -, Ireland, 1879, 1879, SUMT.

SULLIVAN, CORNELIUS, 16, M, Laborer, -, Ireland, 243, 228, CHAS+. In HH of John Conners m 30 born Ireland.

SULLIVAN, DANIEL, 23, M, Laborer, -, Ireland, 205, 184, CHAS.

SULLIVAN, EUGINE, 50, M, Laborer, -, Ireland, 205, 184, CHAS. In HH of Daniel Sullivan m 23 born Ireland.

SULLIVAN, FLORANCE, 38, M, Shop keeper, -, Ireland, 144, 144, CHAS%.

SULLIVAN, HANNAH, 25, F, None listed, -, Ireland, 205, 184, CHAS. In HH of Daniel Sullivan m 23 born Ireland.

SULLIVAN, JAMES O., 37, M, Shop keeper, -, Ireland, 92, 84, CHAS+.

SULLIVAN, JULIA, 15, F, None listed, -, Ireland, 1003, 981, CHAS-. In HH of L. Watts f 32 born England.

SULLIVAN, KITTY, 6, F, None listed, -, Ireland, 205, 184, CHAS. In HH of Daniel Sullivan m 23 born Ireland.

SULLIVAN, MARTIN, 35, M, Laborer, -, Ireland, 242, 228, CHAS+.

SULLIVAN, MARY, 22, F, None listed, -, Ireland, 164, 155, CHAS+. In HH of Morte Sullivan m 22 born Ireland.

SULLIVAN, MARY, 40, F, None listed, -, Ireland, 205, 184, CHAS. In HH of Daniel Sullivan m 23 born Ireland.

SULLIVAN, MICHAEL, 34, M, Ditcher, -, Ireland, 1997, 2003, EDGE. Note; out of order after fam. No. 2000. See pg. 131. In HH of James Gearty m 44 born Ireland.

SULLIVAN, MORTE, 22, M, Mariner, -, Ireland, 164, 155, CHAS+.

SULLIVAN, RICHARD, 27, M, Laborer, -, Ireland, 2058,

2061, EDGE.

SULLIVAN, T.J., REV., 39, M, Clergyman, -, Ireland, 480, 446, CHAS*. In HH of Rt. Revd. Jgn. A. Reynolds m 51 born KY.

SULLIVAN, THOMAS, 40, M, Laborer, -, Ireland, 406, 370, CHAS.

SUTHERLAND, ALICE, 27, F, None listed, -, Ireland, 239, 225, CHAS+. In HH of William Sutherland m 34 born Scotland.

SUTTON, MARY, 28, F, None listed, -, Ireland, 597, 555, CHAS+.

SUTTON, MICHL., 28, M, Laborer, -, Ireland, 597, 555, CHAS+. In HH of Mary Sutton f 28 born Ireland.

SWAIN, ANNA, 75, F, None listed, -, Ireland, 2383, 2383, ABB.

SWAIN, NANCY, 64, F, None listed, -, Ireland, 1562, 1562, ABB. In HH of Robert Swain m 80 born SC.

SWANN, CHARLES, 49, M, Planter, -, Ireland, 113, 113, BARN.

SWEENEY, BERNARD, 37, M, Laborer, -, Ireland, 338, 303, CHAS+.

SWEENEY, BRIGET, 16, F, None listed, -, Ireland, 992, 971, CHAS-. In HH of S.B. Bernard m 38 born France.

SWEENEY, ELIZABETH, 30, F, Nurse, -, Ireland, 45, 53, CHAS. In HH of Wilmot DeSanfure m 28, Attorney at Law, born SC.

SWEENEY, ELIZABETH,

40, F, None listed, -, Ireland, 416, 375, CHAS+.

SWEENEY, MARIA, 26, F, None listed, -, Ireland, 338, 303, CHAS+. In HH of Bernard Sweeney m 37 born Ireland.

SWEENY, EDWARD, 29, M, Pavior, -, Ireland, 322, 297, CHAS. In Boarding house.

SWEENY, JOHN, 23, M, Laborer, -, Ireland, 108, 103, CHAS*. In HH of Patrick Keefe m 40 born Ireland.

SWEENY, JOHN, 79, M, None, -, Ireland, 169, 159, CHAS+.

SWEENY, MARY, 40, F, Laborer, -, Ireland, 316, 291, CHAS+. In HH of Owen Sweeny m 33 born Ireland.

SWEENY, OWEN, 33, M, Laborer, -, Ireland, 316, 291, CHAS+.

SWENY, JANE, 74, F, None listed, -, Ireland, 936, 936, YORK. In HH of John Latta m 33 born Ireland.

T

TAFT, ISABELLA, 35, F, None listed, -, Ireland, 610, 568, CHAS+. In HH of A.R. Taft m 40 born MA.

TALLON, E.H., 59, M, Planter, -, Ireland, 578, 578, SUMT.

TALVAND, A.M., 40, F, None listed, -, Ireland, 51, 47, CHAS-.

TARRY, EDWARD, 40, M, Laborer, -, Ireland, 31, 26, CHAS+.

TARRY, MARY, 30, F, None listed, -, Ireland, 31, 26, CHAS+. In HH of Edward Tarry m 40 born Ireland.

TAYLOR, THOMAS, 18, M, Laborer, -, Ireland, 54, 49, CHAS-. In HH of Robert Leckia m 28 born Ireland.

TEARNEY, MICHAEL, 30, M, Laborer, -, Ireland, 934, 911, CHAS%. In HH of Joana Tinen f 28 born Ireland.

TEDMARSH, WILLIAM, 35, M, Laborer, -, Ireland, 88, 80, CHAS+. In HH of Michael Welch m 35 born Ireland.

TEMPLAR, ELIZA, 25, F, None listed, M, Ireland, 55, 50, CHAS-. In HH of Juliet Saxon f 35 mulatto born Ireland {sic}.

TEMPLE, DELIA, 30, F, None listed, -, Ireland, 1213, 1192, CHAS%. In HH of George A. Trenholm m 44 born SC.

TEMPNEY, JAMES, 26, M, City Police, -, Ireland, 64, 57, CHAS+. In HH of P. Natale m 40 born Italy.

TENNISON, WILLIAM, 17, M, Clerk, -, Ireland, 150, 141, CHAS+. In Boarding house.

TERRY, ANN, 23, F, None listed, -, Ireland, 1692, 1692, GREE. In HH of Jabz? Terry m 55 born Ireland.

TERRY, ANN, 90, F, None listed, -, Ireland, 1287, 1287, GREE. In HH of William Nears {Mears?} m 53 born SC.

TERRY, CATHERINE, 30, F, Servant, -, Ireland, 74, 84, CHAS. In HH of W.C. Murray m 40 born England.

TERRY, ELIZA, 17, F, None listed, -, Ireland, 1692, 1692, GREE. In HH of Jabz? Terry m 55 born Ireland.

TERRY, ELIZABETH, 47, F, None listed, -, Ireland, 1692, 1692, GREE. In HH of Jabz? Terry m 55 born Ireland.

TERRY, JABZ?, 53, M, Farmer, -, Ireland, 1692, 1692, GREE.

TERRY, JAMES, 20, M, Laborer, -, Ireland, 1692, 1692, GREE. In HH of Jabz?, Terry m 55 born Ireland.

TERRY, JANE, 19, F, None listed, -, Ireland, 1692, 1692, GREE. In HH of Jabz? Terry m 55 born Ireland.

TERRY, LUCINDA, 13, F, None listed, -, Ireland, 1692, 1692, GREE. In HH of Jabz? Terry m 55 born Ireland.

TERRY, REBECCA, 11, F, None listed, -, Ireland, 1692, 1692, GREE. In HH of Jabz? Terry m 55 born Ireland.

TETLEY, SARAH, MRS., 40, F, None listed, -, Ireland, 125, 125, Beau+. In HH of Samuel Sanders m 54 born SC.

THOMAS, HENRY, 26, M, Laborer, -, Ireland, 400, 383, CHAS-. In Boarding house.

THOMAS, HENRY, 35, M, Laborer, -, Ireland, 401, 384, CHAS-. In HH of Patrick Pardon m 22 born Ireland.

THOMAS, MARY, 30, F, Boarding house, -, Ireland, 400, 383, CHAS-.Occupation: Keeps Boarding house.

THOMAS, MARY, 35, F, None listed, -, Ireland, 351, 351, CHES.

THOMAS, WILLIAM, 30, M, Book binder, -, Ireland, 631, 589, CHAS+. In HH of Jane Thomas f 34 born SC.

THOMASON, THOMAS, 24, M, Shoemaker, -, Ireland, 826, 826, ABB.

THOMERSON, ELLEN-DER, 67, F, None listed, -, Ireland, 1797, 1797, GREE. In HH of Gillion Thomerson m 67 born SC.

THOMPSON, ALEX-ANDER, 72, M, Planter, -, Ireland, 831, 832, FAIR.

THOMPSON, ANN, 20, F, None listed, -, Ireland, 689, 689, ABB. In HH of Richard Thompson m 24 born Ireland.

THOMPSON, JAMES, 40, M, Laborer, -, Ireland, 40, 37, CHAS-.Listed as prisoner.

THOMPSON, JANE, 65, F, None listed, -, Ireland, 1236, 1237, FAIR.

THOMPSON, JOHN, 35, M, Laborer, -, Ireland, 447, 405, CHAS.

THOMPSON, MARY ANN, 35, F, None listed, -, Ireland, 324, 299, CHAS. In HH of William Thompson m 50 born England.

THOMPSON, RICHARD, 24, M, None listed, -, Ireland, 689, 689, ABB.

THOMPSON, WILLIAM, 26, M, Shoemaker, -, Ireland, 559, 559, CHES. In HH of E. ? West 36 m born SC.

THOMSON, CATHERINE, 36, F, None listed, -, Ireland, 357, 319, CHAS+. In HH of John Thomson m 40 born Scotland.

THOMSON, HANNAH, 70, F, None listed, -, Ireland, 596, 596, NEWB.

THOMSON, MARY, 70, F, None listed, -, Ireland, 628, 629, FAIR. In HH of Samuel Thomson m 40 born SC.

TIERNAN, JOHN, 21, M, Driver, -, Ireland, 540, 523, CHAS-. In Merchants Hotel. Occupation: Omnibus Driver.

TIERNEY, BRIDGET, 35, F, None listed, -, Ireland, 206, 188, CHAS*. In HH of James Tierney m 40 born Ireland.

TIERNEY, JAMES, 40, M, Laborer, -, Ireland, 206, 188, CHAS*.

TIERNEY, MARY ANN, 13, F, None listed, -, Ireland, 206, 188, CHAS*. In HH of James Tierney m 40 born Ireland.

TIGNE?, HUGH, 45, M, Laborer, -, Ireland, 1143, 1144, FAIR.

TIGNE?, {NO NAME}, 40, F, None listed, -, Ireland, 1143, 1144, FAIR. In HH of Hugh Tinge? m 45 born Ireland.

TIMMONS, JOHN, 26, M, Clerk, -, Ireland, 540, 523, CHAS-. In Merchants Hotel.

TIMS, SARAH, 27, F, None listed, -, Ireland, 1224, 1225, FAIR. In HH of Charles Tims m 36 born SC.

TINEN, JOANA, 28, F, None listed, -, Ireland, 934, 911, CHAS%.

TNOKY, C.M., 46, M, Artist, -, Ireland, 504, 504, FAIR. In HH of J.F. Gamble m 42, hotel keeper, born NC. At the

Winnsboro Hotel.

TOBENS, CATHARIN, 23, F, None listed, -, Ireland, 538, 530, CHAS%. In HH of Richard Tobens m 40 born Ireland.

TOBENS, RICHARD, 40, M, Farmer, -, Ireland, 538, 530, CHAS%.

TODD, JANE, 79, F, None listed, -, Ireland, 28, 28, LAU. In HH of Patrick Todd m 82 born Ireland.

TODD, JOHN, 58, M, Farmer, -, Ireland, 165, 165, LAU.

TODD, OLIVE, 70, F, None listed, -, Ireland,706,710, AND.

TODD, PATRICK, 82, M, Farmer, -, Ireland, 28, 28, LAU.

TODD, ROBERT, 35, M, Merchant Clerk, -, Ireland, 1971, 1794, EDGE.

TODD, SAMUEL A., 67, M, Farmer, -, Ireland, 255, 255, LAU.

TODD, SAMUEL R., 42, M, Merchant, -, Ireland, 459, 159, LAU.

TOLLY, JOANA, 19, F, None listed, -, Ireland, 174, 157, CHAS. In HH of A.C. Smith m 45 born SC.

TONEY, ELLEN, 21, F, Servant, -, Ireland, 70, 80, CHAS. In HH of Mr. Rot. Smith m 60 born SC.

TONEY, WILLIAM, 12, M, None listed, -, Ireland, 119, 112, CHAS*. In HH of Dennis Canan m 35 born Ireland.

TOOLE, PETER, 24, M, Mariner, -, Ireland, 237, 222, CHAS-.Poor House.

TOOLE, PETER, 25, M, Laborer, -, Ireland, 312, 296, CHAS-. In HH of Bernard Connely m 26 born Ireland.

TOOLEY, ANN, 5, F, None listed, -, Ireland, 370, 339, CHAS. In HH of Maurice Tooley m 40 born Ireland.

TOOLEY, CORDELIA DAMERIS, 28, F, None listed, -, Ireland, 370, 339, CHAS. In HH of Maurice Tooley m 40 born Ireland.

TOOLEY, HARRIETT, 9, F, None listed, -, Ireland, 370, 339, CHAS. In HH of Maurice Tooley m 40 born Ireland.

TOOLEY, JOHN, 7, M, None listed, -, Ireland, 370, 339, CHAS. In HH of Maurice Tooley m 40 born Ireland.

TOOLEY, MARY JANE, 3, F, None listed, -, Ireland, 370, 339, CHAS. In HH of Maurice Tooley m 40 born Ireland.

TOOLEY, MAURICE, 40, M, Boot maker, -, Ireland, 370, 339, CHAS.

TORBIT, JOHN, 60, M, Farmer, -, Ireland, 10, 10, CHES.

TORBIT, MARY, 55, F, None listed, -, Ireland, 10, 10, CHES. In HH of John Forbit m 60 born Ireland.

TORLAN, ELIZA, 24, F, None listed, -, Ireland, 733, 713, CHAS-. In HH of C.S. Maule m 45 born Scotland.

TORRAH, EON, 31, M, Laborer, -, Ireland, 2052, 2058, EDGE. In HH of Jas. Linch m 28 born Ireland.

TRACEY, JAMES, 49, M, Laborer, -, Ireland, 680, 692, RICH.

TRACEY, JULIA, 26, F, None listed, -, Ireland, 680, 692, RICH. In HH of James Tracey m 49 born Ireland.

TRAPP, LOUISA, 22, F, None listed, -, Ireland, 272, 272, CHAS%. In HH of John D. Aiken m 30 born SC.

TRAPP, SARAH, 25, F, None listed, -, Ireland, 323, 323, CHAS%. In HH of James K. Robinson m 40 born SC.

TROY, HANNAH, 35, F, None listed, -, Ireland, 1066, 1044, CHAS%. In HH of Thomas Troy m 40 born Ireland.

TROY, JAMES, 11, M, None listed, -, Ireland, 1066, 1044, CHAS%. In HH of Thomas Troy m 40 born Ireland.

TROY, JANE, 13, F, None listed, -, Ireland, 1066, 1044, CHAS%. In HH of Thomas Troy m 40 born Ireland.

TROY, THOMAS, 40, M, Gardenir, -, Ireland, 1066, 1044, CHAS%.

TRUESDELL, JOHN, 81, M, Farmer, -, Ireland, 463, 463, KERS.

TURNER, ELIJAH, 40, M, Farmer, -, Ireland, 1395, 1395, SPART.

TWEED, R.L., 34, M, Mechanic, -, Ireland, 86, 86, KERS.

TWOHILT, DANIEL, 30, M, Store keeper, -, Ireland, 385, 347, CHAS+.

TWOHILT, HONORA, 25, F, None listed, -, Ireland, 385, 347, CHAS+. In HH of Daniel Twohilt m 30 born Ireland.

TWOHILT, JOHN, 18, M, Engineer, -, Ireland, 385, 347, CHAS+. In HH of Daniel Twohilt m 30 born Ireland.

V

VALENTINE, WM., 50, M, Planter, -, Ireland, 1566, 1566, SUMT.

VAUGHAN, THOMAS, 54, M, Schoolmaster, -, Ireland, 287, 287, COLL.

VINCOMB, HENRY, 28, M, Ditcher, -, Ireland, 285, 285, CHAS3. In HH of Sookey Bunch f 50 born SC.

W

WABBLE, MARY, 25, F, Servant, -, Ireland, 882, 840, CHAS+. In Charleston Hotel.

WADDELL, JOHN, 49, M, Gardner, -, Ireland, 534, 570, RICH.

WADDELL, SAMUEL, 32, M, Mechanic, -, Ireland, 436, 447, RICH. In Boarding house.

WADE, WILLIAM, 22, M, None listed, -, Ireland, 328, 328, YORK. In HH of Owen Matthews m 41 born Lancester Dist., SC.

WAGNER, MARY, 21, F, None listed, -, Ireland, 47, 43, CHAS$. In HH of John Ewing m 50 born MA.

WALACE, JAMES, 68, M, None, -, Ireland, 200, 200, LEX.

WALKER, DAVID, 71, M, Teacher, -, Ireland, 1020, 1020, CHES. In HH of J.A. Walker m 34 born Ireland.

WALKER, ISAAC, 57, M, Waggoner, -, Ireland, 482, 497, RICH.

WALKER, J.A., 34, M, Physician, -, Ireland, 1020, 1020, CHES.

WALKER, JANE, 82, F, None listed, -, Ireland, 72, 72, PICK+.

WALKER, MARY, 72, F, None listed, -, Ireland, 1020, 1020, CHES. In HH of J..A. Walker m 34 born Ireland.

WALKER, SALLY, 62, F, None listed, -, Ireland, 1588, 1588, YORK. In HH of Margaret McLean f 47 born York Dist., SC.

WALKER, THOMAS, 69, M, Farmer, -, Ireland, 1752, 1752, GREE.

WALKER, THOMAS, 70, M, Farmer, -, Ireland, 943, 943, CHES.

WALKINSHAND, WILLIAM, 57, M, Sadler, -, Ireland, 104, 97, CHAS-.

WALLACE, ANN, 20, F, Nurse, -, Ireland, 99, 111, CHAS. In HH of F.J. Porcher m 30 born SC.

WALLACE, JAMES, 66, M, Farmer, -, Ireland, 1007, 1007, YORK.

WALLACE, JANE, 50, F, None listed, -, Ireland, 2272, 2272, ABB.

WALLACE, JANE, 87, F, None listed, -, Ireland, 184, 184, YORK*. In HH of Robert Love, Jr. m 33 born York Dist., SC.

WALLACE, JOANA, 22, F, None listed, -, Ireland, 893, 873, CHAS-. In HH of O. Chisolm m 33 born SC.

WALLACE, MARY, 61, F, None listed, -, Ireland, 1007, 1007, YORK. In HH of James Wallace m 66 born Ireland.

WALLACE, MICHART, 25, M, Drayman, -, Ireland, 853, 811, CHAS+. In HH of Bernard Carrol m 45 born Ireland.

WALLACE, MIKE, 30, M, Laborer, -, Ireland, 31, 27, CHAS$. In HH of E. Reynolds m 33 mulatto born Ireland.

WALSH, EDMUND, 28, M, Clerk, -, Ireland, 374, 383, RICH.

WARD, THOMAS, 30, M, Laborer, -, Ireland, 400, 383, CHAS-. In Boarding house.

WARD, WILLIAM, 28, M, Laborer, -, Ireland, 400, 383, CHAS-. In Boarding house.

WARNOCK, SAMUEL, 32, M, Silversmith, -, Ireland, 53, 53, NEWB.

WARNOCK, SHANNON, 1, F, None listed, -, Ireland, 53, 53, NEWB. In HH of Samuel Warnock 32 m born Ireland. Shannon's age listed as 11/12.

WARNOCK, SUSANNA, 25, F, None listed, -, Ireland, 53, 53, NEWB. In HH of Samuel Warnock 32 m born Ireland.

WATERS, DAVID SENR., 57, M, Mechanic, -, Ireland, 492, 492, CHES.

WATSON, WILLIAM, 51, M, Farmer, -, Ireland, 568, 568, YORK.

WATT, WILLIAM, 81, M, Planter, -, Ireland, 14, 14, FAIR.

WEBB, HENRY, 20, M, Stone cutter, -, Ireland, 124, 115, CHAS+. In Boarding house.

WEBB, MARIA, 50, F, None listed, -, Ireland, 109, 104, CHAS*. In HH of Walter Webb m 50 born Ireland.

WEBB, WALTER, 50, M, Gardener, -, Ireland, 109, 104, CHAS*.

WEIR, MARY, 49, F, None listed, -, Ireland, 1787, 1787, ABB. In HH of Thomas Weir m 86 born Ireland.

WEIR, THOMAS, 86, M, Farmer, -, Ireland, 1787, 1787, ABB.

WELCH, BRIGET, 26, F, None listed, -, Ireland, 540, 506, CHAS*. In HH of Catherine Green f 39 born Ireland.

WELCH, ELIZABETH, 25, F, None listed, -, Ireland, 883, 860, CHAS%. In HH of George H. Winges m 21 born SC.

WELCH, JOHN, 21, M, Laborer, -, Ireland, 464, 461, CHAS%. In HH of Thomas Cantwell m 45 born Ireland.

WELCH, JOHN, 35, M, Farmer, -, Ireland, 987, 964, CHAS%. In Boarding house.

WELCH, JOHN, 43, M, Planter, -, Ireland, 749, 749, BARN.

WELCH, JUDY, 40, F, None listed, -, Ireland, 1682, 1682, ABB.

WELCH, KYRON, 11, M, None listed, -, Ireland, 1682, 1682, ABB. In HH of July Welch f 40 born Ireland.

WELCH, MARGARET, 18, F, None listed, -, Ireland, 464, 461, CHAS%. In HH of Thomas Cantwell m 45 born Ireland.

WELCH, MARGARET, 34, F, Servant, -, Ireland, 31, 31, CHAS!. In HH of Alexr H. Bowman m 47 born PA. Eliza Clare Bowman age 9/12 yr.

WELCH, MARIA, 8, F, None listed, -, Ireland, 1682, 1682, ABB. In HH of July Welch f 40 born Ireland.

WELCH, MICHAEL, 35, M, Mariner, -, Ireland, 88, 80, CHAS+.

WELCH, NANCY, 25, F, None listed, -, Ireland, 76, 76, FAIR. In HH of George Welch m 29 born SC.

WELCH, PATRICK, 22, M, Drayman, -, Ireland, 123, 114, CHAS+. In HH of James Armstrong m 33 born Ireland.

WELCH, SUSAN, 27, F, None listed, -, Ireland, 123, 114, CHAS+. In HH of James Armstrong m 33 born Ireland.

WELSH, ANNA, 25, F, None listed, -, Ireland, 1056, 1034, CHAS%. In HH of Michael Welsh m 31 born Ireland.

WELSH, DOROTHY, 28, F, None listed, -, Ireland, 1056, 1034, CHAS%. In HH of Michael Welsh m 31 born Ireland.

WELSH, ELIZA, 40, F, None listed, -, Ireland, 28, 28, RICH. In HH of Michael Welsh m 31 born Ireland.

WELSH, JERRY, 9, M, None listed, -, Ireland, 1056, 1034, CHAS%. In HH of Michael Welsh m 31 born Ireland.

WELSH, MARGARET, 6, F, None listed, -, Ireland, 1056, 1034, CHAS%. In HH of Michael Welsh m 31 born Ireland.

WELSH, MICHAEL, 31, M, Laborer, -, Ireland, 28, 28, RICH. Date 1849 by name of Michael Welsh.

WELSH, MICHAEL, 31, M, Laborer, -, Ireland, 1056, 1034, CHAS%.

WEST, JANSASA, 34, F, None listed, -, Ireland, 405, 405, UNION. In HH of George West m 29 born SC.

WHAM, BARBARA, 42, F, None listed, -, Ireland, 1665, 1665, GREE.

WHAM, JOSEPH, 75, M, Farmer, -, Ireland, 1666, 1666, GREE.

WHAM, MARY, 40, F, None listed, -, Ireland, 1666, 1666, GREE. In HH of Joseph Wham m 75 born Ireland.

WHIT, JNO., 24, M, Laborer, -, Ireland, 2058, 2061, EDGE. In HH of Richard Sullivan m 27 born Ireland.

WHITE, WM. M., 19, M, Clerk, -, Ireland, 1007, 984, CHAS-. In HH of Wm. Sherrar m 50 born SC.

WHITES, CATHERINE E., 29, F, None listed, -, Ireland, 793, 773, CHAS-. In HH of Robert White m 40 born Ireland.

WHITES, ROBERT, 40, M, Cabinet maker, -, Ireland, 793, 773, CHAS-.

WHITESIDES, MAYOR, 85, M, None listed, -, Ireland, 1088, 1088, YORK. In HH of Mayor Whitsides m 24 born York Dist., SC.

WHITSON, JANE, 40, F, House Keeper, -, Ireland, 102, 114, CHAS. In HH of Henry H. Raymond m 28 born SC.

WHITTY, CATHERINE, 9, F, None listed, -, Ireland, 346, 308, CHAS+. In Boarding house.

WHITTY, ELIZA, 6, F, None listed, -, Ireland, 346, 308, CHAS+. In Boarding house.

WHITTY, ELIZA, 30, F, None listed, -, Ireland, 346, 308, CHAS+. In Boarding house.

WHITTY, FANNY, 10, F, None listed, -, Ireland, 346, 308, CHAS+. In Boarding house.

WHITTY, FRANCIS, 12, M, None listed, -, Ireland, 346, 308, CHAS+. In Boarding house.

WHITTY, JANE, 7, F, None listed, -, Ireland, 346, 308, CHAS+. In Boarding house.

WHITTY, MARY, 4, F, None listed, -, Ireland, 346, 308, CHAS+. In Boarding house.

WIGG, JANE PATTERSON, 50, F, None listed, -, Ireland, 175, 175, Beau+. In HH of W.H. Wigg m 41 born SC.

WILEY, JOHN, 73, M, Planter, -, Ireland, 1148, 1149, FAIR.

WILEY, MARGARET, 20, F, None listed, -, Ireland, 109, 120, CHAS. In HH of Mary Wiley f 60 born Ireland.

WILEY, MARY, 60, F, None listed, -, Ireland, 109, 120, CHAS.

WILEY, SAMUEL, 34, M, Shop keeper, -, Ireland, 1092, 1069, CHAS-.

WILLIAMS, ESTHER, 35, F, None listed, -, Ireland, 741, 741, ABB. In HH of Timothy D. Williams m 64 born Wales.

WILLIAMS, MARY, 29, F, None listed, -, Ireland, 2329, 2329, ABB. In HH of Alexander W. Williams m 32 born Ireland.

WILLIAMS, THOMAS, 30, M, Laborer, -, Ireland, 40, 37, CHAS-.Listed as prisioner.

WILLSON, THOMAS, 58, M, Farmer, -, Ireland, 828, 829, AND*.

WILSON, ANGUS, 27, M, Teacher, -, Ireland, 864, 844, CHAS-.

WILSON, BETTY, 72, F, None listed, -, Ireland, 2341, 2341, ABB. In HH of William B. Bowie m 38 born SC.

WILSON, CYNTHEA, 36, F, None listed, -, Ireland, 421, 380, CHAS+. In HH of Adam Wilson m 40 born Scotland.

WILSON, DAVID, 56, M, Farmer, -, Ireland, 233, 233, CHES.

WILSON, ELIZA, 39, F, None listed, -, Ireland, 539, 522, CHAS-.

WILSON, ELIZABETH, 70, F, None listed, -, Ireland, 732, 732, ABB.

WILSON, EPHRAIM, 63, M, Bricklayer, -, Ireland, 161, 161, CHES.

WILSON, FRANCIS L., 28, F, None listed, -, Ireland, 488, 484, CHAS%. In HH of John Wilson m 38 born Ireland.

WILSON, JANE, 68, F, None listed, -, Ireland, 1204, 1204, LAU.

WILSON, JAS., 23, M, Laborer, -, Ireland, 2057, 2060, EDGE. In HH of Michael Corner m 27 born Ireland.

WILSON, JOHN, 38, M, Store keeper, -, Ireland, 488, 484, CHAS%.

WILSON, NANCY, 65, F, None listed, -, Ireland, 732, 732, ABB. In HH of Elizabeth Wilson 70 born Ireland.

WILSON, NANCY, 68, F, None listed, -, Ireland, 2348, 2348, ABB.

WILSON, P., 66, M, Farmer, -, Ireland, 4, 4, CHES.

WILSON, ROBERT, 48, M, Mechanic, -, Ireland, 985, 985, LAU.

WILSON, ROBT.., 28, M, Planter, -, Ireland, 49, 49, KERS.

WILSON, THOMAS, 25, M, None, -, Ireland, 40, 37, CHAS-. Listed as prisioner.

WILSON, THOS., 28, M, Boot maker, -, Ireland, 47, 47, KERS

WILSON, WM., 44, M, Farmer, -, Ireland, 634, 634, CHES.

WINDHAM, W.G., 52, M, Laborer, -, Ireland, 625, 583, CHAS+.

WINGES, CATHERINE, 20, F, None listed, -, Ireland, 883, 860, CHAS%. In HH of George H. Winges m 21 born SC.

WINGES, GEORGE H., 21, M, Weaver, -, Ireland, 883, 860, CHAS%.

WINN, ELIZABETH, 3, F, None listed, -, Ireland, 1206, 1185, CHAS%. In HH of Cornelius Desmond m 50 born Ireland.

WINN, MARGARET, 6, F, None listed, -, Ireland, 1206, 1185, CHAS%. In HH of Cornelius Desmond m 50 born Ireland.

WINN, MARY, 35, F, None listed, -, Ireland, 1206, 1185, CHAS%. In HH of Cornelius Desmond m 50 born Ireland.

WINN, NICHOLAS, 40, M, Laborer, -, Ireland, 1206, 1185, CHAS%. In HH of Cornelius Desmond m 50 born Ireland.

WINTERS, BRIDGET, 37, F, None listed, -, Ireland, 732, 723, CHAS%. In HH of Hugh Winters m 40 born Ireland.

WINTERS, EDWARD, 17, M, Laborer, -, Ireland, 732, 723, CHAS%. In HH of Hugh Winters m 40 born Ireland.

WINTERS, HUGH, 40, M, Laborer, -, Ireland, 732, 723, CHAS%.

WINTERS, SIMON, 13, M, None listed, -, Ireland, 732, 723, CHAS%. In HH of Hugh Winters m 40 born Ireland.

WIRE, JAMES, 66, M, Farmer, -, Ireland, 870, 870, ABB.

WISS, MARY, 51, F, None listed, -, Ireland, 1793, 1793, ABB. In HH of Emanuel Wiss m 52 born NC.

WITHERS, MARTHA, 38, F, None listed, -, Ireland, 269, 269, YORK. In HH of John S. Withers m 49 born York Dist., SC.

WITHERSPOON, HENRY, 6, M, None listed, -, Ireland, 83, 83, KERS. In HH of Jas. K. Witherspoon m 33 born NC.

WITHERSPOON, JAS., 10, M, None listed, -, Ireland, 83, 83, KERS. In HH of Jas. K. Witherspoon m 33 born NC.

WITHERSPOON, JOHN, 8, M, None listed, -, Ireland, 83, 83, KERS. In HH of Jas. K. Witherspoon m 33 born NC.

WOOD, JAMES, 10, M, None listed, -, Ireland, 1106, 1083, CHAS-. In Charleston Orphan House.

WOOD, JAMES, 40, M, Ditcher, -, Ireland, 878, 878, NEWB.

WOOD, JANE, 49, F, None listed, -, Ireland, 1106, 1083, CHAS-. In Charleston Orphan House.

WOODBURN, ANGNES, 70, F, None listed, -, Ireland, 840, 840, CHES. In HH of Saml. Woodburn m 48 born Ireland.

WOODBURN, SAML., 48, M, Farmer, -, Ireland, 840, 840, CHES.

WOODSIDES, JAMES, 20, M, Laborer, -, Ireland, 271, 252,

CHAS+. In HH of Mary Campbell f 49 born Ireland.

WOODSIDES, JAMES, 50, M, Farmer, -, Ireland, 1775, 1775, GREE.

WOODSIDES, JOHN, 22, M, Laborer, -, Ireland, 271, 252, CHAS+. In HH of Mary Campbell f 49 born Ireland.

WOODSIDES, NANCY, 70, F, None listed, -, Ireland, 1721, 1721, GREE.

WOORSEN, SARAH, 28, F, None listed, -, Ireland, 473, 470, CHAS%. In HH of Lambert Woorsen m 35 born Ireland.

WORKMAN, ANN, 30, F, None listed, -, Ireland, 385, 385, ABB. In HH of John Workman m 28 born Ireland.

WORKMAN, JOHN, 38, M, Overseer, -, Ireland, 385, 385, ABB.

WORKMAN, ROBERT, 11, M, None listed, -, Ireland, 385, 385, ABB. In HH of John Workman m 28 born Ireland.

WORKMAN, ROBERT, 69, M, Farmer, -, Ireland, 380, 380, LAU.

WRARY, JOHN, 24, M, Laborer, -, Ireland, 2057, 2060, EDGE. In HH of Michael Corner m 27 born Ireland.

WRIGHT, ELLEN, 21, F, None listed, -, Ireland, 394, 396, AND. In HH of Oliver H. Wright m 26 born SC.

WRIGHT, JAMES, 70, M, Farmer, -, Ireland, 276, 276, EDGE.

WRIGHT, MARY, 56, F, None listed, -, Ireland, 31, 31,

YORK+. In HH of William Wright m 50 born Yorkville, SC.

WRIGHT, SARAH, 60, F, None listed, -, Ireland, 596, 596, NEWB. In HH of Hannah Thomson f 70 born Ireland.

WYLEY, ELIZABETH, 29, F, None listed, -, Ireland, 42, 42, YORK*. In HH of Nancy Wyley f 65 born Ireland.

WYLEY, JOHN, 22, M, None listed, -, Ireland, 42, 42, YORK*. In HH of Nancy Wyley f 65 born Ireland.

WYLEY, LEE, 21, M, None listed, -, Ireland, 42, 42, YORK*. In HH of Nancy Wyley f 65 born Ireland.

WYLEY, NANCY, 27, F, None listed, -, Ireland, 42, 42, YORK*. In HH of Nancy Wyley f 65 born Ireland.

WYLEY, NANCY, 65, M, None listed, -, Ireland, 42, 42, YORK*.

WYLEY, ROBERTSON, 20, M, None listed, -, Ireland, 42, 42, YORK*. In HH of Nancy Wyley f 65 born Ireland.

WYLEY, WILLIAM S., 35, M, None listed, -, Ireland, 42, 42, YORK*. In HH of Nancy Wyley f 65 born Ireland.

WYLIE, SAM, 64, M, Farmer, -, Ireland, 31, 31, CHES.

Y

YARBOROUGH, NANCY, 57, F, None listed, -, Ireland, 23, 23, FAIR. In HH of Henry Yarborough m 58 born SC.

YOUNG, ANDREW, 17, M, None listed, -, Ireland, 93, 93, FAIR. In HH of Ann Young f 53 born Ireland.

YOUNG, ANN, 53, F, None listed, -, Ireland, 93, 93, FAIR.

YOUNG, JAMES, 42, M, Farmer, -, Ireland, 969, 1012, PICK.

YOUNG, JAMES, 75, M, Farmer, -, Ireland, 407, 409, AND.

YOUNG, MARIA, 50, F, Teacher, -, Ireland, 227, 227, BEAU. In HH of David McElheran m 50 born Ireland.

YOUNG, MARIA, 50, F, Teacher, -, Ireland, 227, 227, BEAU. In HH of David McElheran m 50 born Ireland.

YOUNG, ROSETTA, 23, F, None listed, -, Ireland, 93, 93, FAIR. In HH of Ann Young f 53 born Ireland.

YOUNG, THOMAS L., 19, M, Apprentice, -, Ireland, 544, 544, FAIR. In HH of James McCreight m 51 born Ireland.

Unknown First Names:

_____, **CATHERINE**, 17, F, None listed, -, Ireland, 415, 374, CHAS+. In HH of Caroline Segee f 30 born Ireland. {Note: Catherine's surnamed was covered with tape}.

_____, **CATHERINE**, 25, F, None listed, -, Ireland, 415, 374, CHAS+. In HH of Caroline Segee f 30 born Ireland. {Note: surname covered with tape}.

Name Index

A

Abbott
  Eliza E., 44
Abels
  Robert S., 1
Abrahams
  Alexander, 170
Adams
  James, 1
  W.J., 1
Adger
  J.B., 122
  John, 88
  Joseph E., 2
Agnew
  Enoch, 2
  Robert, 159
Aiken
  David, 77
  John, 2
  John C., 185
Allen
  William, 2
Allison
  James, 3
Amiel
  John, 37
Anderson
  William, 165
Armstrong
  Jesse K., 4
Arnold
  C.M., 97
Ashby
  Lewis P., 4
Asheford
  John, 131
Ashley
  Nat., 144
Ashton
  William, 9
Avelhie
  P.A., 109

B

Bailey
  Robert, 69
Baker
  Richard, 154, 161
  Thomas E., 10, 104
  Thos., 159
Barber
  Ann, 29
Barkerloo
  William, 2
Barkley
  S.G., 5
Barnwell, Jr.
  Edward, 33
Barr
  James, 130
Bates
  Clark, 72
Beach
  Joseph, 49
  Sylvister, 101
Becaise
  Benj. B., 156
Beggs
  Thomas, 88
Belcher
  Robert, 15
Bell
  Alex, 40
  Thomas R., 6
Belmain
  William, 7
Belton
  George, 140
Bennett
  William, 114
Bernard
  S.B., 45, 68, 96,
    118, 151, 181
Berry
  John, 167
Billings
  David, 65
Bird
  Joseph, 16
Black
  George, 143, 176

  Joseph, 8
Blacklock
  J.F., 46
Blackwood
  G.G., 9
Blease
  Thomas W., 93
Boland
  George, 149
Bowers
  Wm., 45
Bowie
  William B., 189
Bowman
  Alexr. H., 187
  Eliza., 187
Boyd
  H.K., 92
  James, 13
  John D., 129
Boyone
  Thomas, 105
Brady
  Catherine, 174
  John, 75, 100
  Patrick, 95
Brandt
  H.F., 31
Bremar
  John, 11
Brenan
  Luke, 12
Brennock
  Wm. M., 15
Brice
  Alexander, 12
  John, 165
  Robert, 130
Bristol
  T.M., 112
Broadfoot
  Frances L., 24, 25
Brown
  Geo., 51
  John, 90
Bruns
  H., 18
Bryan
  Andrew, 23, 146

195

Feaster
  J.C.C., 106
Ferguson
  Perry, 120
  W.C., 29
Figeroux
  B., 121
Finley
  W.P., 154
Finney
  James, 93
Fitzpatrick
  James, 81, 84, 120
Fitzsimmons
  M., 35
Flagg
  Eliza, 2
Flahartey
  Dennis, 65
Fleming
  Elliza, 173
Flinn
  John, 125
Fogartie
  A., 137
Forbit
  John, 184
Fowler
  Joseph, 155
  William H., 28, 42,
    43, 59, 78, 89,
    93, 94, 96, 118,
    123, 140
Frazier
  Malcolm, 38
Frean
  Thomas, 178
Fryer
  Helena, 42
  Joseph, 67

G

Gainbow
  W.H., 49
Gallagen
  Patrick, 68
Gallaway

Mary, 168
Gamble
  James, 90, 91, 145
  J.F., 129, 171, 183
Garren
  Michael, 69
Garrity
  Edward, 62
Garvin
  John, 111, 112
Gascoin
  Washington, 41
Gatewood
  W.C., 133
Gearty
  James, 101, 119
Georty
  M.L., 63, 118
Gilbert
  A., 161
Gilleland
  Mary, 126
  William D., 111
Gilman
  Samuel, 116
Gilmer
  James G., 71
Glover
  Charles J., 179
Goodman
  Irwin P., 72
Gordon
  Catherine, 3
  David, 89
  John, 69
  Robert C., 73
Gorman
  Richard, 73
Gowen
  Patrick, 74
Grady
  James, 125
Graham
  Archibald, 75
  Mary, 3, 179
Grammer
  Samuel S., 144
Gravelly

John, 83
Gray
  Abasolam, 139
  Miles J., 56
Green
  Agnes, 76
  Catherine, 187
  John, 75
  Owen, 75
  Patrick, 75
Gregg
  E.M., 23
Griffith
  R.J., 76, 177
Grove
  Charles, 110
Guerard
  Ann, 147

H

Haddon
  John T., 77
Hagnes, Major
  P., 6, 13, 22, 29, 81,
    97, 113, 144,
    147, 154
  William C., 85
Hagnes or Hayes, 6
Haley
  John, 31, 32, 58,
    59, 93
Hambleton
  William N., 20
Hamilton
  Alexander, 53
  D.H., 34
  William K., 78
Harbeson
  John, 67
Hardin
  Frances, 129
  Francis, 27
Hardlan
  Hugh M., 2
Hare
  John, 22
Harmon

196

Preston, 80
Harrison
    Martha, 33
Hart
    Hamilton S., 109
    H.N., 29, 83
    S.N., 115
Hasact
    Larry, 82
Hatch
    Lewis, 33
Hayden
    H.S., 3, 28
Hayne
    Emeline, 119
    R.B., 137
Haynie
    David, 82
Hays
    Mary, 5, 77
    Thomas H., 82
Heffernon
    Patrick D., 83
Hener
    Hugh, 82
Henry
    Edward, 160, 178
    Mary, 131
Herbert
    William, 25, 60,
        124, 159
Hewot
    Joseph, 110
Heyward
    James J.B., 113,
        163
Hill
    Ebenezer, 85
    James L, 86
    James W., 158
    John, 20
    William H., 90
Hillborn
    Ebenezer, 83
Hindman
    J.A., 85
Hodges
    Samuel A., 157

Hogan
    Michael, 54
    Patrick, 26, 82
    Richard, 85, 143,
        144
Hogg
    Alexander, 86
Holden
    Daniel, 86
Holland
    John P., 101
Hood
    Elizabeth, 51, 87
Houerton
    J.L., 9
Huger
    Arthur M., 76
Huger, Jr.
    D.E., 113
Hughes
    John H., 88
Hurley
    John, 123
Hutchenson, Hon.
    T.L, 65
    T.L., 91, 92

I

Ingraham
    John, 89
Irwin
    Arthur, 90
    Samuel, 37

J

Jackson
    David F., 159
    William F., 41
Jamerson
    John, 90
Jeannerell
    Mary, 70
    Michael, 71
Jefcoat
    U. \W?\, 66
    W., 61, 66
Jenkins

John, 14, 45, 49,
    86, 118, 119,
    143, 144, 151
Jennings
    William, 16
Jervais
    Eliza, 82, 123
Jleffe
    Charles, 90
Johnson
    Adna, 56, 61, 67,
        141, 146
Johnston
    John, 90
    Samuel, 91
Jones
    Edward C., 146
    James, 69
Jordan
    Hiram, 100
    Thomas, 92

K

Kaicy
    Jas., 96
Karvin
    James, 28, 56
Keefe
    Patrick, 48, 85, 111,
        181
Keenan
    Michael, 73, 130
Keller
    F., 174
    J., 174
Kelly
    Peter, 24, 41, 72,
        108
    Thomas, 95
    William, 95
Kennedy
    Ellen, 3, 97
    James, 68, 86, 146
    John, 96
    Michl., 96
    Tim, 96, 128
Kenny

Sarah, 122
McAllister
   John, 97, 139
McAndrew
   James, 66
McCarey
   James, 148
McCarley
   James, 122
   Robert, 122
McCarrel
   James, 34
McCarthy
   Dennis, 122
   D.L., 9, 133
   James, 122, 124
   Michael, 122
McClain
   Andrew, 124
McClintock
   W.R., 124
McClinton
   A.S., 93
   Mathew, 125
   Samuel B., 125
McClure
   Tho. H., 164
   William, 41
McComb
   Robert, 125
McConnly
   Minor, 4
McCoone
   James, 126
McCormick
   John, 27, 71, 132
   William, 121, 131
McCrale/McCrate
   John, 42, 83, 126,
     170, 177
McCreight
   James, 102, 192
McCullough
   A., 127
   Joseph, 163
McCusker
   E., 115
McDavid

Allen, 128
McDonald
   J., 84, 165
McDonnagh
   John, 128
McDowel
   George W., 129
McDugal
   David, 104
McElheran
   David, 129, 192
   W.C., 134
McElleron
   Charles, 50, 75, 165
McElrone
   Hugh, 52, 130
McGary
   Patrick, 130
McGill
   J.B., 97
McGinnis
   Mary Ann, 137
McGladney
   William, 131
McGraw
   Michael, 163
McGuire
   Henry, 10, 56, 160
McIlwain
   John, 73
   Thomas, 87
   William, 147
McKeown
   H.C., 134
McKuon
   Mary, 17, 162
McLaughlin
   Edwd., 23, 27, 151,
     152
McLean
   Margaret, 186
McLeod
   J.W., 9
McLosh
   Joseph, 82
McLuchlin
   Jane, 135
McManus

John, 120
McMillan
   Thos., 136
McMullan
   William, 168
McMurray
   Michael, 59, 96, 97,
     101, 105, 108,
     109, 134, 154
McNamara
   Hugh, 23, 47, 85,
     92, 101, 114,
     128, 177, 178
McNeil
   Grace, 138
   Thomas, 137
McNeill
   Arthur, 138
   Mary, 105
McNetty
   Timothy, 63
McPherson
   James, 139
Means
   Albert, 37
Mears/Nears
   William, 182
Melton
   Wm. M., 119
Meran
   Patrick, 69
Meredith
   R., 148
Meyer
   Herman, 51
Meyrs
   J.J., 140
Middleton
   O.H., 64
Milling
   David, 89
Mills
   Otis, 55, 106, 140
Mitchell
   Martha, 100
Moise
   J., 21, 131
Monroe

Silcore
 Daniel H., 63, 174
Simms
 James, 125
Simons
 Harris, 106, 107,
  174
 Marie Ramsay, 29
Simpson
 Robert, 175
 Thos., 20
Sims
 C.S., 28, 161
Slattery
 Piercy, 151
Small
 Ann, 177
Smith
 A.C., 184
 Ann P., 120
 Barbary, 27
 Charles, 71
 Edward, 22
 Elesinga W., 75
 John L., 168, 177,
  178
 Johon W., 177
 Richard, 15
 Rot., 184
 William A., 177
Snider
 James J., 108, 178
Spear
 James E., 114
Spencer
 Jackson, 178
 Thomas, 178
Steckeley
 John, 117
Stein
 James N., 46
Stephenson
 George, 179
Sterling
 James, 177
Stevens
 J.H., 19
 Jose, 2, 76

Stevenson
 Robert, 179
Stewart
 Esther, 9
Stokes
 David, 109
Stoop
 Hugh, 29
Stratton
 William, 4, 7
Street
 Henry C., 104, 107
Sullivan
 Richard, 78, 188
 Thomas, 6, 33
Sutherland
 William, 181
Swain
 Robert, 181
Sweeney
 Bernard, 16, 101,
  128, 130, 132,
  148, 163
 Elizabeth, 30, 31
 Owen, 160
Sweeny
 John, 24, 42, 67

T

Taft
 A.R., 181
Tarry
 Edward, 182
Tash
 A.R., 145
Taylor
 Emeline, 15
 James, 165
 Thomas, 117
Theus
 F.W., 48, 128
Thomas
 Jane, 183
 Mary, 136
Thomerson
 Gillion, 183
Thompson

John, 46, 66
 William, 183
 William B., 164
Thompson, Gov.
 M., 139
Thomson
 Hannah, 191
 John, 183
 Samuel, 183
Tims
 Charles, 183
Tinen
 Joana, 95, 98, 182
Torbit
 Thomas, 127
Torlay
 Mary, 109
Trenholm
 George A., 182
Trouchlue
 Caroline, 165
Tunno
 Rachael (black), 4

V

Vironee
 W., 154

W

Waddell
 Eliza B., 6
Walker
 George, 146
 J.A., 120
 Joseph, 95
Watson
 Dunham, 95
Watts
 L., 71, 118, 119,
  130, 180
Welch
 George, 187
 Judy/July?, 187
 July, 114
 Mary, 86, 99
 Michael, 33, 132,
  187

202

West
    E.?, 183
    George, 37, 188
Whiting
    E.M., 179
Whitside, Mayor, 188
Wigg
    W.H., 188
Wiley
    Samuel, 178
Williams
    Timothy D., 189
Willis
    John G., 23, 108
Wilsman
    James, 67
Wilson
    Adam, 189
    Eliza, 71
    Hugh, 150
    J., 150
Winges
    George H., 80, 165,
        187, 190
Winters
    Hugh, 138
Wiss
    Emanuel, 190
Witherspoon
    Frances, 57
    Jas. K., 190
    John S., 190
Wittpin
    Frederick, 43
Woorsen
    Lambert, 191
Workman
    John, 142
Wright
    Oliver H., 191
    William, 191

Y

Yarborough
    Henry, 191
Young
    John, 7, 44

Youngue
    John L., 55

Z

Zerbet
    Henry, 164

§

: * Mulattos listed:

*DaCosta: Henry,
    James, Joseph,
    Louisa R., Louisa
    V., Thomas,
    W. P, William
* Flaharaty, Edward
*Gorcian, Fanny,
    Jane
* Quigly, Charles
* Reynolds, E. Elza,
*Saxon, Eliza, Ella,
    Julia, Juliet
*Templar, Eliza

§§

Occupation Index

A

Accountant, 7, 35, 74
Agent, 170
Agent, RR, 171
Apprentice, 192
Artist, 129, 183
Attendant, 40, 61, 79, 103, 130, 150, 167
Attorney at law, 181

B

Baker,
4, 5, 42, 79, 83, 127, 137, 150, 159, 170, 177
Bar keeper, 50, 144
Blacksmith, 6, 37, 39, 55, 81, 88, 99, 100, 103, 111, 112, 115, 129, 134, 142, 148, 150, 166, 170
Boarding house, 56
Book binder, 183
Book seller, 76
Bootmaker, 39, 61, 63, 65, 73, 117, 130, 147, 148, 166, 184, 189
Brickmaker, 127
Brickmason, 65, 91, 115, 133
Bricklayer, 3, 7, 14, 21, 34, 48, 50, 55, 64, 72, 87, 88, 98, 99, 121, 122, 140,
146, 150, 161, 170, 189
Broker, 47, 120, 125, 169, 170
Builder, 47, 48
Butcher, 96, 97, 148, 156

C

Cabinetmaker, 5, 9, 63, 81, 140, 188
Capt. U.S.A., 51
Carpenter, 5, 7, 8, 16, 17, 18, 23, 24, 27, 45, 46, 52, 54, 61, 68, 77, 85, 93, 98, 111, 117, 125, 143, 152, 155, 157, 159, 162, 165, 169, 179
Carriage maker, 93, 136, 179
Carter, 14, 165
Caster, 140
Catholic Minister, 5
Chemist, 125
City Police, 3, 39, 89, 97, 124, 154, 182
Clergyman, 150, 169, 181
C l e r g y m a n , Episcopal, 178
Clerk, 2, 4, 7, 15, 20, 21, 25, 27, 31, 40, 42, 43, 45- 47, 55 - 57, 59, 62, 65, 66, 67, 69, 70, 75, 77 - 79, 82, 89, 90, 92, 94, 96, 98,
100- 103, 105, 106, 115, 119, 120, 124, 125, 128, 129, 133, 135 - 137, 139, 141, 144, 145, 146, 147, 148, 150, 153- 160, 164, 168, 169, 172- 174, 177 - 179, 183, 186, 188
Clothing Store, 20, 167
Coach maker, 37, 53
Coachman, 22, 33
Coalpasser, 57, 85, 117, 132, 144
Conductor, 84
Conductor RR, 66, 128
Confectioner, 117
Constable, 97
Cook, 154
Cooper, 16, 45, 53, 139
Cotton buyer, 68
Cotton gin maker, 41
Cotton weigher, 136

D

Dentist, 151, 165
Digger, 95
Ditcher, 20, 26, 37, 40, 46, 56, 59, 61, 62, 66, 70, 77, 78, 80, 93, 101, 103, 105, 107, 114, 124, 159, 165, 174, 180, 185, 190
Drayman, 7, 10, 18,

§

Place Index

§

www.ingramcontent.com/pod-product-compliance
Lightning Source LLC
Chambersburg PA
CBHW070417270326
41926CB00014B/2829